# BABY-FACED
# ASSASSIN

# BABY-FACED
# ASSASSIN

## THE BIOGRAPHY OF MANCHESTER UNITED'S
## OLE GUNNAR SOLSKJAER

IAN MACLEAY

JOHN BLAKE

Published by John Blake Publishing Ltd,
3 Bramber Court, 2 Bramber Road,
London W14 9PB, UK

www.blake.co.uk

First published in hardback in 2007

ISBN: 978-1-84454-460-8

British Library Cataloguing-in-Publication Data:
A catalogue record for this book is available from the British Library.

Design by www.envydesign.co.uk

Printed in Great Britain by William Clowes Ltd, Beccles, Suffolk

1 3 5 7 9 10 8 6 4 2

Photographs courtesy of Clevamedia,
Empics/PA, Rex Features and Getty Images.

Papers used by John Blake Publishing are natural, recyclable products made
from wood grown in sustainable forests. The manufacturing processes
conform to the environmental regulations of the country of origin.

# Contents

# Take On Me

**'Ole Gunnar Solskjaer – the sub from hell.'**
**SIR ALEX FERGUSON**

He had scored better goals for Manchester United – goals that had won the Champions League and goals that had knocked their bitterest rivals Liverpool out of the FA Cup. Goals that had secured the Premier League title, like the one at Southampton in the season after they had landed the Treble. He had also scored international goals in World Cup games for Norway. 'The Baby-Faced Assassin' they called him, with more hits than the Sopranos; no one ever asked him how much he detested it.

The goal he scored that balmy night, though, in the autumn of 2006 against Celtic in the Champions League was his favourite. It was the first goal he had scored at Old Trafford for over three years, during which his career seemed in ruins. Paul Scholes had snapped up a loose pass from Gravesen and fed Saha; the Celtic keeper Boruc blocked the shot but Ole was on hand to sweep home.

Everyone had conceded that his career was over, even his manager, the man who had discovered him, nurtured him and watch him grow into one of the deadliest strikers in the modern game. Only Ole had believed that he could turn things round; he knew he had not lost his talent or his nerve. That is what drove him on and renewed his determination to achieve a miraculous recovery.

Ole Gunnar Solskjaer's winning goal against Celtic at 8.47pm on 13 September 2006 was the high spot of the most remarkable comeback in the modern game. It showed that the years of protracted frustration and pain had not broken him. On the contrary, his greatness as a player was about to flower anew.

Lester Piggott won the Breeders' Cup Mile within two weeks of his return to racing following his time in prison. Rocky Balboa made a wonderful comeback in the movies with another blockbuster of a bout; Sylvester Stallone reminded us in his ground-breaking return that it is not how hard you punch but how hard you take a punch that matters. This was never truer than in Ole's case. When he scored on that Wednesday evening against Celtic, Old Trafford roared its approval. United's Number 20 thrust his fists triumphantly into the air. This was just like Rocky did on the steps of the Art Museum in Philadelphia, one of the most iconic moments of modern cinema. Ole's goal will go down in United folklore in similar fashion.

A few nights later, the late-night news round-up ran the usual depressing film snippets of some of the daily events that make up our 21st-century world – a bombing in Iraq, for example, was accompanied by the standard-issue images of death and destruction. Among the onlookers gazing at the burning aftermath of the bombing, the camera lingered on a young boy wearing a red shirt emblazoned with white 'AIG' lettering. Among the carnage, a scrap of normality, a reminder of the global community, and how football has the power to transcend vast differences in ideology and culture. Ole Gunnar Solskjaer is part and parcel of that spirit of genuine sporting endeavour, reaching out to diverse communities around the globe. His efforts, and those of his team, have been hugely appreciated by those who simply love football, and appreciate the spirit and skill with which Ole represents his club and country. As an ambassador for the beautiful game, Ole is an example of all that football could hope for – committed, skilful, loyal and blessed with a perpetually youthful image ... he has become an integral part of the modern history of Manchester United, and a player who has earned respect from fans and footballers alike.

To discover how Ole became this universally-acclaimed global figure, playing for his national team and, arguably, for the greatest club side in the world, we have to travel back in time to 1973, and to Kristiansund, a small town by the coast of More og Ramsdal in the middle of Norway.

Ole was born on 26 February 1973, a year which turned out to be a significant one in world history – Britain joined the EEC, the Watergate scandal broke, famine was rife in Ethiopia and the Yom Kippur War erupted following the invasion of Israel by Egypt and Syria. Manchester United at that time were ailing, having dropped stone-like to 18th position in the old First Division. Bobby Charlton played his last game for United at Chelsea, his stunning flood of goals having now dwindled to a trickle.

Bobby was one of the 'golden triangle' of Charlton, Law and Best who had taken United to stellar heights in the late 1960s. Best's once insatiable desire to drink and party had given way to the paranoia and self-loathing that destroyed his glittering career. Within a year, Denis Law, now at Manchester City, was to back-heel the goal that relegated the club and end the fiasco of their declining years. It was the most symbolic goal in the history of both Manchester clubs. *Et tu, Brute*.

Ole always loved football – his team of choice, like many Scandinavian football fans, was Liverpool – and particularly scoring goals. His family moved when he was four to Clausenengen and, at the age of seven, he joined his local team with the same name. The youngster liked it so much he stayed there for the next 15 years.

Liverpool at that time were the team of the subsequent decade with a galaxy of star names. The men from Anfield went on to dominate the league in a similar fashion to Manchester United's stranglehold of the 1990s. Just like today, all the top English games were shown in Norway and the public followed them with great interest. Ole's favourite players were the heroes he saw on TV at the time, with Kenny Dalglish, the Liverpool superstar, a particular favourite of his. The Scottish international was the first player to score 100 league goals on both sides of the border. Commentators subsequently noted some similarities in style between the two, particularly the bewitching footwork and icy coolness in front of goal.

Both were very stylish players and deadly goalscorers. One of Ole's earliest football memories was watching Dalglish on TV scoring the goal that retained the European Cup for Liverpool in 1979. It was a wonderful, deft, first-time chip with just enough power to find the far corner of the net. In his back garden, young Ole would spend hours practising and developing his own football technique. One of his favourite party pieces was to stab down on the ball to refine the chip reminiscent of King Kenny's against Bruges. Little did he realise that the skills he was perfecting would one day help him score the winner in the most prestigious Cup competition in Europe.

Other heroes of Ole's were Marco van Basten, the Dutch superstar striker, whose wonderful career was derailed by an ankle injury, and Zico, the Brazilian ace.

Another vivid memory of Ole's was of the 1982 World Cup played in Spain. Although they went out to eventual winners Italy, the Brazil side were one of the most attractive teams to ever grace the World Cup. Their style and panache captured Ole's imagination and made a lifelong impression on him.

The football stickers and bubble-gum cards of soccer stars of that time were avidly collected by Ole and traded with his chums at school. Ole's favourite cards were of the Liverpool players, particularly in different strips. His most prized was one of Kenny Dalglish in the 1981/82 all-yellow away strip with the liver bird badge.

In an interview with the Manchester United fanzine *Red News*, Ole discussed the somewhat sensitive subject of the fact that he was a Liverpool fan as a youngster. 'You know, when you are back home and you watch games on TV and you tend to support the team that is winning, so in the '80s Liverpool were winning. Kenny Dalglish, he was the best player I thought, then Marco van Basten and Zico but, in England, Liverpool won so you get caught up in the moment.

'But now ... Actually, in Norway, I used to support a team that was an enemy of the team I signed for in Norway. It is just the story of my career. I signed for United and obviously you become a United supporter. I feel that I am part of the history of the club and you get to learn about the club when you are here for such a long time.'

Ole's father wanted to take him to England to see a Liverpool game, and they planned to stand on the Kop together. Coping with the heaving masses on the terraces held no fear for the Ole's father either – he had been the Greco-Roman Wrestling Champion of Norway from 1966–71.

Ole trained as a wrestler, too, but there was only one sport for him. He inherently sensed his future lay in football and worked even harder on his game. A large proportion of his time was spent on shooting practice. He learnt the basics early on, making sure that he shared equal time between accuracy and power. A full-size goal in his local park provided him with an ideal place for shooting practice, where the young Ole realised that 'sticking the ball away' was the key to it all. The Brazil and Dutch teams he had seen on TV were perhaps the greatest proponents of attacking football. They all played 'the proportion theory'; to players like Zico, it was nearly always better to take responsibility and have a strike at goal. Ole's gift for goal-scoring was never manufactured, though – he was born with it, but his years of hard work honed it to near perfection. As his career developed and his fame grew, it became more apparent that, as a player, Ole was a natural, and simply loved perfecting every aspect of his game – he was a true one-off.

Ole was highly intelligent, mastering the English language, which was taught in all Norwegian schools, at a young age. This gave him an increased knowledge of British culture and heightened his love of the English game. His swiftness of mind was also evident whenever he had a ball at his feet. If the sociologists are to be believed, studies have shown that attacking players have a greater capacity for creativity than their defensive counterparts. And, true to form, Ole seemed to draw upon an animal cunning as part of his game, demonstrating the guile of a natural predator. Logic also played its part – in the early days in Norway, he concentrated on ground shots. The higher the shot, he reasoned, the earlier the keeper could see it.

In his first junior matches, the eight-year-old was now playing against boys twice his age. This was of great assistance to him in his subsequent career; it taught him not to be intimidated by more physical opponents and gave him confidence in his own ability.

Trond Solli is from Frei, a small island outside Kristiansund and is two years younger than Ole. They played together at Clausenengen, and he recalls, smiling at the memory, the first time their paths crossed. 'Ole was a unique talent from when he was a little child. I lived in Frei, and played for their team. One day, we played against Clausenengen with Ole in the team. Ole was then about nine years old and I was about seven. We lost 5-0 that day, and Ole scored all five goals. That is something – scoring so many goals, in one game, so young. I think that he kept being good, because he was always serious about his football. He was always focused on his football during his childhood. There are not many good, young players that can do that. He was a great talent when he was a little child. He scored goals all the time, all the time training very hard, and he always seemed to want to be better and better. He did a lot of extra training also when he was very young. All the people knew that this boy would be a very good football player.

'Later, I moved to Kristiansund and I began playing for Clausenengen, too. We all thought that Ole was a great player and a great man. He was never arrogant, always behaving very well. We liked playing with Ole. His talent was unique, his skills as a goal-getter were unique and he did it. He became a good football player, one of the best in Europe.'

When Ole was 15, his football development had slowed slightly and he was thinking about quitting football to concentrate full-time on his studies. When asked what he would have done if he had not decided to be a footballer, Ole would always tell people that he would have become a number-cruncher. It is doubtful whether he would have had so much fun, though. Most of his friends had dropped football in favour of their studies, having found it too demanding at such a young age.

Ole still retains many of his friends from those times, an important factor in how he has managed to remain so grounded and capable of dealing with the pressures of playing for the most famous club in the world. The sheer intensity of being part of the Manchester United set-up, and the burden of expectation that goes with it, must have been intolerable at times and generally unappreciated by those outside that world. When describing the events leading up to his Champions League-winning goal, Ole told the Manchester United *Opus*, 'I called one of my closest friends back in Norway. He could not make it to Spain, so I wanted to check if he was going to watch the game. He said, "Yeah, but I am going to have to leave 15 minutes from time." [He is a nurse and had the night shift.] I told him he had to watch the whole game. "Get someone to step in for you for an hour," because I had this feeling something big was going to happen to me.'

How many players a few hours away from the biggest game in their life would take the time to ring a friend to ensure that they could count on their support – and then insist that they turned up an hour late for their night shift?

Another friendship that Ole struck up was with Oyvind Leonhardsen whom he met at a Soccer School and later played with at Clausenengen. Oyvind went on to play for Wimbledon, Liverpool and Tottenham and had a fine career in the Premiership. The bond that had been forged in Clausenengen was strengthened when they met up again in England. A little naïve when they arrived in England, many of their contemporaries were unable to carve out a career in the unforgiving environment of first-class football.

Ole's other major interest in life was music. Around the time of his Manchester United first-team comeback, he was sighted leaving the Manchester Apollo after attending a gig by Jack White's supergroup The Raconteurs. Another of his current favourites are the Arctic Monkeys, but his tastes were formed when he was growing up in Norway. The Rolling Stones, David Bowie and Guns 'N' Roses were top of his hit parade, and Elvis Presley is his all-time hero.

At 17, Ole resembled a Patricia Highsmith version of gilded youth, the epitome of Scandinavian cool; his male-model glamour and remarkable talents were soon being noticed. Ole made his début for Clausenengen in 1990 when, in what was to become a trademark role, he came on as sub for the last ten minutes. It was another year before he was able to establish himself in the first team. Clausenengen were an amateur side and there was no money; when he first started playing for them, the club's average crowd struggled to top three figures. It never occurred to Ole at the time that he could have actually earned in living in the game. He was too content to learn his craft and, despite becoming a bit of a local celebrity, he shunned the limelight. The goals continued to flow, though, so much so that in 109 games for the Third Division side, he racked up an amazing 115 goals.

In 1992/93, Ole was conscripted by the Norwegian Army to serve one year's National Service. For a short while, his football ambitions were put on hold. He was stationed in the south of Norway and still travelled back to Clausenengen from his posting to play for them. To maintain his fitness, he trained and worked out when not on duty. A request by Ole to train with Lillestorm was abruptly turned down. It was a rash decision by the high-profile Norwegian club because they lost the possibility of securing one of the deadliest marksmen in Europe.

Eirik Havdahl is a freelance football writer who lives in Norway and has been watching English and Norwegian football for over 30 years. A connoisseur of the brilliant Chelsea side of the early 1970s, Eirik was brought up on the skills of Alan Hudson and Charlie Cooke. Still a die-hard fan, he travels to Stamford Bridge regularly to watch the heirs to the throne of the 1970s King's Road peacocks. A keen student of the domestic game, he regards Ole as the world's most famous living Norwegian. 'Solskjaer is perhaps the most popular Norwegian in the world of all time. He is more popular than Henrik Ibsen and Thor Heyerdahl. His goal in the Champions League final against Bayern Munich in May 1999 is known by more people around the world than Ibsen's *Peer Gynt* I think.'

Clausenengen won promotion to the Second Division mainly on the back of Ole's goals which were starting to attract media attention. In 1994, he scored 31 out of the total of 47 goals scored by them. That was when he was picked to play for the Norwegian Under-21 squad for the first time. It was a great achievement by him, as he was the only player chosen from the Norwegian Second Division to represent his country at that level. The first glimmers of his huge potential were starting to show. As in any league in the world, scouts from the larger clubs would always come sniffing around when a promising youngster emerged, particularly if he was a prolific goalscorer.

Molde FK signed him for a fee in the region of £16,000, probably the best deal ever struck in the history of Norwegian football as the youngster was destined to succeed. The city of Molde had a population of approx 25,000 and was situated between Bergen and Trondheim. Nicknamed the 'City of Roses' because of its beautiful flowered gardens, it suited Ole to move there because of its proximity to Kristiansund. Ole was part of a very close family and wanted to keep any upheaval to an absolute minimum.

A well-known tourist resort, Molde's most famous visitors included German Kaiser Wilhelm II and the author Henrik Ibsen. The city was perhaps best known for hosting Europe's oldest jazz festival, at which one of Ole's musical heroes, Bob Dylan, had performed. In the middle of his prolonged absence from the game, Ole lifted his spirits by seeing Dylan in concert in Manchester.

Molde FK were one of the oldest-established clubs in Norway, having been formed in 1911. Interestingly, they had been first called the 'International' because they played against visitors from the cargo and cruise ships that docked there. Their average gate was about 14,000. Ole was only there for a season-and-a-half, but it was a perfect base for him to extend his experience and develop his skills.

In his first season at Molde, Ole was the club's top goal

scorer with 21 goals, raising his own and the club's profile considerably. Molde's owners, entrepreneurs Kjell Inge Rokke and Bjorn Rune Gjelsten, similarly looked to try their luck in the English leagues, when they became involved with Wimbledon FC for a period before the south Londoners crashed and burnt. Molde finished as runners-up to the mighty Rosenborg, the superpower of Norwegian football and a formidable adversary. Molde was managed by Age Hareide who had played in England for Manchester City and Norwich City. Hareide, who also managed the national team, quickly realised the quality of player he had in Ole and used him as the focal striker in a three-pronged attack.

Hareide was quoted as saying of Ole, 'He has such balance, that he could have played in a suit', and his instructions to the team were simple – try and create as many chances as you can for the scoring genius. At the time, Ole played with two other well-known Norwegian strikers, Arild Stavrum and Ole Bjorn Sundgot, the latter having had a spell playing for Aberdeen.

Ole's first taste of European competition came when Molde FK participated in the now defunct European Cup Winners' Cup. They played against Paris St Germain and were not overawed. That initial experience of European action whetted Ole's appetite for regular participation against the cream of Europe.

All the while, Ole's exploits on the pitch were inexorably moving him further and further into the limelight, and into the sights of some very influential movers and shakers in European football, as well as the national team coach. He had scored 13 goals in 19 Norwegian Under-21 games and was rewarded with his first full cap against Jamaica. The match was a friendly played in Kingston and Ole scored on his début on 26 November 1995. Ole's next international goal was at Windsor Park, Belfast, when he scored in Norway's 2-0 win.

It was then that he went into overdrive as his next two goals for Norway were to propel him into the stratosphere. Azerbaijan were the visitors to the Ullevaal Stadion in Oslo and Ole grabbed the headlines with another two goals. In the *Red News* interview, Ole explains what happened in the aftermath of that match: 'They [United] were going to watch Ronnie Johnsen playing for Norway and in that game I scored two goals ... Jim Ryan called the gaffer that night and said we have not got anything to lose. "He is not going to be expensive, he scored two great goals, let us just take a chance, put him in the reserves for a year and see how he develops."

'When they called me, obviously you cannot say "No". Coming here, I had to wait because the clubs were discussing the fee. We went by private plane with the owners of Molde, we came over here and they were speaking to Martin Edwards and while that was happening I just went to see one of the tour guides at the museum. He took me on the trip and said, "So you are a supporter then? You like United?" and I said, "Actually, I am going to sign for them today."

'He gave me his pen, so I signed the contract with his pen. I can not remember his name, but I have met him a couple of times, so he enjoyed that. I had lunch with the gaffer – fish and chips or something – and that was it. They sent me away for two weeks to have a holiday and then come back and start training.

'I am a lad from Kristiansund who played for his local

team until he was 22 and then suddenly was to be part of the history of Manchester United.'

Molde lost their greatest-ever player but, in 1998, a new, state-of-the-art stadium was inaugurated. The funds received from the Solskjaer transfer and other stars like Jo Tessem went towards the cost, together with a massive donation from Messrs Rokke and Gjelsten.

The transfer took a while to complete, during which time Ole's girlfriend Silje Lyngvaer had to switch her studies to Manchester University. Eventually, the deal was done and Ole went off to Manchester to embrace a new career and a new city. Soon, the people of Manchester were to embrace Ole without reservation. For the Norwegian striker, it was the start of one of the most exciting roller-coaster journeys in the history of the game.

# 2

# Ole Gunnar who?

'Manchester United always had great entertainers, great individuals, great stars... players who fitted into the pattern I was always trying to perfect, yet who could produce something from nothing, or who made people gasp or laugh with the sheer enjoyment of seeing something different, something surprising, something creative, something extraordinary, something exciting for its sheer impudence or audacity, something graceful, explosive, beautiful.'

**SIR MATT BUSBY**

Manchester is second only to London in the glamour stakes. In football terms, they have been about equal in terms of success, although no London club has ever won the pre-eminent European club competition – the former European Cup, or its subsequent reincarnation into the Champions League.

Originally, there were two Manchesters – the first was a Roman fort built at Castleford and the second grew around the cathedral which formed the medieval town. At the time of the Norman Conquest in 1066, the region was Anglo-Saxon and known as 'Mamecaster'. It was not until much later, towards the end of the seventeenth century, that it mutated into Manchester. For centuries, the community remained just a small market town with an annual fair, but all that changed when, in the late eighteenth century, almost

75 per cent of the country's cotton industry was based in the region. The reason was simple – the damp climate (for which the area has become well known) was highly conducive to cotton spinning. Thus the town grew and grew into a world-famous industrial city.

Manchester is known to many because of its association with *Coronation Street*, the longest-running soap opera on television, now showing four nights a week. Numerous pop groups have also grown up in the city, including the Hollies and Herman's Hermits in the 1960s; the Fall, 10CC and the Buzzcocks in the 1970s; Joy Division/New Order and the Smiths in the 1980s; the Happy Mondays and Oasis in later years. At Christmas 2006, the most successful boy band of all time, Take That, were staging one of the biggest comebacks in the business with a Number One single and album.

It was football, though, that captured the imagination of most of the population throughout those decades, and it still continues to do so. The Manchester that Ole arrived in, in 1996, was different to the one he still resides in over a decade later. On 16 June 1996, a 3,000lb IRA bomb – the biggest ever on the mainland – exploded in a lorry parked outside Marks & Spencer on Corporation Street. It was a miracle that nobody was killed – it was the eve of Father's Day and the shops were packed – but over 200 people were injured and over 75,000 square feet of retail and office space needed to be reconstructed. Manchester was shaken to the core, but the city fought back and was successfully regenerated, bigger and better than ever, in the subsequent years.

Ole was not the only signing that summer; the other players who joined the club were goalkeeper Raimond van der Gouw from Vitesse Arnhem for £200,000; forward Jordi

Cruyff from Barcelona for half a million; fellow Norwegian international defender Ronny Johnsen joined from Besiktas in Turkey for £1.4 million; and the Czech winger Karel Poborsky was acquired from Slavia Praha. Poborsky had been one of the outstanding successes in Euro '96 and great things were expected from the player nicknamed 'The Express Train'. The main reason for his huge impact was a perfect lob, apparently defying the laws of physics, over the Portuguese goalkeeper in the quarter-final.

The infusion of new blood brought a more competitive edge to Sir Alex's squad; he was only £2.6 million adrift on his dealings following a similarly extensive clear-out. With gate receipts of £9.7 million, there were still some pennies left in the red-and-white coffers. The big transfer story that dominated the headlines that busy summer, though, was the chase for Alan Shearer who had decided to head for the exit door at Blackburn. A mini-Abramovich of his day, the late Jack Walker had brought Shearer to Blackburn in 1992 from Southampton for £3.6 million. Under the Svengali management of Ole's hero, Kenny Dalglish, the team that Jack built won the Premiership in 1994/95, pipping the Red Devils by one point. To add insult to injury, United had been Shearer's biggest suitors at the time and Ferguson was particularly unhappy that they did not land him first time around. The euphoria subsided as the bubble burst at Ewood Park and, within a few years, Walker died and the gravy train was derailed. Shearer wanted to move to a bigger stage and there was none so grand as the Theatre of Dreams. It appeared to be an ideal move but, instead, Shearer opted to bring his killer instinct to Newcastle. In Michael Crick's book, *The Boss*, Ferguson is quoted as saying, 'I had this terrible gut feeling all along it wouldn't happen simply because Jack Walker hates United.'

Shearer eventually became a legend on Tyneside as he took his rightful place among the all-time great Newcastle centre-forwards, alongside the fiery Scot Hughie Gallacher, Malcolm McDonald and Jackie Milburn, whose record of 200 goals for the Magpies Shearer surpassed. Unfortunately for the Geordie superman, despite his undoubted success on the pitch, other than acclaim, Man of the Match awards and some gongs from fellow professionals, Shearer did not win so much as an egg cup at Newcastle, while his Norwegian adversary amassed more medals than General Patton. Shearer played against United in the Charity Shield game at Wembley, but he didn't get a look in as United powered to an easy 4-0 victory.

Ole's first game for United was at Old Trafford on 13 August 1996 in a friendly against the ultra-glamorous Inter Milan. Paul Ince had left United in the summer to join Milan, with part of the complicated transfer deal including home and away fixtures against the Italian side. The purchase of Ince had been funded by the sale of Denis Bergkamp to Arsenal. United lost 1-0 to the Nerazzurri but the flaxen-haired Solskjaer looked impressive.

The Premiership started in anger on 17 August and United travelled to Selhurst Park to play Wimbledon. That match proved to be the making of a new national hero, and offered a defining moment in the history of the premiership – Beckham scored his 'wonder goal' that day, chipping Neill Sullivan from near the halfway line. Ronny Johnsen challenged for the ball, which broke for McClair, who slipped a pass through to Beckham. Seeing Sullivan off his line, Beckham attempted the impossible. Goal of the season, scored in the first match of the season. Surprisingly, it was shunned for the *Match of the Day* award with the honour strangely going to Matt Le Tissier. Becks's gem put United 3-0 up and another legend was born as he offered a tantalising indication of what was ahead. For his sheer talent, looks and style on and off the pitch, the tabloids and magazines would hound him from that day on. Ole had a similar, profligate talent, but was to become a far more low-key, undramatic media darling. For the Norwegian youngster, the football always came first.

Ole let his feet do the talking when he came on as sub against Blackburn Rovers on Sunday, 25 August 1996 and scored the first goal of his Manchester United career. Rovers had taken the lead through Shearer's replacement, Warhurst, but the hyperactive Cruyff smartly equalised. Rovers' classy midfielder Bohinen restored Blackburn's lead with a stunning goal, offering the crowd of over 50,000 a great spectacle. Ole had come on for defender David May and equalised within nine minutes, with virtually his first touch of the ball. The move had been brilliantly engineered by Cantona, ably assisted by Cruyff.

Solskjaer has many great memories at United, but still insists that the one that has given him the most joy was his first goal in United colours. The sight of the exuberant Cantona running to congratulate him is particularly cherished.

Sir Alex told David Meek of the *Manchester Evening News*, 'The Norwegian's first goal sounds the bell that there is another player coming along at Old Trafford who is going to be a real star. He amazes me. My intention that season, as I explained to him when he joined us, was that he should spend this season learning about how we play. Perhaps, I said, he would get a few games in the Coca-Cola Cup, or the odd appearance here and there. "Let's see how you go," I said, but from the first training session he made everyone sit up and take notice. The improvement he makes each week is startling. As they say in football, a player's goals will pick him. This has been an excellent start on top of all the scoring he has been doing in training.'

When a striker joins a new club, it is so important to get a good start and set a benchmark, as opposed to marking time on the bench. The best thing any centre-forward can do is to score early on, which immediately relieves the pressure. The Ukrainian striker Andriy Shevchenko is a perfect example. Since his fantastically expensive £30.8 million transfer from AC Milan to Chelsea a decade after Ole's move to England, Shevchenko struggled to make an impact, scoring a meagre five goals in his first nineteen games. The tabloids were hinting that he was grossly overpriced and that the bespoke predator was in decline as he struggled to adapt to the pace and power of the Premiership. Ole was lucky in one respect – when he arrived at the Theatre of Dreams, he was a complete unknown, and the expectations of colleagues, the fans and, indeed, the gaffer, were nothing compared to those later heaped upon the shoulders of Shevchenko.

Apparently free from the debilitating nerves that inhibited many of his colleagues, Ole's first appearance set the tone for many subsequent appearances. He coolly stepped on the pitch and immediately did what was required of him, plundering a vital goal which saved the game. 'Cometh the hour, cometh the man... ' In Ole's case, this is particularly true.

The first United strip that Ole wore in the heat of battle was the darker red ensemble worn with the large print of the badge. His collar was faded black-and-white with a small red devil button on the neck.

Brian McClair – or 'Choccy' as he is known to all Reds' fans – played in the Blackburn match and wrote in his *Odd Man Out* book, 'The new personnel will take some settling in. Ole Gunnar Solskjaer has not required much time to do that, however. He wants to shoot from everywhere and he has a good eye for goal, fortunately for us in this match.'

A huge Champions League tie beckoned against Scudetto superstars Juventus in Turin, but first there were two away fixtures in the Premier League to contend with. Ole came on as a sub in both of them, a pedestrian 1-1 draw with Derby, in which he replaced Cruyff, and a 4-0 romp at Leeds, in a switch with Poborsky. Ole replaced the same player when he came on in the Stadio delle Alpi against Juventus after 76 minutes. It was Sir Alex's last throw of the dice but came a little too late. United gave a creditable performance against Italian football's 'Old Lady', winners of the Italian League 23 times. They went down to a solitary goal by the talented Croat striker Alen Boksic after 33 minutes.

Marcello Lippi's reigning European Champions deserved their narrow win. Zinedine Zidane controlled the midfield in his best display since his summer move from Bordeaux. Zidane, who had lost weight and gained confidence since his transfer, completely outshone his compatriot Cantona, whom he had replaced in the French team. Juventus played with a fluid 4-3-2-1 line-up.

United were the first English team that Juventus had played in a competitive match since the Heysel disaster in 1985. They opted to play Cantona in the lone striker's role, a tactic still fashionable with Chelsea and Drogba a decade later. For United to progress in the competition beyond the group stage, they had a mountain to climb –Fenerbaçe, the Turkish Champions, and Rapid Vienna were their other opponents.

After United's exploits in Europe, it was back to the Premiership and, at the opposite end of the spectrum, a home fixture against Nottingham Forest. Ole scored his second goal for the club to equalise after Haaland had put Forest ahead. A colleague of Ole's in the Norwegian national team, Haaland was later to become embroiled in one of the most controversial incidents of recent years with Roy Keane. Giggs and Cantona (twice) weighed in with further goals as United ran out comfortable 4-1 winners. No European hangover, then, for Ferguson's men in red.

On that day, some other famous sons of Manchester were also making the news. Oasis created outrage at the MTV awards at New York's Radio City Music Hall, when, during the band's performance of 'Champagne Supernova', Liam Gallagher spat on stage, threw a beer can into the crowd and swore at them. Premiership footballers and rock stars had a lot in common, it seemed.

Sir Alex was introducing Ole sparingly, giving him a run-out of 45 minutes against Aston Villa in the Midlands. The important home game with Rapid Vienna followed on the Wednesday and the United boss wanted to assess the fitness of Andy Cole, who replaced Ole. Cole's future strike partner, Dwight Yorke, was on the opposing side that day. The Tobago-born forward looked a threat as the game fizzled out into a 0-0 bore draw.

Ole scored his first (and that season's only) Champions League goal when he opened the scoring against Rapid Vienna at Old Trafford. It was a vital strike, with the other rising star in the United galaxy, Beckham, sealing the victory with the second. The win stabilised United's bid to qualify from Group C. The wily Vienna coach Ernst Dokupil tried to outwit Sir Alex, but Vienna's European Cup star, Christian Stumpf, only made a fleeting appearance.

Ole's rich vein of goals continued as he struck twice in the 2-0 victory over Tottenham the following Saturday. In the Spurs side that day, the former Nottingham Forest striker Teddy Sheringham, Sol Campbell and Israeli international Ronnie Rosenthal took the field. Ole looked every inch the complete striker as he notched his fifth goal in a handful of appearances. Not until Walker in the Tottenham goal had committed himself, did Ole take his chance, although Brian McClair wrote in his book that Ole had slipped and Walker had missed the ball as a result. Whatever the circumstances surrounding the goal, the figures were stacking up nicely to reinforce Ole's status as one of the Premiership's deadliest strikers. He was proving a real handful for defences and, after the game, Sir Alex told the *Manchester Evening News*, 'That boy is starting to make the hairs on the back of my neck stand up. I don't want to get carried away, but it's difficult to overestimate how good he could become one day.'

Beckham scored the only goal of the game after 23 minutes in the home match against Liverpool. The clash between the two titans going head to head was dubbed 'Red October' by the media. The man from Kristiansund, who had a huge part in the goal, was replaced by Giggs with ten minutes to go. For the first time at Old Trafford, Ole failed to score, but he kept Liverpool's back three of Scales, Matteo and Babb at full stretch. A considerable achievement, in fact, as Ole had been taken off in his previous match for Norway and was carrying a knock.

The young Norwegian was back to his best in Turkey

when United took on Fenerbaçe, with Ole setting up both goals in an exciting 2-0 victory. Cantona's free-kick sent Solskjaer away, who put in Beckham to fire the Reds ahead. The Turks tore into United and only some good goalkeeping by Schmeichel kept them in front. Then Solskjaer's imaginative back-heel found Cruyff, who squared the ball for Cantona to curl a left-foot shot beyond keeper Rustu. Ole's simple and deliberate back-heel was yet another example of his ever-growing repertoire of skills, and his ability to think quickly and improvise on the spur of the moment. The volatile Turks (famous for their 'Welcome to Hell' placards) hurled abuse and stoned the team bus on the way back to the airport, and some were even spotted wearing Leeds shirts to wind United up even more.

Then United's form slumped dramatically as they lost the next four matches, three of them in the Premiership. It was their worst losing streak since April 1992, when Leeds had deprived them of the title. A decade on, a run like that would have almost certainly cost them any chance of winning the League. At Christmas 2006, with United and Chelsea both locked in combat for the title, both sides had only lost twice each all season. Once again, the curse of playing a Premiership game close to a Champions League fixture reared its head, as Newcastle crushed United 5-0 at St James' Park.

Cantona had a poor match; his distribution, the key to his game, was shocking. The previous March, Eric's deft poacher's goal on Tyneside had set United up for the title. It was Sir Alex's heaviest beating as a manager and still is.

Ole, who was substituted by Scholes in the Geordie rout, was given a few days' break and flew back to Norway. There he was honoured as the Norwegian Player of the

Year, with the award presented by Sir Alex Ferguson who flew over specially to honour his golden boy and to offer his own assessment of Ole's value to the team.

Then there was another savage beating in the Premiership as Southampton crushed United 6-3. Roy Keane, sporting a goatee beard á la George Michael, was sent off after 20 minutes for a second bookable offence and the roof finally fell in as Ostenstad hit a hat-trick on a horrendous afternoon for United.

The south coast was an unhappy hunting ground for United because the previous season they had lost 3-1. It was memorable because it was after that game that Sir Alex blamed their infamous grey kit on the defeat. At half-time, he ordered that they change to the blue-and-white striped outfit, because he believed that the grey shirts were too hard to pick out. That colour combination was never worn again and it was estimated that the club lost in excess of £200,000 because of it. The blue-and-white shirt incorporated the name of every past and present United player and, by a strange quirk of fate, it was worn again in the 6-3 massacre as, due to a mix-up, the standard white/black away kit clashed with the Saints' colours. The joke among the United fans was that United's blue-and-white striped kit merged with hundreds of Tesco carrier bags being brandished by Saints fans, rendering the Old Trafford side invisible.

Ole spoke to the *Red News* about the aftermath of the two bad defeats, observing, 'I remember the day after, we had a meeting... Just conceded eleven goals in two games. That was one of the things with the gaffer – there is never a panic button. He has been through everything before, so it settled us down. "Do not panic... we have lost two games but it is just six points."'

United lost their proud unbeaten home record in Europe when they lost 1-0 to the unfancied Fenerbaçe on 30 October. A late breakaway goal from Bolic, which took a deflection off David May, was enough to smash the record which had stood for 40 years. A few minutes earlier, Solskjaer had been sent on for Cruyff but that night he could do nothing to save the game. Jay Jay Okocha played up front for Fenerbaçe and was a constant threat to United with his highly mobile, muscular style of play. Okocha was later to grace the Premiership playing at Bolton for Sam Allardyce. The technical levels of the Turkish defenders seemed very high and they were well organised, with United giving away possession far too often.

The pressure mounted on United and Ferguson in particular, who was celebrating ten years in charge. Sir Alex told the *Mail on Sunday*, 'Fourteen dismal days in ten fantastic years. So much for my sense of timing!'

Having won the Double the previous season, the knives were out for the young side. Ruud Gullit's Chelsea added to Sir Alex's woes when they won 2-1 at Old Trafford a few days later, the first Premiership team to win there in 36 games, only a mere two results short of the club record. It was a poignant time for the west London team as their young vice-chairman, Matthew Harding, had been tragically killed in a helicopter accident a few days before. If Harding had lived, the history of Chelsea might have been significantly different, with Mr Abramovich's deep pockets being attracted elsewhere.

The line-up which finished the Fenerbaçe game started the Chelsea match with Solskjaer and Scholes up front with Cantona in his preferred central role. Schmeichel was culpable for both goals, fumbling Duberry's downward header from a Wise corner for the first. Then Schmeichel hesitated as Gianluca Vialli's run beat the offside trap and presented him with a simple controlled strike past the stranded goalkeeper. Solskjaer was pressed hard by wing-back Dan Petrescu and could make little progress against the Chelsea defence, modelled in those days on Arrigo Sacchi's Milan rearguard. Ole's crisp pass to Poborsky was volleyed in for a late consolation.

The corner was turned with a crucial, solitary-goal victory over Arsenal at Old Trafford. Ole played in a three-pronged attack alongside Giggs and Poborsky, with Cantona lying deep. The goal was a messy affair, with Nicky Butt's shot deflecting in off Nigel Winterburn. The only incident of real note in the match was the first-half contretemps between Schmeichel and Arsenal striker Ian Wright. A complaint was made to the FA that the Danish goalkeeper had racially abused Wright after he had been booked for a challenge on him. Schmeichel vigorously denied the allegation and the bad feeling between them continued over the years. The two would later work together as pundits on BBC *Match of the Day*.

With their 40-year record in tatters, United lost their second home tie in Europe in succession going down 1-0 to Juventus in the return-leg meltdown. It was a typical Old Trafford European night of huge passion, emotion and noise played out in front of 53,529 expectant fans. The Italians scored through a Del Piero penalty after he had been brought down by Nicky Butt just inside the penalty area. United were reeling, having had to re-organise their system after just 12 minutes when Phil Neville limped off with a hamstring injury. Of particular concern to Ferguson that night was the yo-yoing form of Eric Cantona, particularly in the Champions League. Of the forwards, Ole was the pick of the bunch, and all but equalised with a great diving header that just failed to beat Angelo Peruzzi.

The last time Juventus had played at Old Trafford they had almost won, with only an equaliser by the late Alan Davies saving the game. Lippi was delighted that his rebuilt side were the first Italian club to win at the Theatre of Dreams, and in the second half they had to withstand almost constant pressure from the home side; the Italians rode their luck, but also played textbook Italian defensive football.

Sir Alex was upset at losing but was pleased to have been part of such an epic match. He told the *Football Italia* magazine, 'Juventus were fantastic and proved why they are European Champions. Their work ethic was superb, every player earns his money, they have experience and threats in all the right places. It was no disgrace to lose to them.'

Ole did not play in the next game at Middlesbrough which ended in a 2-2 draw. A disputed 'Boro penalty cost United the points, the spot kick being awarded by Alan Wilkie, the referee who had sent Cantona off at Selhurst Park on the night of the extraordinary kung-fu kick.

The Norwegian crowd-pleaser was back on the score sheet against Martin O'Neill's Leicester when he fired in the second goal in a 3-1 victory, having come on as a substitute for Jordi Cruyff. American keeper Kasey Keller defied United for 75 minutes until Nicky Butt breached the defence. Ole looked particularly sharp, perhaps as a result of Sir Alex having increased the time in training devoted to shooting practice. It was a hard-fought result because, a few nights earlier, United's team of youngsters and squad players had been dumped out of the Coca Cola Cup by the same team – Leicester City. Martin O'Neill had made a good start to his managerial career and, at the end of the season, his young side won the competition by beating Middlesbrough.

The win over Leicester heartened United for their trip to the Ernst Happel Stadium in Vienna for their return with Rapid. The pre-match press conference was attended by a smart-looking Ole who made a fine job of dealing with the media in one of his first appearances in front of their massed ranks. As always, the handsome striker conducted himself with great humility, understated humour and dignity, the perfect ambassador for his new club. It turned out to be a good trip for the British team as they cruised into the quarter-finals with an effortless 2-0 victory. Giggs scored the first from Cantona's pass early on to settle their nerves and quieten the crowd. Twenty minutes from time, the influential Frenchman scored the second from a chance engineered by Beckham. Only Ivanov kept Rapid afloat with a series of brilliant interceptions.

The increasingly dazzling Solskjaer put in a display as assured as his performance earlier in front of the cameras. Juventus went on to beat a leaden Fenerbaçe 1-0, guaranteeing United's qualification from Group C with nine points, despite losing three matches in the group.

Then United travelled down to Upton Park to take on West Ham at a ground where they had not lost since 1992. Ole led the line with Cantona given a roving role. Beckham put them ahead with a fine goal but faded; Ole put them two up with a neat goal from a superb pass from Cantona, briefly displaying his golden touch. They appeared to be cruising to an easy three points but, ten minutes from time, hard man Julian Dicks blasted the Hammers back into the game when he converted a penalty which almost took Schmeichel's head off. It set up a grandstand finish and, after a sustained bombardment of Schmeichel's goal, the home side grabbed a point when the substitute Romanian Florin Radiciou equalised after a rare mistake by Ronnie Johnsen.

The Reds always found a hostile atmosphere awaiting them in the East End and the West Ham side – like many who played Manchester United – always seemed to raise their game when roared on by their fanatical supporters. United had lost the 1994/95 Premiership title to Shearer's Blackburn side when they failed to win at Upton Park on the last day of the season. On this occasion, as their luxury coach headed back to Manchester, it stopped by some lights close to a pub frequented by fans in claret-and-blue. When the lights changed and the coach sped off into the mild December night, a hail of bottles smashed against the side of the bus. It was like being back in Turkey.

The next away game was to a nondescript Sheffield Wednesday which ended in United's third successive away draw in the Premiership. It was a poor match and Ole was given no space by a rugged Wednesday defence well marshalled by Des Walker. Scholes equalised for United in the second half, but Sir Alex was growing increasingly displeased with the erratic form of his defence. In the first 17 Premiership matches, they had already conceded 25 goals; Chelsea in 2004/05 conceded just 15 league goals, the lowest ever by a team in the top flight, and they also managed to keep a record 25 clean sheets.

The United front line, though, posed few problems for Sir Alex and, four days before Christmas 1997, the Reds trounced Peter Reid's Sunderland 5-0 at Old Trafford. Ole scored his second brace of the season with Cantona also scoring twice, one of them a penalty.

## OLE GUNNAR WHO?

Ole grabbed the vital first goal after 35 minutes to open the floodgates. Once again, the Norwegian led by example for that opening goal. Sir Alex Ferguson thought that his young protégé would have to learn his trade gradually in England, and was prepared to allow him some time to adjust to the demands of the English game. By Christmas, though, Ole had already done enough to prove to the Old Trafford faithful that he was already the complete striker.

If any more proof were needed, Ole scored again away to Nottingham Forest in another match that was little more than shooting practice for United. Ole had spent his first Christmas Day in Manchester having a quiet meal with his girlfriend. In the evening, the team assembled at a hotel in Nottingham in readiness for the Boxing Day clash at the City Ground.

Beckham put United ahead with another fine goal and Butt doubled their lead with a well-taken strike. Ole claimed a simple third goal on what was to prove to be a happy hunting ground for him. The chance was set up by Cantona who had driven a shot against the bar after taking a fine ball from Beckham. Always looking for a half chance, Ole pounced for a Christmas present of a goal.

Ten years earlier, Ferguson had told the *News of the World* that any player he signed for United 'must possess a special kind of presence, arrogance and stature.' Those qualities were certainly applicable to Cantona, and the young Ole Gunnar Solskjaer, perhaps substituting arrogance for extreme self-confidence, had the other two qualities in spades. The rest of the teams in the Premiership were certainly taking note of his dynamic impact. Ferguson was telling everyone in the media who would listen that Ole had been a revelation and could only improve. Before the

Sunderland game, United had been at the generous odds of 7-1 to retain their Premiership title, but now they were slashed to 3-1.

Cantona scored a penalty to beat his old team Leeds in the next home game, to gain maximum points over the holiday period. Ole was replaced by Andy Cole, who was making a comeback after pneumonia and then breaking his leg in a reserve match. This had occurred in a clash with Neil Ruddock, the former Millwall and Liverpool stormtrooper and future *I'm a Celebrity, Get Me Out of Here* contestant. Ole had a tough game opposite former Chelsea defender and hardman Aussie Tony Dorigo.

Another Australian player, goalkeeper Mark Bosnich, gave a master class in the art of goalkeeping when he starred for Aston Villa as they prised a point away from United at Old Trafford in their next game. Ole had a superb drive magnificently saved by Bosnich in the first half, and it turned out to be the Midland club's second 0-0 draw of the season against United. A wide-eyed Bosnich got into the Australian Junior team at 12 years old where he was spotted by United and subsequently played for the youth team. He then made his début against Wimbledon in April 1990 as a non-contract player. Due to work permit problems, he reluctantly returned to Australia and, shortly afterwards, he married an English girl and returned to England to sign for Aston Villa rather than United, much to Ferguson's chagrin.

Next came a couple of games against Tottenham, the first being at home in the FA Cup then away in the Premiership. In the Cup match, Andy Cole started and was subsequently replaced by Ole. United comfortably won 2-0, with goals from the young guns Scholes and Beckham.

Ole scored the first goal in the next match at White Hart

Lane. A brilliant, high-speed passing move involving Scholes, Neville, Keane and Cantona provided Ole with the opportunity. It was his third Premiership goal of the season against the north London side who were already coveting the Norwegian predator. Spurs chairman Alan Sugar had at that time been highly critical of some of the foreign imports who had joined the Premiership, but Ole was no glory-seeker simply out to make a quick few quid and disappear back home.

Tottenham equalised through Allen after a rare mistake by Roy Keane, but David Beckham, an increasingly influential presence in the team, won the points with one of his ferocious, long-range net-busters.

Around that time, Kevin Keegan resigned from Newcastle. The previous season, United had beaten them to the title by four points. Newcastle had, at one stage, held an 11-point advantage, but Ferguson's side had relentlessly eroded the lead. That season, Keegan succumbed to the media pressure and his detractors as Newcastle battled to keep pace with the leaders.

Ole scored again in the second half of the next fixture at Highfield Road against Coventry in a 2-0 victory. 23,083 fans watched him score the second goal in a victory that enhanced their title hopes. The goal was a masterpiece of relaxed precision, the true mark of a born goalscorer.

Wimbledon then visited Old Trafford in the Fourth Round of the FA Cup. The media were of the opinion that United had no real interest in the competition, their objectives being to retain the title and attempting to win the Champions League. To go for the Treble looked beyond the resources of even the mighty Reds; in his diary for that season, Sir Alex admitted it would be almost impossible.

Their starting line-up included the youngster Casper and the veteran Brian McClair. Wimbledon put up stubborn resistance and, with 15 minutes left, Ferguson threw on his strikers Cole and Ole in an attempt to break the deadlock. In the last minute, Scholes headed home Cantona's cross but, in injury time, Robbie Earle, now yet another TV pundit, plundered an equaliser.

For the third time that season, United then found themselves playing in their next Premiership fixture the same team that they had just faced in a Cup game. Ole was probably United's best player, according to Sir Alex Ferguson, though he did not score in the 2-1 victory. In a thrilling game, the striker could have scored a first-half hat-trick, hitting the bar twice. From the second of these strikes, Andy Cole scored the winner from the rebound. Cole's spatial awareness instinct was similar to that of Ole, in that the excellent positions he took up created many openings for goals.

The win put United back at the top of the Premiership for the first time since the opening few weeks of the season. Another 2-1 home victory over Southampton strengthened their position. Selhurst Park was the next venue where United were involved in their replay with Wimbledon. Ferguson's team dominated the tie and should have gone through, but slid out of the Cup to a goal from Wimbledon's Gayle. It was a clear indication of where Sir Alex's priorities lay for that season.

With a free weekend because of the Internationals, Ole went to Cyprus to celebrate the 10th Anniversary of the United Supporters' club. Despite having only been at the club for a few months, he was turning out to be a wonderful ambassador. His clean-cut image, affable manner and wry humour was a PR consultant's dream.

## OLE GUNNAR WHO?

Then it was back to London for two vital fixtures against Arsenal and Chelsea. The Highbury game was played on a Wednesday night and United came out worthy 2-1 winners. Ole started up front with Cole and the pairing dovetailed brilliantly, both scoring. Ole claimed the first with a neat finish; Cole then put United two up, before Bergkamp pulled one back. The fall-out from the Schmeichel–Wright clash continued, with the Arsenal striker's allegations adding an extra tension to the already volatile atmosphere.

Chelsea were held 1-1 at Stamford Bridge three days later. Zola gave Chelsea an early lead but Beckham equalised with a great volley, and then Ole was denied a goal by Hitchcock's smart save. United did well to come away from London with four points out of six against the capital's two strongest teams.

A Champions League quarter-final loomed against Porto, managed at that time by Antonio Oliveira. What José Mourinho would have made of Porto's performance at Old Trafford would have been interesting, as the Portuguese side were blown away 4-0. It was a scintillating display by United which was beyond even Ferguson's highest expectations, as the Portuguese side were unbeaten in their previous Champions League matches that season. Ole did not score in the game, the goals going to May, Cantona, Giggs and Cole. It was a marvellous team performance against one of the sides fancied to win the tournament. The basis of Porto's previous success had been their formidable defence, but it crumpled under the sustained pressure of the red tide that was simply too powerful for them. Goalkeeper Hilario joined Chelsea ten years later when Petr Cech was injured, but that night he had no chance with any of the goals.

The result hammered out a warning to the rest of Europe that United had a genuine chance of winning the Champions League. It was probably the best result Sir Alex Ferguson had secured so far in Europe with United.

Shuffling his cards, Ferguson put Ole on the bench for United's next game away to Sunderland, along with his strike partners against Porto – Cole and Giggs. They had run themselves into the ground and Ferguson wisely rested them. Once again, though, the post-Europe hangover struck and United went down 2-1 to the eventually relegated Wearsiders. It was a poor performance, with United only managing to score through an own-goal. Even the most ardent United fan would have agreed that it was a dire performance.

The Reds quickly bounced back with an easy 2-0 victory over Sheffield Wednesday. Ole was replaced by Scholes who had a brief run out following a cartilage operation, which also involved removing a cyst.

The same substitution was made in the return match with Porto, Scholes coming on for Ole. The game ended 0-0 in the Estadio das Antas; after a nervous opening spell, United settled to put in a controlled performance. Cushioned by a four-goal lead, they cruised into the semi-finals of the Champions League. There was no celebrating for the team on the way home, though. They had partied rather hard after the 4-0 result over Porto and paid the price with their lacklustre display at Sunderland. Now, a difficult game at Goodison Park awaited them in a couple of days. The pugnacious, precocious Rooney was yet to explode on the scene, but in Duncan Ferguson they had a striker of awesome power and intelligence.

Ole gave United the lead at Everton when he scored on 38

minutes from a breakaway. Nothing looked on for him, but he lashed in a great shot to beat Everton keeper Gerrard. Cantona made it 2-0 from another breakaway to set the seal on a solid victory.

Before the first game against Borussia Dortmund in the semi-finals, United had a home game against Derby. They went down 3-2 in a shock defeat, but it turned out to be their fifth and last loss in the Premiership that year. Ole was sent on by Sir Alex with United trailing by two goals. He had an immediate effect and a superb pass set up Eric Cantona to reduce the arrears. Sturridge put Derby 3-1 up with a soft goal, and Ole cut the deficit again with United's second. United played the remainder of the game in or around the Derby box but could not force the equaliser.

The result was not a good omen for the trip to Germany. Things became worse for United when Schmeichel suffered a back injury and missed the game. Dortmund had built a reputation as being a tough side to break down, and were superbly coached by Ottmar Hitzfeld. United had their chances, though, with Nicky Butt hitting a post, and Beckham firing in a great shot which beat their goalkeeper Klos but a defender cleared off the line. An under-energised Cantona also missed a good chance and it looked likely that United would be returning to Old Trafford with a pleasing 0-0.

Roy Keane, in his autobiography, describes what happened next. 'Fourteen minutes from the end, Eric jumps out of a tackle in midfield. His challenger, Tretschok, breaks forward and shoots... the ball takes a deflection off Gary Pallister's foot. Back of the net. Perhaps that's the moment Eric's future was decided.'

Van der Gouw could not be blamed for the goal. In the

first 20 minutes, he collided with Pallister and was groggy for the rest of the half. Ole found his chances limited and, once again, Cole came on to replace him. The defeat was a setback, but Sir Alex was of the view that the Dortmund lead could be overturned in the second leg.

It was then back to business in the Premiership, with Blackburn at Ewood Park. Beckham, who had a disappointing match in Dortmund, was rested and Ferguson opted for Ole and Cole up front. Blackburn stopper Hendry had a hernia problem and Sir Alex wanted to put him under severe pressure. Cantona missed an early penalty but Cole stole the show, scoring the first and laying on goals for Scholes and the enigmatic Frenchman.

Then it was off to Anfield for the game that could virtually clinch United the title. United won 3-1, with Gary Pallister scoring twice from set pieces, in a match that did not feature Ole. The result put them five points in front of both Liverpool and Arsenal with a game in hand on both. The Keegan-less Newcastle were nine points adrift. United now needed just to hold their nerve and pick up points from their last four games to bring the title back to Old Trafford.

The great win on Merseyside should have been the springboard for a glorious victory against Dortmund. United opted for three up front again – Cole, Ole and Cantona – whereupon the critics attacked Ferguson, accusing him of being too reckless. No doubt about it, it turned out to be a calculated gamble. Keane missed the game because of a yellow card he picked up in Germany, and Giggs was another absentee with a stomach problem.

Dortmund scored an early goal that killed off United's hopes of an appearance in the final. Lars Ricken gleefully scored with a soft shot that deflected off Pallister's toes –

he'd had little luck against Dortmund either in Germany or at home. Schmeichel could only watch in horror as the ball skewed off Pallister and flew into the net. United now needed three goals to progress but, despite a sustained effort, the score remained the same. At half-time, Ferguson focused his hair-dryer tirade at the hapless Schmeichel for his error, but subsequently apologised when it became apparent that the shot had been deflected.

The Germans defended superbly in the second half with the marvellous Jürgen Kohler at the heart of everything. The Scot, Paul Lambert, anchored the midfield and Ole was unable to create an opening. It was a hugely disappointing result as United were convinced they had the firepower to overcome Borussia Dortmund, who were clearly a team firing on all cylinders that year. Having overcome the English Champions-elect, they went on to overwhelm Zidane's Juventus 3-1 in the final in one of the biggest upsets in the history of the tournament.

There were four games left in the Premiership, to be played over a period of eight days, in good old English football tradition! The first was a tricky away trip to play Leicester at Filbert Street. United had to get something out of the game to shake off the after-effects of their European disappointment. Sir Alex's fear was of a catastrophic collapse that may leave them without a trophy.

On Saturday, 3 May, the weather was unusually warm, reaching nearly 30°C. Ole had a brilliant game, scoring twice from Andy Cole assists to grab an invaluable point after his lacklustre side had trailed 2-0 to Leicester's early strikes. The result left them needing three points from their last three games, all at home.

Ole saved United again in the next game against relegated

Middlesbrough, which ended 3-3. The Norwegian scored the third goal, United again having trailed by two goals at one stage. 'Boro, over the years, had become a bit of a bogey team for the Reds. The elegant young Brazilian, Juninho, gave 'Boro an early lead before Roy Keane belted in the equaliser. Juninho inspired them with a terrific performance to set up further goals for Emerson and Hignett, with Gary Neville hauling United back into the game with their second goal. Ole's equaliser effectively won United the title because, the next night, West Ham drew with Newcastle and Wimbledon beat Liverpool.

The penultimate game for the Reds was a home tie against Newcastle. Ole came on as sub against the Geordies, but the game fizzled out into a 0-0 draw. The last match of the season was a 2-0 win over West Ham, whose side included Rio Ferdinand and the former Palace/Charlton manager Ian Dowie up front.

There was a carnival atmosphere at Old Trafford throughout the game and Scholes set up the victory with the first goal. Ole did not get a chance to add to his 18 Premier League goals in 25 games, but he was still top goalscorer, finishing well ahead of Cole and Cantona.

In his autobiography, Peter Schmeichel was quick to praise Ole. 'He didn't hesitate to accept the challenge. He had a great season and finished convincingly as our top scorer.' Schmeichel, apparently, was keen to go up front for United but the chance never presented itself in the game. Schmeichel has already scored a goal against Rotor Vologrod in September 1995, when he'd headed home a corner to save the game, but it was Alex Stepney, the former Chelsea keeper, who starred in the 1968 European Cup Final, who was the first Reds goalkeeper to get on to the score sheet, converting a penalty against Leicester City in a September 1973 home defeat. The fans were desperate to see their Danish hero gambolling around in the West Ham penalty area, but nobody in the 55,249 crowd that afternoon would have guessed that the next time Schmeichel went rampaging in an opponent's six-yard box just how dramatic the outcome would be.

Scholes was replaced by Cruyff, who scored the second goal. Once the final whistle had been blown, Ole was awarded his first winner's medal. There is a great picture of the newly-crowned Champions with the young Norwegian, scarf draped around his neck, proudly looking at his medal; meanwhile, David May sprayed his team-mates with champagne in best Formula One fashion.

The days of wine and roses never last long. Keane said the elation lasted until they got back into the dressing room. The euphoric mood was quickly dispelled when the news broke that Eric Cantona was to quit the game. It shook the football world and dominated the sporting headlines for days to come. In 185 appearances for United, he scored 82 goals as they won four titles and two FA Cups. To lose a player of that quality was a huge blow to Sir Alex Ferguson's five-year plan to reign supreme over the Premier League and emerge triumphant in the Champions League. After four-and-a-half years at the Theatre of Dreams, the double-winning Footballer of the Year quit for a variety of reasons... one of them being that he wanted to become an actor.

To this day, Cantona has not been fully replaced by United. Despite the brilliance of Ronaldo and the potential of Rooney, no player has had the impact on the club that Eric had. Only Ole and Giggs are the last men standing from that era. Ole only played for one season with Cantona, but had the partnership continued, who knows how many goals would have been scored and how it would have developed.

*Red News* once asked Ole who had been his biggest influence from all the stars he had played with at United. He said, 'It is different from different parts of my career, but obviously Eric Cantona. In my first season, he was fantastic, I learnt a lot from him. I benefited from him maybe more as a player than from anyone else.'

At the peak of his United reign, there were 25 different types of Cantona t-shirts, and *Eric the King* was the biggest-selling player's video in history. In *Gladiator*, Oliver Reed tells Russell Crowe that he was the most successful gladiator of his era not because he was the greatest but 'because he was the one that the crowd loved the best'. To the fans who idolised Cantona, he was the best; he was also the most outstanding player of his generation. The fulcrum of the side, Cantona guided United to four titles in the five seasons he played at Old Trafford. On the single occasion that they failed to win the league (losing the title to Jack Walker's Blackburn), Eric had to serve an eight-month ban following his kung-fu kick on a fan at Crystal Palace. Throughout the 1996/97 season, his form had visibly dipped and perhaps he thought that his powers were on the wane. A few days away from his 31st birthday, Cantona possibly sensed that his advancing years in football terms would deprive him of the rebel streak that gave him his unique spark.

The philosopher Eric was the complete opposite of ice-man Ole. Cantona was totally at the mercy of his impulsive, hot-blooded nature, while Ole was always in control of his emotions in even the most stressful of situations. Yet if any

## OLE GUNNAR WHO?

United player in the subsequent decade has earned a similar level of respect from the fans, then surely it is Ole.

Two of the reasons Cantona gave for leaving were that the United board were unadventurous in not purchasing world-class stars and that he did not like being a pawn in the global merchandising operation. Edward Freedman, then in charge of marketing at the club, had aggressively used Cantona's image and persona in a manner unlike any previous footballer. Everything from sweat shirts to pens, from calendars to ties, was stamped with the great man's name or face, and sold. Freedman's gift was that he saw the commercial potential in his global icon, even right from the time of his transfer from Leeds.

In the wake of the Frenchman's highly emotional exit, Ferguson's immediate problem was to find a replacement of similar calibre. In June 1997, he turned to Teddy Sheringham, then at Tottenham, whom he purchased for a cool £3.5 million. The player was 31 – slightly older than Cantona – and many eyebrows were raised at the time among United fans. If the imaginative Sheringham had done one thing in his career, though, it was to make a mockery of the calendar. Ten years on, Teddy was still causing Premiership defences a great deal of trouble for West Ham.

In every great partnership, there tends to be the one who takes the glory and the one who makes the glory possible. Sheringham was Morecombe to Ole's Wise, or, if you prefer, Teddy was McCartney to Ole's Lennon.

It would be fair to say that, despite some hugely important contributions, Sheringham never adequately filled the void left by Cantona's retirement. But then, which player could? Up until then, Teddy's silverware consisted of winning the Full Members' Cup with

Nottingham Forest in 1992 and, until his transfer to Old Trafford, the high spot of his career had been a glorious Euro '96. Chosen by his ex-Spurs boss Terry Venables, the ex-Millwall striker had scored twice in the 4-1 mauling of Holland. The abiding memory of that beautiful evening was the third goal he laid on for Alan Shearer with a delightful side-foot pass. It encapsulated Sheringham's supreme attributes – the ability to spot an opportunity, and an awareness of space. That is what impressed Sir Alex most and led to his eventual acquisition.

In his autobiography, Sheringham described United as 'a world club, a club for the world'. And, as if to reinforce his status as a member of that exclusive club, Sheringham made a dramatic appearance on his first day's training when he turned up in a red Ferrari, dressed head to toe in designer threads, looking like he had stepped off the set of *Miami Vice*.

There was a tension between him and Keane dating back to their time together at Forest. In his autobiography, Keane made the valid point that, while they did not get on personally, it never affected their business arrangement, Sheringham's being to make and score goals. Ole had no personality clashes to deal with – he just kept his own counsel and did what he did best, hitting the back of the net.

Sheringham's début for United was in the 1997/98 Charity Shield against Chelsea, who had won the FA Cup the previous season by beating Bryan Robson's Middlesbrough 2-0 at Wembley. Teddy endeared himself to the fans with a flare-up in the match against the combative Dennis Wise. One memorable image from that match – that football fans up and down the country secretly enjoyed – was of Sheringham grabbing the diminutive Wise by the throat after a midfield clash.

## OLE GUNNAR WHO?

United won the Charity Shield – soon to become the Community Shield – for the last time in the 20th century after a penalty shoot-out. Mark Hughes, the ex-United gladiator, put Chelsea ahead, but Ronny Johnsen equalised and that was how it stayed after 90 minutes. Roy Keane, Paul Scholes, Dennis Irwin and Nicky Butt all scored from the spot for the Champions, which was enough. The brilliant Schmeichel psyched out Roberto Di Matteo and Frank Sinclair, who fluffed their spot-kicks. In retrospect, it's strange to consider that, despite a highly successful career in front of goal for United, Ole has never scored from the spot for the Reds in a first-team game. Extraordinary, when you take into account the coolness and accuracy he brings to the business of converting chances into goals.

After the success of the Charity Shield, the serious business of the 1997/98 Premiership season began. In his first season, Ole had scored 18 goals, making a significant contribution to his new club's retention of the Premier League title. In doing so, Ole had begun to carve a name for himself in the hearts of the Old Trafford faithful and, more importantly, in the mind of Sir Alex Ferguson as he looked to the various domestic and European campaigns facing his team the following season. If Ole could just continue in his rich vein of form, then he'd certainly feature as a crucial element in Sir Alex's supreme red machine.

# 3

# Salford Lads Club

'Ole sat on the bench more often than not...
he never complained and, when called upon to do the
business, obliged more often than not. In a team game –
which for all the hype about individuals, soccer is, and will
always be – a professional like Ole is priceless.'

**ROY KEANE**

Salford Lads Club is situated at the end of Coronation Street (there is such a place), a Number 33 bus ride from Piccadilly Gardens. The area was the backdrop for the classic 1987 video 'Stop Me If You Think You've Heard This One Before' by The Smiths, featuring the legendary Mancunian bard Morrissey. The group posed together outside the club for the inside sleeve of their seminal *The Queen is Dead* album in 1985, and one of the club's former members was Graham Nash, a founder member of the Hollies and, later, of the supergroup Crosby, Stills, Nash and Young. The Salford Lads Club is still going strong today, and offers girls and boys the chance to enjoy sporting or charitable activities, and pursue excellence in a safe and secure environment.

## BABY-FACED ASSASSIN

Having had a dream start to his Manchester United career, that continual pursuit of excellence was very much on the young Ole's mind as the 1997/98 season began. To put it another way, the difficult 'second album syndrome' is a music biz cliché that relates to a new artist who has experienced some early success. When the first wave of initial triumph has subsided and the artist or band has to follow it up, then the difficulties can often arise. The same is true for football – when a young player has made an impact in his first season, then he finds it increasingly difficult to maintain that level of consistency and improvement. Ole was there for the long haul, and was determined that his initial success would turn out to be a great deal more than just a flash in the pan. By the end of the 2006/07 season, he would have completed his 11th campaign at Old Trafford and, at a cost of just over £130,000 a season, it would prove to be a fantastic return on his £1.5 million fee.

However, that was all to come – the 1997/98 season would prove to be very challenging to both him and the club. The spine of the team he was part of could almost have come directly from the Salford Lads Club as well, because it included many youngsters from the class of '92 – David Beckham, Paul Scholes, the Nevilles and Nicky Butt. Other wannabes at that time were Pilkington, Clegg and Curtis. Injuries, though, disrupted the season and United let a 12-point lead slip to the eventual champions Arsenal. It was only the second time since 1988/89, when they finished a disappointing 11th in the league, that the Reds had failed to capture any silverware. It was a season of promise, though, in many respects and, at one stage, the unprecedented Treble looked within their grasp... then everything fell apart.

Ole's first game of the season came in an exciting 2-2 home draw with Chelsea at Old Trafford at the end of September. The ever-sharp Norwegian scored a late, crucial equaliser after Mark Hughes's initial strike and then a scrappy own goal had given Ruud Gullit's side the advantage. Scholes scored United's first in a bad-tempered match. At half-time, the handbags and fists flew in a tunnel brawl, and then Keane was booked in the second half. It was a warm, late summer's evening and the pulsating game was savoured by the 55,163 crowd.

The goal Ole scored that night figured in his personal choice of top five goals in the *Manchester United Annual 2007*. He remembered, 'Beckham sent a cross-field pass over from the right to where I was stood on the edge of the box. I took one touch to the right and then curled the ball into the far top corner. It was something I'd been practising in training so it was a great feeling to see it fly in.'

Teddy Sheringham described it as a 'wonder goal' in his autobiography. Rather prophetically he also wrote, 'Ole is always likely to do this.'

Ole was a first choice again for the trip to Leeds where he played alongside Sheringham as they went down by a solitary goal scored by David Wetherall. The striking partnership looked a bit lightweight that day as the Champions crashed to their first defeat of the season. It was a costly afternoon, though, because they lost the services of Keane for the rest of the season. The new United captain had been involved in a running feud with Alfie Haaland all afternoon. The Leeds manager, David O'Leary, had detailed the Norwegian to man-mark Keane for the entire game to try and nullify the influence of the Irishman. In the closing minutes, Roy Keane lunged towards Haaland but his studs caught in the turf and his cruciate ligament snapped.

Keane told the media that he could actually hear the ligament tear as he went down. It was a terrible blow to both player and club. Paul Gascoigne, arguably the finest talent produced in the British Isles since George Best, had never been the same player after he sustained a similar injury against Keane's old side Nottingham Forest in the FA Cup Final. Keane did not return for the rest of the season, making only nine appearances; his loss, like that of Cantona's to the side, was so significant that United's hopes for the season were almost dashed there and then.

Ole was also in the opening line-up for the visit to Old Trafford of the newly promoted Barnsley side. United put them to the sword 7-0 but, strangely enough, Ole did not figure among the scorers. Cole plundered a hat-trick, Giggs (plagued by hamstring problems all season) chipped in with two, Scholes scored one of his more straightforward goals and Poborsky, shortly to join Benfica after failing to establish himself, scored his last goal for the club. It was the club's biggest win since Cole had scored five times against Ipswich in the 9-0 victory four years earlier.

Teddy Sheringham was named as a substitute that day, which displeased him. When he broached the matter with Sir Alex, he was told that the gaffer wanted to play Ole and Cole up front as they needed match practice together.

Ron Wallwork was also named as a sub that day; he had been voted Best Young Player and was expected to make the same impact as his contemporaries, Beckham and Scholes. Possessed of a talent that screamed prodigy, fame somehow eluded him and he played just a handful of senior games. Loaned to Royal Antwerp, he was banned for life after an alleged attack on a referee. A Belgian Court later reduced the sentence to a three-year suspension of which two were probationary. In December 2006, he was stabbed seven times in the Sugar Lounge in Manchester.

Ole's modest lifestyle, free from controversy and excess, was the bedrock on which he built his long and successful career. The temptations open to a young man with money in his pocket in a city like Manchester are manifold, and some – George Best being a prime example – were not strong enough to resist those temptations.

United were at home again the following week against Sheffield Wednesday and the goalfest continued as they steamrollered the Yorkshire club, winning 6-1. The Sheringham–Solskjaer partnership looked a well-oiled outfit. The deadly duo seemed to have built up an innate understanding of the other's game and thinking, and complemented each other accordingly. Both scored twice, and their fellow strike partner Cole scored a fifth.

Suddenly, United couldn't stop scoring, and Sheringham scored twice more in the following match at Highbury. Unfortunately for United, Arsenal scored three times and United lost valuable points and a psychological advantage to the only team to threaten their supremacy in the 1990s. Teddy was in trouble for kissing his badge and was accused of inciting the Arsenal fans.

Sir Alex's young side were made of stern stuff, though, and their response was to bounce back in impressive style by winning their next six Premiership games. Wimbledon were thrashed 2-5 at Selhurst Park and then Blackburn were crushed 4-0 at Old Trafford. Ole had a field day, scoring two goals. His sniping runs caused panic all afternoon and the shell-shocked Rovers defence imploded, adding two own-goals. Sir Alex lavished praise on Ole in the press call afterwards, and even in the early stages of his United career, it was obvious that the manager and his young striker were very much on the same wavelength – score more than the opposition, and you'll win.

Ferguson himself had had limited success as a striker for Glasgow Rangers. Former Scotland Boss Craig Brown, who played in the same Scottish schoolboys side as Sir Alex, once said of his team-mate, 'Fergie was what you would euphemistically call a hard player...'

A comparison could be drawn with the former United and Scotland striker Joe Jordan, who earned a reputation as one of the hardest, most physical players of his era. Both were cast from the mould of the old fashioned centre-forward, in complete contrast to Ole who, although more than able to look after himself, relied on stealth, skill and speed to score his goals. Perhaps to the ex-Dunfermline forward, Ole was the striker that he always wanted to be.

Further wins followed over Liverpool, Aston Villa, Newcastle and Everton. Ole featured in the Villa game but was finding it hard to dislodge the Cole–Sheringham combination as the starting strike partnership. Sheringham was slowly finding his feet but Cole's confidence had come flooding back. As Sir Alex rotated the squad for the hectic Christmas fixture list, Ole started at Coventry on 28 December 1997. That was the day that United's winning streak came to an end when the Sky Blues beat them 3-2. Although it was the third game of the punishing Christmas schedule, it was very energetic and exciting. At one stage, United were 3-0 down but Sheringham pulled one back and, when Ole slammed in the second, it set things up for a grandstand finish. Coventry, managed then by Gordon

Strachan, held on for the points and, surprisingly, that was the last goal Ole was to score that season in the Premiership.

A few days later, United went to the FA Cup holders, Chelsea, in the Third Round and won a memorable game 5-3. In a rain-lashed Stamford Bridge, Cole and Sheringham started up front. By the time Ole had come on for Scholes after 72 minutes, they were already 4-0 up and coasting. Within two minutes of the change, Sheringham had headed in United's fifth. The first four had been shared between Beckham (scorer of the first two, one of which was a breathtaking free-kick) and Cole. The ex-Newcastle man's fearsome pace proved too much for Frank Leboeuf, John Terry's predecessor. Cole was again in blistering form, his second goal of the match being the pick of them as he effortlessly beat the Dutch keeper De Goey. Cole had already rattled in 19 goals, 17 of them scored in the previous 16 games.

It was an utter humiliation for Ruud Gullit's side; they simply had no answer to the ruthlessness of their opponents' finishing. The Chelsea coach sent Vialli (soon to replace him at the helm) on for Ole's Norwegian colleague Flo. The Ex-Juve striker salvaged some pride for Chelsea as he grabbed a couple of late goals but, by that time, thousands of Chelsea fans had already departed for home.

In the late 1990s, the disparity between the sides was immense. United had a talented squad that could afford to keep a striker as prolific as Ole on the bench. The Chelsea squad of that era lacked similar strength in depth. All that was to change with the Russian Revolution, but it is interesting to note that, ten years on, Ole is still very much on the scene – Yorke, Sheringham and Cole were all eventually replaced by Rooney, Saha and Van Nistelrooy.

Ole, of all the strikers, was clearly always the favoured, reliable provider in Sir Alex's mind, and too valuable a commodity to let go.

After the complete and utter destruction of Chelsea, the red machine looked on course for yet another Double; Arsenal were 12 points adrift of United in the table at the turn of the year. Their Cup hopes were high also, although the United manager was in those days giving off the distinct impression that the oldest Cup competition in the world had became almost an unnecessary distraction. Sir Alex had no time for replays, for example. In the post-match press conference, he was joking about sending Schmeichel up front for the last ten minutes if the game was level. 'No draws,' he told the *Sunday Times*, 'no draws.'

A draw never looked likely in the Fourth Round when Walsall were the visitors to Old Trafford; they were soundly beaten 5-1. Ole scored twice to brighten an otherwise dour match, scoring his first ever goals in the famous competition. In the Premiership, though, United lost games just before and after the Walsall rout as the wheels started to fall off their Treble bid. Disappointing 1-0 defeats to middle-of-the-table sides Southampton and Leicester sounded a warning.

In those types of games, Keane was most missed because he galvanised his team-mates during difficult periods, and made sure that no complacency set in. Keane was making a slow but steady recovery, but coupled with Ryan Giggs's absence with a torn hamstring, the squad was badly hit that season by long-term injuries to their key men. The loss of their talismanic Frenchman was becoming more noticeable. As they frittered away points in the home game against Bolton, the fans rued Cantona's decision to turn his back on the game.

A famous Manchester fan and bookie, Fred Done (owner of the Bet-Fred chain of betting shops), had already paid out on bets that United would retain their Premiership title, but it was anything but a forgone conclusion. Arsenal, under their new manager, the shrewd Arsène Wenger, were emerging as serious challengers and, even though Wenger was new to the demands of the English game, he was proving a worthy opponent to Sir Alex.

Barnsley were drawn against United in the Fifth Round of the FA Cup to be played on the day after St Valentine's Day. After the seven-goal massacre inflicted upon them in October, it looked like an easy passage to the quarter-finals. The men from Oakwell had learnt quickly, though, and it was a major surprise when they forced a replay. Sheringham scored United's only goal of the game, in which Ole did not play a part. Neither did he play in the replay, although a young Norwegian did start the game for United up front – Erik Nevland. Barnsley played with tremendous spirit in the rematch, and ended up knocking United out of the Cup.

Another exit occurred a few weeks later from the quarter-finals of the Champions League against AS Monaco. United had qualified easily from Group B, topping the group with five wins and suffering only one defeat, a narrow 1-0 away defeat to eventual runners-up and old adversaries, the 'Old Lady' of Italy, Juventus. Ole played in that match, gaining valuable European experience against the skilful, well-drilled Italians.

Monaco were regarded as the weakest side left in the competition and on paper it looked like a nailed-on passport to the semis for United. Once again, the Reds were to go out to a team that they really should have beaten. The previous season, Sir Alex was of the view that his side had been too cavalier in their approach to the Borussia Dortmund match. This time round, he preached caution and took a defensive-minded side to the less-than-glamorous Stade Louis II. A nervous United came away from the Riviera with a goalless draw, a very unsatisfactory scoreline because it meant that Monaco would only have to score one goal at Old Trafford, or manage a score draw, to be guaranteed a place in the next round of the competition.

The Monaco ground was curiously constructed on top of an underground car park which meant that the pitch was always hard. In an attempt to disrupt Monaco's free-flowing style as much as possible, Ferguson instructed the ground staff to flood the Old Trafford pitch, which would hopefully suit his players more.

The plan backfired, though, because Monaco grabbed an early lead through David Trézéguet, the classy French striker who later played for Juventus. The goal stemmed from an error by Nicky Butt who lost possession and subsequently incurred the terrifying wrath of his manager. It was unfortunate for Butt, who had performed splendidly in midfield all season after the loss of Keane.

Ole equalised for United with his last goal of the season. It was not enough, though, and, once again, United were knocked out of Europe on away goals. It was particularly distressing for Sir Alex that the teams who had ended United's run in the competition during that period – Galatasaray, Gothenburg, Volgograd and Borussia Dortmund – were not of the same calibre as the élite clubs who might have presented more worthy opposition – Barcelona, Juventus or AC Milan, for example. No doubt about it, though – for some of United's players, and Ole particularly, the experience they had had so far would stand them in very good stead for the future.

Another factor in United's demise that season was the injury list – apart from the big two of Keane and Giggs, also absent from the second leg against Monaco were Pallister, Gary Neville, May and Scholes.

Keane had been openly critical of Eric Cantona's performances in Europe and remarked that he could not recall one match-winning performance by him in the Champions League. Sir Alex Ferguson realised that night that if United were to scoop the biggest prize in European football, then he would have to extend their scope and modify the tactics. Fortunately for him, he could still rest secure in the knowledge that his Norwegian striker could take chances at any level, in any situation.

A few days before the Monaco exit, United had been beaten 0-1 at Old Trafford by the rampant Arsenal side who were now on course for a Double of their own. Ole was on the bench for this game and watched Arsenal winger Marc Overmars score the only goal of the game. Sir Alex had long been an admirer of the Dutch player and this irritated him even more. The previous summer, attempts had been made to sign Brian Laudrup, Glasgow Rangers' brilliant striker, and Bayern Munich's tough defender Markus Babbel. Both deals had failed to proceed for financial reasons, which added to Ferguson's frustrations. If the squad had been strengthened by those acquisitions, there was every chance that they would have retained the title and won a major trophy.

There was one more disappointment for Ole as United's season slowly died on its feet. For the only time in his career, he was sent off. In the drawn home game against Newcastle, he was red-carded for a professional foul on Robert Lee. It was a deliberate foul to prevent a goal and, as Ole trudged off the field, he received a standing ovation from the United fans. It was an extraordinary act of faith by them, acknowledging the sacrifice Ole had made for his side and also the affection that they held him in. It was another example of the strengthening admiration and respect the fans had for their Norwegian striker.

Ole discussed the incident with *Red News*. 'Next morning, I did not think I was going to stay at the club for so long! I was in the gaffer's office and he was really slaughtering me for doing that because it was very unsporting and I can understand that. We lost the league by one point that year and all I was thinking was "Stop him before he gets inside the box". Then, we could still win it. I still felt we could win this game on the counter-attack.

'I can understand the supporters' point of view but, as a role model, as young players in Norway look up to me, it is not the right thing to do.'

Arsenal had completed the double over United and went on to win the title by a solitary point. They won their last ten Premiership games and completed the domestic double with victory over Newcastle in the FA Cup Final. Schmeichel wrote in his autobiography, 'The 1997/98 season turned into a slightly disjointed affair for us. We allowed ourselves, for example, to be beaten seven times, twice at home... And with statistics of that kind, you do not become English champions. Disappointment was hanging in the air; that kind of achievement [finishing second] does not really count at this stage of Manchester United's history.'

At the end of the campaign, they were mentally shot by their exertions which had, in the final reckoning, proved too demanding. Sir Alex quickly reacted with a spending spree of Russian billionaire proportions to bolster his squad. He spent £28m purchasing the Swedish winger Jesper Blomqvist from Parma, defender Jaap Stam, and Dwight Yorke from Aston Villa, for a then British record of £12.6 million. Other targets that summer were Patrick Kluivert, Gabriel Batisuta and the young Brazilian demi-god Ronaldo. The budget constraints and wage structure prevented their purchase.

Tottenham bid £5.5m for Ole in the summer but he declined to move to London, opting to stay at United, despite the intense and now increased competition for a place. Ole had finished the season with a haul of nine goals – six in the Premiership, two in the FA Cup and one in the Champions League – in a total of 19 starts and 11 substitutions. It was his lowest tally before his injury problems but, the following season, he was to double that figure and play a huge part in what would turn out to be one of United's most memorable seasons.

# 4

# There Is a Season

**'He has the best movement inside the penalty box of any striker I have had during my time at United.'**
**SIR ALEX FERGUSON**

O n the autumn day in November 2006 when United pummelled Portsmouth 3-0 to celebrate Sir Alex's 20th anniversary and jump clear of Chelsea, the world-famous singer Tony Bennett appeared on the *Parkinson* show. Parky talked of the certain period in the late 1950s when American music was dominated by fantastic crooners and musicians like Frank Sinatra; he called it the 'Renaissance' period, comparing their explosive talents and achievements to those of the great artists like Michelangelo.

The 1998/99 season could be called the Manchester United equivalent of the Renaissance, because that was when they scooped the unthinkable grand slam of the Premier League Championship, the FA Cup and the holy grail – the Champions League. The immortal Treble.

Although it was United's supreme achievement, the

debate as to whether or not it was won by the greatest ever team to wear the red and white is still open. One thing is sure, though – the Treble-winning side were inducted into the Manchester United Hall of Fame that season. Purists will insist that the 1968 side that won the European Cup for the first time, including Best, Law and Charlton, was the ultimate dream team. The stellar heights attained by the 1993/94 Double-winning side was a wonderful achievement undoubtedly, and the likes of Cantona, Hughes and Kanchelskis had a wonderful balance of flair and solidity, but nobody can argue with the supreme glory that was dramatically etched into United folklore by Ole's winner in the Nou Camp in the Champions League Final. For that alone, forever more, Ole Gunnar Solskjaer's name will be chanted with utter devotion by the Old Trafford faithful. But as a crucial part of the squad as a whole, Ole contributed so much more than that one, single moment of inspiration.

If Keane and Giggs were the mind and body of United, then Ole was the soul. Ole told *The Opus*, 'It is strange to think that I will be an old man, and I will be meeting United fans, and they will still want to talk to me about that goal, but I have got used to it. I always get asked questions like, "How does it feel? You were the one that won it." It wasn't me who won it, it wasn't my touch, it's what the team did over the season... but never mind.'

The perfect season started in a very low-key fashion. United were soundly beaten 3-0 in the Charity Shield by the current Double-holders Arsenal. The first European fixture was against LKS Lodz of Poland in a first-leg, second-qualifying-round tie played in mid-August. The Old Trafford side had gained entry into Europe that season by the back door. Sir Alex had allegedly even contemplated turning down the invitation to enter Europe as he felt that the Champions League should really only do what it said on the tin – offer a competitive arena for the Champions only.

The ill-fated Jaap Stam, a £10.75 million acquisition from PSV Eindhoven, slotted neatly into the back four against Lodz. Ryan Giggs, throwing off his injury problems of previous seasons, opened United's account for the season after 16 minutes. It was a bright start for him and he never looked back. Andy Cole then headed the second after 81 minutes and, in the next minute, Ole came on for Paul Scholes. The game ended with a 2-0 score line and that was the final aggregate score as the teams played out a goalless draw in Poland a fortnight later. Ole came on for Giggs after 65 minutes and was yet to make a senior start, a point made by Sir Alex in the press conference.

Sandwiched between the Lodz games were two draws in the Premiership at home to Leicester 2-2, and away to West Ham 0-0. Leicester had given United a real scare, having led 2-0 until late in the game. Only a stoppage-time, trademark Beckham free-kick had salvaged a point, and saved the blushes of a rather insipid display up front.

Ole started against Charlton and starred in an effortless 4-1 victory over the south London side. All five goals came in a frantic half-hour period; Kinsella shot Charlton in front after 32 minutes, but Ole equalised seven minutes later with his first strike of the season. Dwight Yorke, making his home début, was key in a fluid passing move that put Ole through on goal. The Charlton fans moaned afterwards that it had been a lucky bounce that enabled Ole to pierce the defence and score with a well-taken shot. Yorke got into the act himself scoring on either side of half-time, and Ole completed the rout with a delicious, close-range diving header after 63 minutes. Ferguson then shuffled the pack by substituting Ole and Yorke to bring on Sheringham and Cole.

That game, Ole donned the famous red Umbro strip with the 'Sharp' sponsorship logo, traditional white shorts and black socks. This was a revolutionary kit made from Umbro's 'Vapatech moisture management fabric'. The collar was of particular interest as it included the unique locking zip mechanism. The United fans loved it because it featured the Umbro diamond on both shorts and sleeves; the Manchester United board loved it because it had global appeal.

Ole had a hand in setting up Yorke's opening goal against Coventry at Old Trafford a few days later. Ole's clever flick enabled Giggs to cross a fine ball. The Coventry keeper Hedman (later to join Chelsea) could only palm it to Scholes whose prompt return pass was smashed in by Yorke. The game was eventually won 2-0.

A marvellous game with Barcelona was to follow. United were drawn with the Catalan Champions in Group D, nicknamed the 'Group of Death', along with Bayern Munich and Brondby. Ole played for 55 minutes before being replaced by Nicky Butt. A magnificent first-half display by the Reds encapsulated why Ferguson's side had a growing belief that it could be their year to reclaim the trophy first won by Matt Busby's all-stars.

Beckham's pin-point crosses from the right tormented the Barça defence for the entire game. It was that display which first highlighted Beckham's qualities to the other Spanish giants, Barcelona's bitterest enemies, Real Madrid. Ole headed a Beckham cross against the bar early on which set the tempo for the game. After 17 minutes, Giggs headed another Beckham cross home and, eight minutes later, the elegant Yorke scissor-kicked overhead another perfect Beckham cross. Ruud Hesp, the Barça keeper, somehow parried the shot, but Scholes nonchalantly poked home the rebound.

That was how it stayed at half-time, but in the second half the virtuoso elements of Barcelona's marvellous attacking ensemble swept them back into the game. Rivaldo – then at the height of his powers – grabbed control of the game; first, he caused havoc in the United defence and created a goal for his fellow Brazilian Anderson. Later, Rivaldo's mazy run into the box then won a penalty, from which Barcelona levelled.

Beckham put United in front with another marvellous free-kick that even the Barcelona fans openly admired. Barça equalised when Ole's replacement, Butt, handled on the line and Luis Enrique converted their second spot-kick of a memorable evening. It was a firm rebuttal to anyone who thought it would be a sterile clash.

Ole did not feature in the next match, a 3-0 drubbing at Arsenal. Feeling the hangover of the tumultuous Barcelona match, United, playing in their all-black strip, were no match for a rampant Arsenal, fired up by an early Tony Adams goal.

The black kit was highly controversial. When the Premiership was formed, the refs were given a new ensemble. No longer could the famous 'bastard in the black' be chanted at the man in the middle. United were now able to play in Armani's favourite colour and it was hugely popular with the fans, possibly because it could be worn more easily with normal day-to-day clothes. Umbro originally saw the black outfit as a training kit and the shirt featured ribbed panels on the sides.

## BABY-FACED ASSASSIN

The Norwegian was back in the starting line up for the home clash with Liverpool and had a part in setting up the first goal. It was his low shot that American keeper Brad Friedel fumbled. After some haphazard defending, the ball was eventually scrambled away for a corner. Beckham's inswinging corner caused problems and, eventually, a penalty was given against Jason McAteer for a deliberate handball. Dennis Irwin converted the spot-kick.

Andy Cole replaced Ole after 70 minutes and, 10 minutes later, knifed his way to the by-line for Scholes to run in his cross for the second goal. It was a vital win which kept United in touch with the leaders Aston Villa, whom they trailed by six points. Huge game followed huge game, with United travelling next to Germany for the Group D clash with Bayern Munich. They came away with a 2-2 draw and were only deprived of a superb win by a rare lapse by Schmeichel in the dying seconds. Ole remained on the bench throughout the maelstrom. United had only two points from their two group games so far. Barça led by four points and Munich had three, so to qualify from the group still looked a monumental task.

Ferguson rearranged his strike partnership again and decided on the duo of Cole and Yorke to grab the goals in the next few games. And grab them they did, in a 3-0 romp at bottom club Southampton and a 5-1 thrashing of Wimbledon.

Brondby were pole-axed 2-6 in a rain-swept Copenhagen as United stormed their way forward in Group D. It was a record away win in the Champions League. Ole came on after 61 minutes with United already having scored five. Within a minute, Ole scored as he burst on to a Yorke pass to fire home. Bayern's narrow win over Barcelona meant that United had a great chance of qualifying... if they could get a result at the Nou Camp.

Ole was included in the team that played in the Worthington Cup home tie against Bury, which actually turned out to be the only competition that they did not win that season. The team was a mixture of hardened pros like Phil Neville, should-have-beens like Jordi Cruyff, and wannabes like Jonathan Greening.

The game turned out to be a personal duel between Ole and Dean Kiely, the heroic Bury keeper. The Republic of Ireland international defied United with save after gymnastic save, most of them thwarting decent efforts from the Norwegian striker. Kiely was finally beaten in the 106th minute of the game by Ole's low drive, which spun off his gloves on to the post and into goal.

For connoisseurs of football, these types of games are sometimes more interesting than the bread and butter of the Premiership. Greening, who created Ole's goal, is now plying his trade at West Bromwich Albion after a spell at Middlesbrough, having been signed by Steve McClaren. Wes Brown, now an England regular, came on as sub in that game, having earlier made his full league début against Wimbledon.

Erik Nevland scored the second; he had been signed from Viking Stavanger and was hailed as the new Solskjaer. Unfortunately, that was his only 15 minutes of fame with United and he returned to Viking where he had a successful career. Nevland's two goals in Viking's famous victory over Chelsea in 2002 always guaranteed him a soft spot in most United fans' hearts.

The red machine then rolled on to Goodison Park, where they beat Everton 4-1. The Blues, at that time managed by Walter Smith, had put together a run of ten unbeaten games but were simply brushed aside by their Lancashire neighbours. Dwight Yorke notched up his eighth goal in twelve appearances as Ole looked on from the bench.

Brondby took another battering as United scored five times without reply in the return fixture at Old Trafford. Three goals in the first quarter-of-an-hour tore the heart out of Schmeichel's old side. Ole came on for Cole after 53 minutes, and the Yorke–Cole partnership continued to prosper as they both finished up on the score sheet that night. With Bayern Munich winning in Barcelona, the bookmakers made United favourites for Europe's top prize.

The Worthington Cup could never be described as one of European football's most glamorous competitions; it was famously dubbed the 'Worthless' cup by Ray Winstone in the highly-rated football film *All in the Game*. Sir Alex told David Meek of the *Manchester Evening News*, 'I respect sponsors who put money into football and the Worthington people are entitled to get a proper return on their investment. I am sure they look at the teams I put into the competition and question why one or two of the more familiar names are missing. I have a lot of sympathy with that view but, at the same time, I have to consider my requirements and use my own judgement of the English game to determine my selections.'

His selections for the home tie with Nottingham Forrest paired Ole alongside Jordi Cruyff. Jordi was a very unlucky player, burdened by having the most famous name in European football and a career decimated by niggling injuries. He was actually saddled with his father's Christian name, but chose instead to be known by his second name – Jordi – the patron saint of Catalonia. Throughout his spell at Old Trafford, he tried to free himself of his father's shadow, playing his own style of football, but the greatness that was part and parcel of his family name could never really be shrugged off.

Hendrik Johannes Cruyff emerged as a world star in the early 1970s as his team Ajax won the European Cup three years running, while the superstar Dutchman won the European Footballer of the Year award three times. What made him so special? Johan Cruyff was a ballet dancer on the field, naturally right-footed, but he liked to play on the left. He scored goals and made goals, a supreme artist with instant control and fierce shooting power. He was also recently chosen by the magazine *Nieuwe Revu* as the greatest ever Dutch player.

Almost as successful as a coach, he led Barcelona to four championships and a European Cup. In more recent times, he had a spat with José Mourinho over Chelsea's 'negative' tactics in their memorable clashes with Barcelona. Jordi was himself a fan of his father, and told Martin Samuel of the *Sun* about the undeniable greatness of Johan: 'Training at Barcelona, sometimes my eyes nearly fell out of their sockets. Sometimes, I had to stop and stand still when I saw what he could do with a football.'

Jordi showed touches of his father's brilliance when he split the Forest defence after 57 minutes with a wonderful through ball. Ole had beaten the offside trap and raced through with exhilarating acceleration to beat the veteran goalkeeper Dave Beasant with a low drive.

Two minutes later, the Cruyff–Solskjaer combination struck again. Jordi dribbled through midfield and found Ole, who raced behind the Forest back line to tuck the ball past Beasant. Up until then, Forest had enjoyed a fair amount of the play and their manager Dave Bassett made the point that if Ole had been playing for his team, they would have built up a healthy first-half lead. Bassett's side had to be satisfied with a ferocious drive from former England midfielder Steve Stone, but it was not enough to save the game. Ole was delighted at the opportunity the Worthington Cup presented him to showcase his finishing and press his claims as a first-choice striker.

Cole and Yorke retained their places for the next two Premiership fixtures, a 3-2 home victory over Blackburn and a surprise 3-1 defeat at Sheffield Wednesday. Ole made substitute appearances in both games. Around that time, Peter Schmeichel announced his retirement from English football. Schmeichel was arguably United's finest-ever keeper, and was certainly a character to be reckoned with, both on and off the pitch. He was the only player to have a TV soap opera dog named after him, and he has appeared from time to time as an expert football pundit, as well as on the Saturday night TV game show *Strictly Come Dancing*. The tradition of 'larger-than-life' goalkeepers at United was maintained after Peter's departure from the Theatre of Dreams as the colourful Mark Bosnich and the quirky Fabien Barthez attempted to fill the gap.

Then it was back to the Nou Camp, a match that Barcelona had to win to stay in the competition, but United came away with a 3-3 draw in another marvellous European goalfest. Anderson gave the home team a dream start but the Reds fought back twice to take the lead. Rivaldo eventually salvaged a draw with an outrageous bicycle kick. It was back to the Premiership for a home game against their bitter rivals Leeds, then still a powerful force in British football. Their subsequent slide and then plummet into obscurity over such a short period is a stark warning to all clubs of the need for sound financial planning, astute leadership, solid youth policies... and great players who want to give their all to the club. It's debatable now whether the greatness that Leeds once had will ever be recovered.

Sir Alex rotated his squad again, and Ole started the match with Giggs on the bench. Jimmy Floyd Hasselbaink shot Leeds ahead but, with the ref about to blow the half-time whistle, Yorke beat two defenders on the left, and crossed for Ole to bury the ball in the net, driving past Nigel Martyn from an acute angle.

In an eventful match, Martyn suffered a back injury and was replaced by the future England keeper Paul Robinson. Roy Keane scored the second goal, but the talented Harry Kewell cancelled it out when he sprang the United offside trap to score a neat equaliser. Nicky Butt then clinched the points with an unlikely gem.

Ole's dreams of a Wembley Worthington Cup Final evaporated when Spurs knocked the Reds out after a 3-1 defeat at White Hart Lane. It was to be the last game in a Cup competition that they were to lose that season. Ole started against the side he had so nearly joined the season before, and he told *Red News* that he kept the contract signed by Alan Sugar and Martin Edwards. Sugar never did get the chance to fire him!

Sir Alex recalled the time that his Norwegian striker had nearly joined the north London side. He told the *Manchester Evening News*, 'In the close season, Spurs had come in for him... I put the situation to Ole, and he wasn't sure whether he wanted to take up the offer and go. He asked my opinion. I said it was entirely up to him and that I wasn't forcing him out of the door. I told him that he had been a model professional with United and that while I couldn't guarantee him a regular first-team place, I could assure him that he would get plenty of football. He said he didn't want to leave Manchester United.

'"Well, that's the matter over with… " I replied. You could see the uncertainty in the boy and when he asked for my advice… I said I honestly didn't think he should go.'

Ferguson at the time could not have known just how important Ole's decision to stay at Old Trafford could have been. On such moments, football empires are built or lost.

Ferguson fielded a stronger line-up against Tottenham than in the earlier Worthington fixtures with Sheringham, playing against his old side, alongside Giggs. The ex-Spurs hero scored the United goal that evening. George Graham's Tottenham team were worthy winners, though, with David Ginola putting on a performance that showed why he was later to be voted the sports writer's Player of the Year. A remarkable achievement, considering the performances throughout the season of the United superstars like Keane, Giggs and Co, and their Treble achievement, which perhaps came too late in the season to affect the voting. Ginola was a tabloid dream, the Beckham of his day – with model looks, and skills to match, he shone briefly, and was then eclipsed by other, younger players.

Two 1-1 draws followed, in which Ole did not feature. The first was at Villa Park against the league leaders, and then came the crunch group match against Bayern Munich. Roy Keane cracked a fine goal past Oliver Kahn, which was subsequently cancelled out by Salihamidzic for Bayern. A draw was enough for both sides to qualify from the Group of Death, and boot Barcelona out of the competition. The rest of the match was played out tamely in an unreal atmosphere. Bayern finished as winners of the group, while the 20 goals rattled home by United made them top scorers in the competition. Both sides could now concentrate on their domestic fixtures and await the knock-out stages in the spring.

Ole came back for the league visit to White Hart Lane, where they had been dumped out of the Worthington Cup ten days earlier. The Norwegian was determined to make the most of his squad rotation opportunity and grabbed two early goals. The first of these came after 11 minutes; David Beckham floated over a perfect centre and Ryan Giggs' diving header was palmed out by Ian Walker. The ball ran to Ole to lash home, a typical conversion by the striker who made it look so easy.

Perhaps fittingly, that goal was scored at Tottenham because that was the home ground of the player whose Ole's style most resembles – Jimmy Greaves – a legend whose name is so deeply inscribed in the folklore of the game. The Tottenham maestro finished top scorer in the top flight six times in his glittering career. And significantly, the majority of Greaves's goals were scored in the six-yard box where he would slam in rebounds, fumbles, centres and crosses. His positional sense and anticipation were second to none.

Sir Matt Busby in his *Soccer at the Top* book described Greaves by saying, 'No matter what the goalmouth struggle, the nimble, perfectly balanced Jimmy would seem to find himself room for a ballet-dancer's pivot and, in a flash, there would be a lift of that tiny left foot and the ball would be glided into the net. He did everything crisply, neatly.'

The instinctive Ole operates in similar territory, working on the same margins, pouncing on the merest whiff of a chance. Whenever and wherever the ball comes to him, he would instinctively adapt and execute the most efficient outcome. Ole's second goal was vintage Greaves – a perfect cross from Beckham, and Ole nipped in front of Sol Campbell to slip past Walker.

United were coasting thanks to Ole, but five minutes before the break the whole complexion of the game was changed when Gary Neville was sent off for a tackle on Ginola, who collapsed to the ground. Gary had previously received a caution and controversial ref Uriah Rennie had no hesitation in giving him his marching orders.

Sir Alex now had to reorganise his side to accommodate ten men. Ole was substituted at the break and replaced by defender Henning Berg. On a hat-trick, it was a huge blow to lose Ole and United's attacking options were severely restricted in the second half. Tottenham, inspired by Ginola, attacked in waves and two goals from Sol Campbell restricted United to a point as defensive lapses were punished.

Chelsea were the next team to visit Old Trafford; Ole sat this one out as Ferguson opted to pursue his rotation policy. It was another brilliant overseas striker who dominated proceedings that night. Gianfranco Zola, in one of his early games in the Premiership, scored a brilliant late equaliser to deny United further points. Zola worked a one-two with Gus Poyet before deftly chipping the ball over Schmeichel. United had led by a smartly taken Andy Cole shot past De Goey just on the break. Chelsea in the pre-Abramovich era were just starting to make an impact with their first influx of foreign imports and they hit the top spot the following Saturday as United crumbled to a shock defeat at the hands of Middlesbrough.

Brian Robson was back at Old Trafford managing 'Boro. It was one of the few successes during his chequered career at the Riverside Stadium. With less than an hour gone, United trailed 0-3. At that precise moment, the odds of winning the Treble must have been monumental. Butt and Scholes gave the score line some respectability and Solskjaer came on for the last ten minutes as United laid siege to the 'Boro goal but to no avail.

Sir Alex Ferguson missed the match due to a family bereavement, but was later said to be appalled at the Sunday League defending. Already in the season, his team had lost three out of eighteen matches, two of them to 'lesser' sides 'Boro and Sheffield Wednesday. The demands of qualifying from the Group of Death had taken their toll in subsequent Premiership fixtures. The Middlesbrough game was a watershed for United; it was the last Premiership game – indeed, the last game in any competition – that they were to lose that season.

On Boxing Day 1998, Forest came to Old Trafford and were battered 3-0; three days later, United played out a 0-0 draw with Chelsea. Ole did not feature in either game but came on after 70 minutes in the home FA Cup game against Middlesbrough. Once again, fate intervened and the side that had out-fought and out-thought United for long periods a few weeks earlier took another shock lead. Andy Townsend fired them ahead after 53 minutes but, a quarter-of-an-hour later, the quicksilver Cole equalised. Ole replaced the Swede Jesper Blomqvist as the game seemed to be heading for a replay.

Eight minutes from time, United were awarded a bitterly disputed penalty when Butt went down under Maddison's challenge, and Denis Irwin coolly sent 'Boro keeper Schwarzer the wrong way with his spot-kick. This was despite former United star Pallister, who had a fine game for 'Boro, offering some advice to Schwarzer before the vital kick was taken. The ploy to psych out Irwin failed.

Ole sealed the match in the dying seconds when he set up Giggs to crash in the third. Giggs started the move with a razor-sharp run, but it was Ole's perfect return pass in the one-two that enabled the Welshman to score. It was a tremendous start to 1999.

Ole scored his first goal of that awesome year when he came on at Old Trafford for Nicky Butt against West Ham. There were only 12 minutes left and the Reds were cruising with a 3-0 lead. The Cole–Yorke combination had been working well, with Cole slamming home the last two. Ole scored within three minutes of taking to the pitch. This was a rare opportunistic header, only his second of the season, after Giggs' powerful shot had hit the Hammers keeper Hislop and looped up into the air.

Towards the end of the game, Joe Cole made one of his first appearances in the Premiership as a second-half substitute for West Ham. One of Joe's future Chelsea colleagues, Frank Lampard, scored a late consolation for the East Enders.

The big red goal machine then rampaged down to Leicester and butchered them 6-2, with the Yorke–Cole partnership scoring five of them. Yorke notched a hat-trick, and Ole's special services were surplus to requirements.

The next game was the Fourth Round home FA Cup tie against Liverpool, the biggest, bitterest rivals of them all. A victory over Liverpool is, to most United fans, the most treasured of scalps. Although United fans could identify several 'hated' opponents over the years – Manchester City, Chelsea, Leeds – Liverpool were always the real enemy, and the feeling was mutual. The reasons for this date back to the 1960s with the emergence of Liverpool as a dominant force in the game. Inspired by Bill Shankly, the Kop became the most famous home end in football. It was the era of the Beatles and the Mersey sound echoed around the world. United won their first European Cup but the team soon spiralled into decline. For years, the Scousers lorded it over United and some of the most vicious clashes between rival sets of fans occurred between Liverpool and United.

In the 1990s, as the balance of power swung back to United, the enmity was still as strong with feelings running deep. Chelsea were soon to break up the duopoly, but even to this day nothing has replaced the tension, loyalty, passion and hostility that this fixture engenders. Throughout the world, the cities of Liverpool and Manchester were famous for two things – music and football.

Ole was one of the subs as Cole and Giggs continued as the main strike force. It may be interesting to note the starting line-ups. United fielded Schmeichel, Neville (G), Irwin, Keane, Stam, Berg, Beckham, Butt, Cole, Yorke and Giggs; Liverpool went with James, Heggem, Harkness, Carragher, Matteo, Bjornebye, Ince, Berger, Fowler, Owen and Redknapp.

The Merseysiders managed a dream start scoring after just three minutes to send their vast travelling army of fans into paroxysms of delight. The goal incensed Sir Alex because it was down to poor defending – Jamie Redknapp collected a throw-in on the halfway line and fed the ball to full-back Heggem, who scampered down the right before sending a towering lob into the box. Stam and Berg hesitated as if rooted to the spot, and Michael Owen headed past Schmeichel.

Owen at that time was the rising star of the game. Only Beckham had a higher profile after Owen's fabulous goal for his country against Argentina in the previous summer's

World Cup. Michael's strike partner was Robbie Fowler, and there was no doubting the potential in their pairing. Liverpool manager Gérard Houllier had been quoted as saying that he thought his duo of Owen and Fowler could become the most lethal strike force in the Premiership, but Yorke and Cole, Sheringham and Solskjaer eclipsed their efforts.

Like Owen, Fowler had burst upon the scene in a blaze of glory, scoring five goals against Fulham in one of his first games at Anfield. Somewhere along the line, Fowler failed to deliver on his early promise. His career became ravaged by ankle and knee problems, and he was involved in several off-field incidents. In 1999, he was struggling to adapt to the squad rotation system, and had fallen out with Houllier, and his once brilliant career was at a crossroads. In an interview in the *Guardian*, Cantona lamented the decline in Fowler, saying, 'Fowler was so good at 18, and 4, 5 years later, at 23 or 24, finished, not even playing for England, finished. Completely out. Why?'

Onlookers offered up all sorts of explanations – the wrong attitude, media pressure, a personality clash with his manager, getting in with the wrong crowd, not taking the physical or nutritional advice seriously enough, spending too much time drinking and clubbing... or just sheer bad luck. Whatever the real reason – or combination of reasons, Fowler's lifestyle was clearly not helping.

Owen's career was to take a similar downward curve to Robbie – injuries destroyed his career in recent years, and it remains to be seen if he can recapture any of the scintillating form he showed when he ran rampant for England and Liverpool. Owen was a far less controversial character off the field than the Toxteth tearaway, and his consuming interest away from football was horse-racing.

Ole's career was in complete contrast to other players who shared his outstanding ability in front of goal. No modern player was better adjusted to the rotation system, and his personal life was unblemished. A tabloid's nightmare, but a manager's dream.

At the break, the away side still clung to their early, precious lead. Liverpool packed their midfield and the United strike force was stifled and blunted. Dwight Yorke had been the focal point of the attack but was forced deeper by the midfield congestion. Giggs found himself running into defensive walls, where he was picked off by scything tackles. Scholes replaced Butt after 68 minutes, but still Liverpool stood firm against the red onslaught. They had an amazing escape when Keane thundered a shot against the post, the ball taking a wicked rebound and running along the goal line before Liverpool midfielder Paul Ince hacked it clear. United fans thought the ball had crossed the line but the game continued. It was a sweet moment for Ince, who had denied his old club an equaliser, but it appeared to have been a turning point in the game.

Ince had left Old Trafford at the start of the 1995/96 season, at the time of the 'night of the long knives', when Ferguson had also culled the Siberian Express Andrei Kanchelskis and the legend that was Mark Hughes. This was to make room for the golden generation of Beckham, Scholes and their chums. In his autobiography, Schmeichel described Ince's contribution to the team by saying, 'There is no doubt Ince was a good player. But at the same time, I felt he was, to put it mildly, self-centred and arrogant, and his potentially adverse influence on young players in particular was something that I know worried Ferguson. Ince always referred to himself as the "Guv'nor" – in other words, the boss – and he played up to this self-assertion to an almost absurd degree; he had "GUV" written on his boots, and had a number plate made with L8 GUV on it. In the end, Ferguson became so fed up with it that he was prompted to utter the words, "I'll show him who the f\*\*\*ing Guv is!" and he sold him to Inter Milan.'

Ince became the new player-manager of Macclesfield Town at the end of 2006 and the football world wondered how the new 'guv'nor' would fare at the club languishing at the foot of the league.

Keane struck the post again as United became increasingly desperate and time ticked away. Every fumbled pass or mis-directed cross took on enormous significance to the huge crowd. Jamie Redknapp was substituted 20 minutes before time and walked off applauding the travelling Kop as if victory was assured.

Redknapp was the prototype 'Spice Boy' from the class of '93, famous for the white Armani FA Cup Final suits that they sported on the day Cantona fizzed home the winner. Redknapp's career was cursed with endless injuries but he lived the dream, marrying pop star Louise, crowned Sexiest Woman of the Decade in 2004. After retiring from football, he ended up a Sky pundit and magazine publisher.

Gambling heavily, Sir Alex threw on Ole Gunnar Solskjaer and Ronny Johnsen with just nine minutes left, sacrificing two defenders, Irwin and Berg. Ole immediately joined Yorke and Cole up front with Johnsen employed as an auxiliary midfielder. The modified United side battered the Liverpool defence in a frenzied, non-stop barrage. The strength of their attack at last told as Liverpool's well organized marking system imploded. Two minutes from time, Beckham floated over a free-kick, Andy Cole at the far post neatly tapped it back to Dwight Yorke who side-footed in an easy goal. Football can be remarkable in its simplicity at times. The United fans could scarcely believe it, their heroes having looked down and out of the Cup. The ease with which they had equalised made a mockery of what had gone beforehand. A replay at Anfield loomed.

Deep into stoppage time, Jaap Stam punted a high ball into the Liverpool penalty box. The area was packed and it was more in desperation than anything else. His main thought was to waste the remaining time, the realisation that the tie had been saved was uppermost in his mind. Paul Scholes controlled the ball beautifully and moved in on goal. Ole Gunnar Solskjaer had only one thing one his mind at that moment – putting the ball into the Liverpool net. In that split-second, he exhibited the essential qualities of a great predator – quick reflexes, wonderful anticipation and an innate sense of timing. Ole's balance was perfect as he ghosted in to take the ball from Scholes and fire off an instant shot with his left foot, the ball flying past James with unerring accuracy and power. It was vintage Ole, and would set up a vintage season for United.

# 5

# The Immortal Treble

**'Ole is probably the best signing the club ever made. Nicknamed the baby-faced assassin, Ole was both baby-faced and an assassin.'**

**ROY KEANE**

Manchester United hit the top of the Premiership on the last day of January 1999. It came courtesy of a last-gasp winner at Charlton. For the second week running, a last-minute strike defined a key moment of the epic season. This time, Ole did not score the crucial goal, that distinction falling to Dwight Yorke. Ole had come on for Beckham after 71 minutes of a bruising encounter.

Charlton manager Alan Curbishley had tried to curb the goal threat of the United strike force by employing three solid centre-backs. Scott Parker, just breaking into the big time, was sent on shortly after the introduction of Ole with the brief of man-marking the Norwegian dynamo.

Derby were then dispatched at Old Trafford in another solitary goal victory, Dwight Yorke bagging the 65th-minute winner. It was his seventh goal in five games and comparisons were already being drawn with Eric Cantona, particularly because of the brooding looks and turned-up collars.

It was a bad day for Derby because, not only did they lose the game, but they also lost the services of their highly rated manager, Steve McClaren, the future England coach, who opted to go to Old Trafford as the replacement for Brian Kidd, Ferguson's assistant. Ole played the full 90 minutes for only the second time in the Premiership that season.

Ole's next appearance, though, was to turn out to be truly historic. United visited Nottingham Forest and crushed the home side 8-1, still a record for biggest away victory in the Premiership. They also hold the record for the biggest Premiership win the – 9-0 victory over Ipswich Town at Old Trafford in March 1995. Andy Cole scored five in that game, the record for the most goals scored in one match (shared with Alan Shearer, who scored five for Newcastle against Sheffield Wednesday in September 1999). Ole was setting records of his own – albeit unofficial ones – as he'd scored four times in the last 18 minutes that he'd played.

That game, Ole was razor-sharp and in the best form of his life. His performance was little short of amazing. The recent match-winner against Liverpool and the impending strike at the Nou Camp were to become the stuff of legend, but they tended to overshadow his remarkable performance at the City Ground on 6 February 1999. United were already cruising to an emphatic 4-1 victory with the deadly duo of Cole and Yorke having scored two apiece. Ole had replaced Yorke in the 72nd minute and struck his first goal eight minutes later. This made his achievement even more remarkable as he squeezed his four-goal burst into just ten minutes. Beckham set up the first when he found the overlapping Gary Neville out on the right. The England defender's low centre was tapped in at the far post by Ole.

Beckham, with a determined run, then engineered Ole's second and United's sixth two minutes from time. Beckham's superb diagonal through ball found Ole, who ran through the centre of the Forest defence to fire coolly home with a low drive. The hapless Dave Beasant blocked the shot, but Ole picked up the rebound and dribbled around the Forest keeper before lashing the ball into the roof of the net.

As the clock ticked into injury time, Paul Scholes then burst through the middle and fed Ole, who volleyed in his hat-trick. And Forest were made to suffer further humiliation when Butt curled over a centre as the ref put the whistle to his lips to blow for time. Scholes mis-timed his shot but the ball spun back to Ole, who, displaying great poise, drove in number eight.

Including his double in the Worthington Cup game, it was Ole's sixth goal of the season against Dave Beasant, who must have been sick of the sight of the Norwegian striker.

As a demonstration of perfect finishing, Ole's performance during those last ten minutes of the game at the City Ground offers a masterclass in coolness, power, precision and tremendous balance. What continued to set Ole apart from the rest was the fact that he could come on and immediately take chances. Somehow, he could instantly click into the pace of the game, and make the most of the faintest of opportunities. Having spent so much time on the bench, he might be forgiven for allowing his mind to wander, rather than following the action assiduously. But Ole's great skill is to read the game from the sidelines when required, and then use that knowledge to devastating effect when he's brought on.

Mike Phelan, one of the United coaches, highlighted why Ole was the best sub in the game when he told the *Manchester Evening News*, 'Most players on the bench talk and joke amongst themselves, but Ole is involved in the game from the sidelines, looking for weaknesses in opposing defences that he can exploit once the call comes from the manager.'

When Joe Cole missed a crucial chance for Chelsea in the dying moments of their FA Cup semi-final against Liverpool in 2006, many pundits pointed out that the main reason was that Joe had only been on the field for a few minutes. Consequently, he had not been used to the pace of the game or the particular playing styles of individual opponents. Cole had had a brilliant season for Chelsea and, at that time, was a contender for player of the year, but that one instance showed the fine line between success and failure. One can only guess whether Ole might have been instantly more clinical in the same situation.

Ole's achievement could be considered to be even more remarkable given that Ferguson had set up a hierarchy of strikers. At that stage in the season, he was employing Yorke and Cole as his main attacking force for the major games, with Ole and Sheringham as the aces tucked up his sleeve. Everybody knew their role and what was required of them. Compare this to a club like Tottenham during the winter of 2006, when Martin Jol had four attacking players at his disposal – Jermaine Defoe, Robbie Keane, Mido and Dimitar Berbatov. A great deal of confusion had arisen as none of the quartet really knew if they were Jol's first or fourth choice. This led to a great deal of instability and uncertainty, and few goals hit the back of the net as a consequence.

Ole knew the score, and was psychologically robust – whether first choice or warming the bench, he knew what he had to do, and would take every opportunity that arose. End of story.

In his autobiography, Jaap Staam observed, 'That unbelievable scoring spurt may have come as a surprise to the rest of the League, but it didn't to us. Ole does it in training all the time; if you give him space in the box, he will kill you.'

After the Forest rout, United came down to earth with a bang when Fulham visited Old Trafford in the Fifth Round of the FA Cup. Managed by Kevin Keegan, they were blasting their way out of the lower leagues en route to the Premiership. They put up stubborn resistance and only lost by the solitary goal scored by Cole on 26 minutes. Ole, fresh from his glory at Forest, played alongside Yorke and Cole in a three-pronged attack and assisted in Cole's goal, collecting a high cross from Nicky Butt at the far post. Ole cushioned the ball on his foot and cut it back perfectly into the path of Cole, whose shot deflected over Chris Coleman and into the goal. Blomqvist replaced Ole after 68 minutes as the game petered out, with United looking a little lacking in energy.

Ole took no part in the next instalment of the clash of the titans – United v Arsenal at the Theatre of Dreams. Both sides seemed overcome by the tension of the occasion and the game ended in a tepid 1-1 draw. Anelka scored for Arsenal from a chance engineered by Kanu, but Cole headed United level. It seemed like a dress rehearsal for the FA Cup clash later on in the season.

The Red Devils visited Coventry next and came away with three points thanks to a Ryan Giggs goal after 79 minutes. Giggs had come on as sub in the Arsenal game after recovering from the hamstring injury sustained in the Derby game. His first ever appearance for United was when he played against Everton in a 0-2 home defeat in March 1991.

The goal was a gem, starting from Schmeichel's long throw to Yorke, who linked with Giggs and then on to Beckham, the free-flowing nature of the passing a joy to behold. Beckham's cross brushed the head of Coventry defender Richard Shaw, but the ball fell to Giggs, who had run the length of the field from Schmeichel's goal line to score.

Ole had substituted a subdued Yorke towards the end of the game, and Sir Alex kept him in the side for the home clash with Southampton in the next match, where another three points were secured with a 2-1 victory. It took the unbeaten run to a lucky 13, with 11 of them wins. Ole made way for Cole on 68 minutes with the score still 0-0. Keane and Yorke put United ahead, before an extraordinary goal from the stylish Le Tissier reminded everyone of his exceptional maverick talent.

Two more monster Cup ties followed at Old Trafford, the first being the home leg of the Champions League quarter-final fixture against the Italian giants, Inter Milan. United won 2-0, with Beckham and Yorke duplicating the same first-half goals, both being engineered from inch-perfect crosses and a superb flicked header.

Chelsea forced a 0-0 draw in the Sixth Round FA Cup tie against Chelsea three days later. After the battle with Milan, Sir Alex rotated the side as the Premiership leaders faced the stiffest workload of any side in modern times. With Yorke and Cole on the bench, Ole played for all but the last eight minutes when Cole replaced him. Chelsea, inspired by Zola, were unbowed at the end of a gridlocked contest. Di Matteo of Chelsea was sent off in the first half and Paul Scholes was dismissed in the closing minutes.

Three nights later, United broke the deadlock – and Blues' hearts – when they won the replay 2-0. Two goals from Yorke, both set up by Andy Cole, were enough to overcome Vialli's team. Ole came on for Yorke in the closing stages.

The four-point lead over Arsenal was maintained when Andy Cole scored twice against his old side Newcastle at St James' Park. Unusually, Peter Schmeichel went off at half-time with the 'flu as a precautionary measure prior to United's return fixture with Inter in Milan.

Ole played in neither of these matches. A vital goal from Paul Scholes two minutes from time gave United a draw in the San Siro and a place in the semi-finals. It was United's best ever result in Italy, their previous six visits all ending in defeat. The Red Machine moved inexorably towards its destiny in Spain.

Interestingly, 50 per cent of the points dropped by United came in fixtures immediately following European games, so it was increasingly important as the tournament unfolded to remain consistent in the League as well. In the following Premiership clash with Everton, United's League wobbles were non-existent. Ole, playing alongside Yorke and Cole, struck the first goal after 55 minutes in United's 3-1 home victory, following stubborn resistance by the Merseysiders. It was a vital breakthrough because both Arsenal and Chelsea were snapping at United's heels.

The goal that broke the deadlock started when he collected a pass from Gary Neville, whose muscular surge had taken him to the edge of the Everton box, and worked a one-two with Yorke. Ole then spun before expertly firing home a low drive. Neville himself doubled United's lead and Beckham wrapped it up with his first goal in five months. After the match, Ferguson was quick to recognise Ole's contribution, and reinforced the opinion that Ole was critical to his strategic thinking, and was a key element of his ongoing assault on three trophies.

Beckham scored again to grab a point at Wimbledon. With the home European semi-final against Juventus looming, United seemed distracted and unable to summon the fire required to beat the south Londoners. With Jaap Staam missing, Ronny Johnsen played in the heart of the defence alongside his Norwegian international partner Henning Berg. When Ole came on for Blomqvist after 73 minutes, there were three Norwegians on the field.

Wimbledon one day, Juventus the next – psychologically, the difference in class and importance of the games were aspects that needed to be managed carefully by the coaching staff at United. The Reds struggled in the first half to contain the Italian Champions, seeming a little overwhelmed by the size of the occasion. Conte gave them an early lead and only a late goal from Ryan Giggs kept United in the competition. In his autobiography, Roy Keane remembered, 'Juventus was a huge test. We didn't play well. We were on a 20-game unbeaten run in League and Cup. With Inzaghi up front, Zidane, Deschamps and Davids in midfield, and a typically mean Italian defence to back them up, we were not talking Nottingham Forest and 8-1 victories here.'

Sheringham came on for the last 15 minutes and he, more than anyone, put United back in contention. In the 90th minute, he headed down a Beckham cross for Giggs to

*Above*: Ole turns on the speed as Manchester United beat Newcastle United 2-0 to win the FA Cup Final at Wembley Stadium, May 1999, the year of their remarkable Treble.

*Below*: Team-mate Jaap Stam (left) and Ole with the FA Cup on their team's triumphant tour of Manchester.

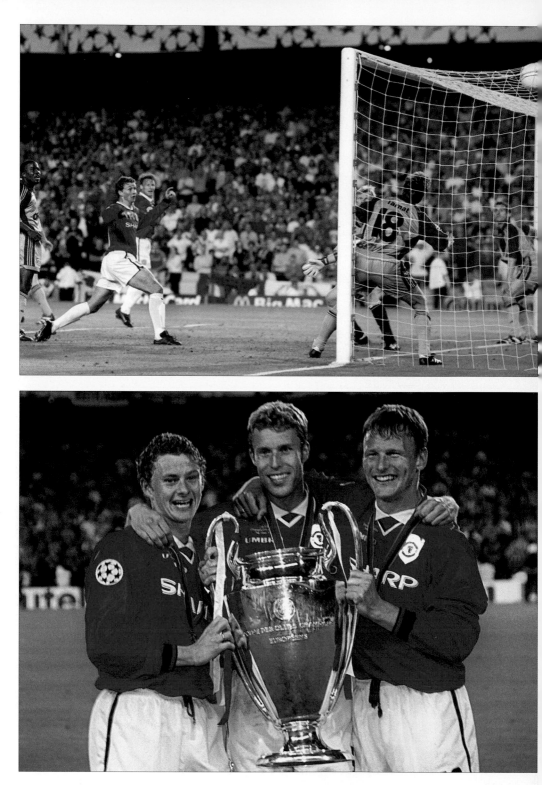

*Above*: Scoring the winning goal for Manchester United against Bayern Munich for the Champions League Cup Final, 26 May 1999.

*Below*: Goal scorers Ole and Teddy Sheringham (right) with team-mate Ronny Johnsen (middle) holding the European Cup.

Pictured here with partner Silje Lyngvaer and Noah after attending Brooklyn Beckham's third birthday party at Manchester's Film Works, March 2002.

Spending quality time with his son: (above) watching his local team in Norway, and having fun on a quad bike (below).

smash into the roof of the net. Manchester United appeared to have a monumental task ahead, having to win in Turin if they were to get to the Final.

Another huge battle presented itself four days later when they fought out a 0-0 draw at Villa Park on 11 April with Arsenal in the semi-final of the FA Cup. Referee David Elleray ruled out Keane's thunderous volley because of a highly debatable offside decision. Ole replaced Giggs in the first period of extra time, and Arsenal's Nelson Vivas was sent off in that period, but United were unable to take advantage.

So it was back to Villa Park on the following Wednesday for one of the most extraordinary FA Cup matches ever played by United. Sir Alex gambled again by leaving Yorke, Irwin, Scholes and Giggs on the bench and rested Andy Cole. Ole was the main striker playing in front of Sheringham, who created Beckham's goal to put United ahead after 17 minutes. Beckham started the move, gathering a loose ball in front of Arsenal's Petit to find Sheringham. He shielded the ball from Tony Adams before turning it back into the path of Beckham who curled a powerful shot into the bottom right-hand corner. Arsenal keeper David Seaman appeared to have it covered at one stage, but the flight of the ball deceived him. The game deteriorated in a spate of bookings and flare-ups, Keane and Butt becoming involved in a war with Petit and Vieira, and little love being lost between Jaap Staam and Dennis Bergkamp.

Ole should have doubled United's lead early in the second half when Keane played him in on Seaman, but, for once, he missed the target as he dragged his shot past the post. That miss proved costly because Arsenal inched themselves back into the game. Marc Overmars came on for Arsenal as they threw everything into attack and forced United back on their heels. Ryan Giggs was thrown into the fray, and then Bergkamp equalised with 20 minutes to go. It was a fortunate goal because Schmeichel could have conceivably saved his right-foot shot but the ball spun off Stam's leg into the corner of the net.

Arsenal were now clearly on top with Bergkamp at the hub of everything. A fierce shot from him was dropped by Schmeichel and Anelka dribbled round him to tap home, but the goal was ruled out for offside. Keane was then sent off two minutes later for chopping down Overmars as he rampaged down the left flank. Already on a yellow for a foul on Bergkamp, the United captain knew Elleray would make him walk.

Once again, the Treble seemed to be slipping away, perhaps never more so than when Arsenal were awarded a penalty in injury time. Phil Neville tripped Ray Parlour in the box and Elleray had no hesitation in pointing to the spot.

In each competition, there was a defining moment when United appeared to have blown it – 3-0 down at home to Middlesbrough was the Premiership low point. When Bergkamp strode up to take the penalty at Villa Park, not only did it look like the Reds were heading out of the FA Cup, but the Premiership again looked in jeopardy. Arsenal had, at that juncture, the psychological advantage. They had already beaten United by 3-0 score lines in the Charity Shield and in their September Premiership Highbury fixture. In addition, they had come away from Old Trafford with a point. With Chelsea only drawing at Middlesbrough the same evening and missing the chance to overtake United, Arsenal remained the only team mentally and physically strong enough to deprive them of the title. If they had beaten United at Villa Park, there was the overwhelming feeling that it would have given them the impetus to go on and snatch the title, leaving United demoralised and vulnerable. The FA Cup was a poor third on a list of priorities, but it was a vitally significant moment on which the rest of United's season depended. If the penalty went in, then there would only be a matter of minutes to salvage the game, and perhaps keep their season on track.

All Schmeichel could think about was saving the penalty. Bergkamp was desperate to score, not only to provide the spring board for a potential Double, but also to bury the ghost of missing the previous Cup Final Arsenal won during their last Double-winning campaign. The Dutch master hit the ball almost perfectly to the left, but Schmeichel flew through the air to turn the ball around the post. It was a great save, possibly one of the best of Schmeichel's long and glittering career, and paved the way for even greater things as the season reached its climax.

There could only be one winner now as the game went into extra time. The United fans sensed it and turned up the volume as Ole was replaced at the start of the first period of extra time by Yorke. Schmeichel was now unbeatable as he foiled Bergkamp again with a full-length save, then beating out what looked like a certain own-goal when Petit's corner was deflected towards the goal by Ronny Johnsen.

Giggs won the match with possibly the greatest goal in the history of Manchester United and certainly the greatest goal in the history (so far) of Ryan Giggs. The goal stemmed from a misplaced pass from the exhausted Patrick Vieira which Giggs gathered. Semi-finals are often won or lost on a mistake, a missed tackle or a misdirected pass, and they usually occur when fatigue sets in, particularly during periods of extra time.

What Giggs created was a thing of great beauty, of footballing poetry almost, producing an astonishing dribble which brought the amazed crowd to its feet. Arsenal were in no great danger at the start of his run; they were back in strength and were ready for anything. Giggs rolled the ball under his left foot, his shoulders swaying, and balanced, weight forward, ready to go either way when the first challenge was made. The Arsenal defenders opted to hurl themselves at him to try and dispossess him, but, one by one, he ghosted through them, almost in slow motion, weaving and twisting his way through the whole Highbury rearguard. Giggs finished with a powerful shot past Seaman into the top, far corner of the net.

Giggs set off in a famous run down the touchline, whirling his white shirt with the red-and-black panels above his head. It was one of the most iconic images of football in the 1990s. Strewn around the pitch was the wreckage of the most famous defence in football, and it heralded the first time that United had beaten Arsenal in seven attempts. That goal also secured Giggs the status of an Old Trafford legend, alongside the likes of Best and Cantona.

Ole was in the side for the home game against Sheffield Wednesday, another domestic Premiership fixture sandwiched between the epic Arsenal replay and the vital return with Juventus. The importance of the Norwegian predator to his side's cause could not be underestimated as he put United ahead after 34 minutes with a typically opportunistic goal. Blomqvist, in for the resting goal hero Giggs, sent over a high centre that found skipper Keane at the far post. The Irishman made a hash of his attempted volley and the ball spun crazily to Sheringham, who tried a quick overhead flick. It fell to Ole, who pocketed yet another goal with a crisp, instant drive into the far corner of the Wednesday net.

Sheringham's assistance was repaid on half-time when Ole turned provider for his partner. Ole fired over a cross that Beckham would have been proud of, and Sheringham put away the second with the help of the post. It was a special goal for him, his 250th in a glorious career.

The Sheringham–Solskjaer combination continued to light up the game. Both players could see opportunities early, find space and fire off speculative shots. Sheringham put Scholes in for the third on the hour, and United cruised to a solid win, maintaining a four-point lead over Arsenal.

The fact that the Solskjaer–Sheringham partnership was as effective as that of Yorke and Cole was a crucial factor in United's march towards the Treble. At the time of writing, it is interesting to note that all of the quartet are still playing top-class football and scoring goals. Sheringham at West Ham entered the records books by being the oldest player to score a Premiership goal, a wonderful header against Blackburn in a crucial relegation battle – he was 40 years and 210 days old at the time. He joined the former United favourites Gordon Strachan and Les Sealey as being in the select band of Premiership players over 40 years of age.

Andy Cole at Portsmouth was still scoring freely after spells at Manchester City and Fulham. Cole also became the second highest all-time Premiership goalscorer behind Shearer and in front of Thierry Henry.

Dwight Yorke is still playing international football for Trinidad & Tobago and was reunited with his former skipper Roy Keane at Sunderland.

Finally, the Champions League was reaching its climax with a trip to the Stadio Delle Alpi for the return with Juventus. The Italians already had an advantage over United by virtue of the away goal and the situation became far worse when Fillippo Inzaghi scored two early goals. He had missed a great chance at Old Trafford to win the game for Juventus, but his brace of goals in Italy appeared to have doomed United to a semi-final exit. Inzaghi, nicknamed 'Super Pippo', is Italy's highest scorer in European competitions. At that point, United looked down and out, although just like the moment when Bergkamp strode up to take the injury time penalty at Villa Park, United found a depth of resilience and belief that enabled them to raise their collective game to a new level.

That night they wore the unique red-and-white strip used exclusively in the Champions League; the socks and the collar on the shirt were the basic white, with no trimmings. Keane's shirt was almost torn from his back by his team-mates when he leapt to head in Beckham's corner to drag United back into the game. Keane was booked soon after; chasing a loose ball from Blomqvist, he collided with Zidane and earned a booking that meant he would miss the final – if there was one.

Yorke made sure there was by equalising from Cole's cross after 34 minutes. Amazingly, United were back in front by virtue of the away goals; Juventus, apparently coasting to the final, were knocked completely out of their stride.

As Keane so eloquently put it in his autobiography, 'They packed it in. Zidane, Deschamps and Davids all went missing. I went for a 50-50 ball against Davids. It was no contest.'

Scholes grabbed the winner six minutes from time in one of the greatest ever performances from United. They had gone looking for the winner throughout the second half, not content to hang on. Ole did not play in the game and did not make any more appearances until the FA Cup Final at the end of May.

Before then, United clinched the first leg of the Treble by winning the Premier League by one point from Arsenal. It was the 12th in their history and Ferguson's fifth win. Arsenal pushed them very hard and United eventually only won by a solitary point. Arsenal briefly overtook them, but a crucial United game in hand made the difference. The Old Trafford side also remained unbeaten for the rest of the season, despite dropping points in away draws against Leeds, Liverpool and Blackburn. The title was clinched in the last game of the season, a tense 2-1 home win over Tottenham. Les Ferdinand had put Spurs ahead, but goals from Beckham and Cole brought the trophy back to Manchester.

Then it was on to Wembley for the second element of the unlikely Treble. Their opponents were Newcastle, managed then by the Dutch legend Ruud Gullit. Rumours were rife that Gullit was in conflict with the iconic Alan Shearer. The famous Geordie side was a cauldron of simmering tensions and seething passions. Ole played in his first Cup Final for United alongside Cole and Giggs, with Yorke and Sheringham on the bench. Bayern Munich awaited them at the Nou Camp four days later, but all their thoughts were on the FA Cup.

Scholes and Keane were out of the reckoning for the Bayern game through suspension, and were anxious to make up for it at Wembley. Keane only lasted eight minutes; already playing with strapping, he was the victim of a hard tackle by Gary Speed that put him out of the game. Butt would have deputised under normal circumstances, but Sir Alex was safeguarding him for the European final. Instead, Sheringham was sent on with Ole moved to the right, switching with Beckham, who now went inside to play in central midfield alongside Scholes.

Even Sir Alex could not have dreamed how well this formation was to work. Within two minutes of coming on, Sheringham scored after a neat triangular move involving Cole and Scholes. The ex-Millwall striker gave Newcastle keeper Steve Harper no chance. The goal settled United, and any doubts or misgivings relating to the loss of Keane were dispelled. Newcastle proved to offer little in the way of competitive challenge – they were weak opponents, one of the poorest sides to appear in a recent FA Cup Final, and as a preparation for the battle that lay ahead it could not have been easier for United.

Seven minutes into the second half, Ole created the goal that killed the game and secured the second part of their Treble. The Norwegian picked up a loose ball and found Sheringham with his back to the Newcastle defence. Sheringham instantly found Scholes, who fired a piledriver of a shot into the back of the net.

United coasted for the rest of the game, with Jaap Stam coming on for Scholes 15 minutes from time. The Dutchman had had problems with his Achilles and was being saved for the Champions League Final, but Ferguson wanted to give him a run-out and a Cup medal. Once the inevitable had occurred, with the game being brought to a merciful end by the referee, Prince Charles presented the Cup to Keane.

Stam was Ole's room-mate and, in his controversial book, he described the post-match events, saying, 'All the celebrations on the pitch seemed to fly by and we left that pulsating cauldron of excitement and returned to the dressing room where I sat next to Ole. "That was brilliant," I told him, "miles better than I expected."

'"You can't beat the feeling of winning here," he admitted.

'"It's odd, though, Ole... I'm from Holland, you're from Norway, and here we are feeling on top of the world about winning a trophy in England."

'Ole laughed. "It's strange, all right, but then how many countries have the FA Cup?"'

Both of their native countries participated in the Champions League, though, but on this occasion the representatives in the Final were English and German. Bayern Munich had fought their way to the Final by overcoming Dynamo Kiev 4-3 in the semis. It was a fine performance, because the Russian side included the Ukrainian Andrei Shevchenko, commonly regarded as one of the finest strikers in the world. United had played Bayern twice already in the competition and had not managed to beat them, with the Germans finishing as group winners. They were a typical German side – well organised, tough physically and mentally and very hard to beat. Steffan Effenberg was the heart of the team, a master of instant, precise control. They were also in the hunt for a Treble of their own, having scooped their domestic trophies.

After leaving Wembley, United decamped to Burnham Beeches where the Double-winning celebrations were very restrained. Everything was geared for the Champions League Final and the recovery of the long-lost trophy. Ole and his pals trained on Sunday morning at Bisham Abbey, the England team's training ground. Then they took Concorde to Spain. The plane was decommissioned shortly afterwards, but Ferguson's grand gesture was the start of the psychological war he was to wage on the Germans. The future kings of Europe were travelling in style – the message was clear: best team in the world flew in the best plane in the world.

They stayed in a beautiful hotel at Sitges, just down the coast from Barcelona, although Ferguson was disappointed at the number of United fans waiting at the hotel. The Old Trafford supremo wanted complete rest and seclusion for his players.

Ole roomed with Jaap Stam as usual. It seemed strange that the club that would hire Concorde to transport its players would then make them share rooms rather than let them have their own space. Stam was quoted as saying that he liked to room with Ole because he did not snore and was very quiet. They spent most of the time watching DVDs and reading thriller novels. Ole said in the *Opus* of the accommodation arrangements, 'I was rooming with Jaap Stam, as usual, and he was taking an afternoon nap. I couldn't sleep, so I watched a bit of a DVD.'

The day before the Final, the United players watched a DVD of Bayern; the tension was gently rising, and thoughts of the Treble were soon forgotten. Beckham, who had been playing brilliantly in the last few weeks of the season, was told that he'd be starting in the middle of midfield alongside Nicky Butt, the pair replacing the engine room of Keane and Scholes. Giggs went to the right, with Jesper Blomqvist coming in on the left. Ole and Sheringham were named as substitutes.

The United fans were officially given 30,000 tickets that night, but in truth there were in excess of 45,000 in the Nou Camp. It seemed to be a sea of red-and-white, and the noise was deafening.

Keane sat next to Scholes and United coach Jimmy Ryan, later describing watching the Reds kick-off as his worst experience in football. The Cork-born captain of Manchester United was prevented from having any influence on the pitch, and watched instead with another two billion people... and the substitutes who might just get a chance to play their part.

Somewhere in the arena, George Best was watching and recalling a spring night 31 years earlier when he had helped United win the Cup.

Sir Alex's parting words to his troops were apparently along the lines of 'no team can beat you if you play at the level you are capable of'. Unfortunately, United played nowhere near that level for most of the game, having got off to the worst possible start by conceding a goal in the first six minutes. Beckham lost possession and Stam bounced off the giant Bayern striker Carsten Jancker as he burst through on goal. Ronny Johnsen then fouled Jancker, and referee supremo Pierluigi Collina had no hesitation in blowing for a free-kick.

It was a huge night for Schmeichel, his last ever appearance for the Reds and wearing the captain's armband in place of Keane. There looked to be no real danger as Basler shaped to take the long-range free-kick. Bayern fashioned the set-piece beautifully, however, with Markus Babbel charging Nicky Butt and Jancker's oblique run pulling Stam out of the wall. Basler struck a swerving drive through the gap which deceived Schmeichel. It could be argued that the Dane's positioning was less than perfect, but he became a virtual onlooker as the ball sailed into the United net.

That was pretty much it for the majority of the match.

United seemed incapable of raising their game, while the Germans were content to sit on their lead. In the second half, with United pushing up for the equaliser, Bayern twice hit the woodwork when they could have killed the game off completely. First, a long run from Basler took him deep into the United half, where he fed the sub Mehmet Scholl, who deftly chipped Schmeichel. The ball drifted over the keeper's head but hit the post and bounced clear.

Then United failed to clear a corner and the bald-headed Jancker executed a daring scissor-kick, which propelled the ball against the bar with Schmeichel beaten. This remarkable good fortune lifted the United fans, who roared their team on even more.

Like their fans, the German team seemed strangely subdued. By the time Sheringham came on for Blomqvist with just over 20 minutes left, United had almost total control of the game, but despite their superior possession, they could make no clear-cut chances. Bayern were holding on for dear life in the closing minutes and Keane was convinced that they had 'gone'.

With nine minutes left, Ferguson sent Ole on for Cole, although this seemed a last, desperate roll of the dice. Still the minutes ticked away, and seemingly the Treble with them. With two minutes left, Basler was substituted by Salihamidzic, the old campaigner milking the moment for all it was worth, having scored what he and most of the two billion watching thought was the Champions League decider. Given what happened next, he would probably never make such overtures to the crowd again in similar circumstances.

The fourth official held up the board to show that there were three minutes of added time left, at which Gary Neville was seen screaming, 'It's not too late.'

# THE IMMORTAL TREBLE

In the last minute of normal time, United won a corner on the left. It was about then that Schmeichel raced up into the Bayern penalty box, desperate to salvage something for United. Sir Alex was horrified at this risk-taking. Keane shook his head, knowing that it had never worked before. This time, though, Schmeichel's presence was enough to unsettle the Germans momentarily. They were probably also thinking that it presented a wonderful opportunity for them to snatch a breakaway goal.

Beckham sent over an immaculate corner, and a Bayern defender sliced his volleyed clearance to Giggs, who tried to thunder it home. The Welshman only managed the faintest of touches, though, and the ball spun to Sheringham. He reacted immediately, and rolled the ball past Oliver Kahn for the equaliser.

The Nou Camp exploded in red-and-white delirium as the disbelieving fans celebrated saving the game. The Germans were completely demoralised by the goal, some players sinking to their knees in despair. Drained by the events, cursing their bad luck, they now had to pick themselves up and try to win the game from an equal starting point.

Bayern kicked off deep into injury time; United regained possession and forced another corner, again on the left. Beckham repeated the trick; if anything, his delivery was even more accurate. The battle-hardened Sheringham leapt to meet it on his forehead, and flicked the ball downwards. Ole was waiting – right place, right time – and thrashed the ball first time into the roof of the net.

In *Opus*, Ole remembered, 'The goal... it's one of those that you score one time out of five. If you score one time out of five, you're lucky, because you haven't practised that finish. You just do it. You just guide the ball on. More often than not, it goes over the bar... And there's a man on the far post so, other times, you won't guide it above him. There were so many things that could have gone wrong with that finish... it was just instinct.'

# 6

# 'You Are My Solskjaer...'

After the dust had finally settled and the unadulterated insanity of those ten days in May finally subsided, one fact remained – Manchester United had done the Treble, and Ole had scored the winner in the match that sealed it.

As John McEnroe so succinctly put it, 'The older I get, the better I get.' In Ole's case, that could be said to be true. Ole claims only to have watched the 1999 Champions League Final once since his supreme moment of triumph. It is rumoured that he does not even own it on DVD. The only record of it in the Solskjaer family is a video kept by his father in Norway. As the technology develops, and old formats become obsolete, soon he will not have the equipment to play it on. The blue biro on the VHS label is fading, but the memory never will.

Ole told the *Sunday Times*, 'When I come on, you can see there's a step, a rhythm in my running. When I'm heavy-legged, you can tell I'm not on song. But entering the field that night I was springy. I was bounding on. Everything felt good and my only thought was positive. Come on, get a goal.'

We know the rest. There are many stories of that magical night in the Nou Camp, and a few surfaced in the aftermath of that glorious triumph, adding to the sense of fantastic, other-worldly myth surrounding the whole event.

Swede Lennart Johannson, the UEFA President, had been asked to go down to the pitch to present the Cup to the victorious Germans. With a couple of minutes left and Bayern Munich still a goal ahead, he made his way down in the lift to the bowels of the magnificent Catalan stadium. As Johannson stepped out of the lift, he saw George Best, who had scored the second goal in extra time of the 1968 European Cup Final, heading out into the evening air. Poor George, a shadow of the fit, dynamic global star he'd once been, must surely have been bitterly disappointed to see his beloved side lose to Bayern Munich that night, and appear so lacking in invention in their quest for goals. Having decided that there was no hope of a reprieve, he headed for the exit.

Shortly after his sighting of Best, the UEFA President made his way up through the tunnel to the touchline. The noise level suggested that the game was over. Glancing upwards, he glanced at the illuminated scoreboard. At first, it did not register with him, but then he realised that it indicated that Manchester United had won 2-1. Disbelieving, he had to check the score with some excited fans, who told him about Ole's fantastic last-gasp contribution.

The German team were devastated; Michael Tarner was waiting for the earth to swallow him up, while Sammy Kuffour punched the ground in despair.

Was it the greatest goal scored in the history of the club?

Not the most spectacular, certainly, but, to this day, it can rightly claim to be the most important because it not only won the Champions League in a fiendishly dramatic final twist, but it also marked the watershed of one of the most exciting periods in English football.

The websites were full of polls for the greatest post-war goal. Top of the élite strikes was Giggs's semi-final Cup-winner against Arsenal, which topped most polls. Cantona's goal at Newcastle was rated very highly, too, and there was one he scored for Leeds against Chelsea in April 1992 in which he chipped the ball over Steve Clarke's head, ran round him and slammed home a sweet volley that people still talk about to this day.

The most savagely hit goal by a United player was scored by Bobby Charlton in the 1967 Charity Shield game against Spurs. A world-class goalkeeper, Pat Jennings was in the Tottenham goal that wonderful August afternoon. It would have taken his fingers off had he even managed to get near it. It must have been an amazing match to witness, as Jennings himself scored during that game with a goal kick that bounced over Alex Stepney's head.

In more recent times, Paul Scholes's goal at Villa Park in the 2006/07 season was worthy of being in such exalted company.

How do you follow a grand slam? After the perfect season, what more could be achieved? Well, nothing – the Quadruple was still something to aim for, but no one would ever consider that to be realistically attainable, given the demands of a full season and the fixture congestion. There is simply nowhere else to go after achieving the Treble. When you reach the top of the mountain, there is only sky.

Sir Alex's most pressing problem prior to the 1999/2000

season was how to replace Peter Schmeichel, who had handed his gloves in after winning the Treble.

They went for Mark Bosnich, who had turned down Juventus to rejoin the club he loved. Rumours were rife that the Australian was caught in the power struggle between Martin Edwards and Ferguson, who had wanted Fabien Barthez, the French international, but Edwards did not want to pay a large transfer fee when Bosnich was available under the Bosman ruling.

The other major event of the summer was the marriage of David Beckham to Victoria Adams. It marked the start of a fairytale that was to lead them from London suburbia, where they both had their roots, to the razzmatazz of Hollywood and LA Galaxy. The young couple chose to live in Hertfordshire and the future England captain had a round trip of over 320 miles to The Cliff training ground. Perhaps it was around this time that the first cracks in the relationship between Beckham and his manager started to show.

The first competitive match of the season was a 1-2 defeat to Arsenal in the Charity Shield. After that, the first game in the Premiership was an away tie at Everton. Ole played in this match, which ended in a 1-1 draw. Yorke put United ahead, but a late headed own-goal from Jaap Stam meant that the points were shared. Then it was five straight wins as the Champions revved up a gear. The first victory was a 4-0 thumping of Sheffield Wednesday at Old Trafford, a game in which Ole scored his first goal of the new season after coming on as sub.

Around that time, the chants of 'Who put the ball in the Germans net? Ole Gunnar Solskjaer... ' could be heard around Old Trafford, and it instantly became a classic. To the United faithful, though, the all-time favourite with the fans when they wanted to praise their Norwegian hero publicly was sung to the tune of 'You Are My Sunshine':

'You are my Solskjaer, my Ole Solskjaer;
you make me happy, when skies are grey.
And Alan Shearer was much dearer
So please don't take my Solskjaer away.'

A fine 2-1 victory at Highbury was the high spot of the mini-run; Keane scored both the goals after Arsenal had taken the lead. The midfield tyro won his personal gladiatorial battle with Vieira as Arsenal slipped to their first home defeat since December 1997. United won six of the first nine games, drawing the other three.

Bosnich suffered a hamstring injury after just two-and-a-half games and was replaced by Raimond Van Der Gouw until Sir Alex purchased Massimo Taibi. The Sicilian was signed for £4.5 million from Venezia and only played four games for United.

The third of them was a 3-3 draw at home to Southampton, in which Ole played. During the match, Taibi allowed a weak shot from Matt Le Tissier to squirm through his legs. Worse was to follow the following week at Chelsea, when United lost their first Premiership game in 10 months, a run of 29 games. The 5-0 score line was their most embarrassing defeat since the kicking they received at Newcastle.

In the first 30 seconds, Taibi misjudged his punched clearance and Gus Poyet's header flew into the net. Shortly after, Chris Sutton scored one of the few goals in his ill-fated time at Stamford Bridge to make it 2-0.

Nicky Butt was dismissed midway through the first half

after a clash with Dennis Wise which ended any chance of a United comeback. Without Keane and Giggs, they could do nothing to stem the blue tidal wave and conceded three further second-half goals. Poyet hit the third after Taibi failed to hold Frank Lebouef's simple ground shot. Then Henning Berg, tormented by Zola all game, turned one of the little Italian's crosses into his own net. Jody Morris scored a fifth goal with a fine shot that went through Taibi's legs. The keeper was subsequently dubbed 'the blind Venetian' by the fanzines, never played for United again and returned to Italy for £2.5 million to join Reggiana.

Ole came on as sub for Cole after 65 minutes, while Beckham was subbed by Teddy Sheringham. Ole almost pulled a late consolation goal back when he hit the side netting with a flashing drive.

Sir Alex's famed 'hair dryer' treatment has become the stuff of football legend. Doug Rougvie, the ex-Chelsea defender, played for the Scot at Aberdeen and once tellingly described his former manager as 'a serial chucker', referring to his propensity to hurl tea cups and plates around when his side under-performed. Just how much crockery was smashed that day is not known – all the players, though, received a severe tongue-lashing, with the gaffer questioning their credentials as holders of the Champions League.

United's defence of their Champions League trophy went smoothly in the first group stage, facing Croatia Zagreb, Olympique Marseille and Sturm Graz. Ole was sub in United's only defeat in the first phase, a 1-0 defeat to Marseille. Roared on by a fiercely partisan crowd, the French side won by a goal from a promising player called William Gallas, the first time that the classy French defender was to clash swords with Ole.

Unlucky that night, and thwarted by some great defending by Marseille, Ole went on to score the winning goal against Sturm Graz in early November at Old Trafford. The goal was superb, a wonderful volley from 30 yards that flew into the net. It put them through to the next stage of the competition, and a double-header against Fiorentina. Once again, Ole was on the bench in Florence. Defensive mistakes from Keane, who had been in brilliant form that autumn, and Henning Berg provided gilt-edged opportunities to one of the best finishers in the game, Gabriel Batistuta, and his team-mate Balbo. They both took their chances well, and United went down 2-0.

November was a massive month for United because they were soon to fly to Japan to play against Palmeiras of Brazil in the Toyota Inter-Continental Cup on 30 November. This was effectively the unofficial World Club Championship, between the Champions of Europe and their South American counterparts. No team from the British Isles had ever won it.

Celtic competed in 1967, when the Cup was decided on points, and had lost to the Argentinian side Racing Club in a play-off. In the second leg in Buenos Aires, the Celtic goalkeeper was hit by a missile and carried off. In the play-off at Montevideo, four Celtic players and two Argentinians were sent off.

The following year, Matt Busby's European Cup winners played another team from Argentina – Estudiantes. In the first leg in Buenos Aires, the European Cup holders lost 1-0 in a brutal hacking match. World Cup hero Nobby Stiles was sent off and Bobby Charlton, George Best and virtually every other player in the team were assaulted. Busby called the referee's judgement that day into question. In the return match, an Estudiantes player called Verón headed an early goal which killed the game. George Best was sent off for fighting and Dennis Law was carried off .Willie Morgan scored late in the game, and it remained at that time the only goal scored in the competition by a British side.

Sir Alex was desperate to win in Japan and took the competition very seriously. The problem for United was the punishing schedule of the English game – the trans-global fixture had to be squeezed in between the demands of the Premiership and Champions League matches. Palmeiras arrived in Tokyo three days ahead of the party from Manchester in an attempt to acclimatise themselves better to the conditions.

Beckham was accosted in true 'Beatlemania' style by the locals at the airport, and the team finally arrived exhausted at their hotel. Ole roomed again with Stam, staying in their hotel suite endlessly surfing the channels despite the exotic locality. The hotel was superb, with Spanish marble showers and penthouse villas. Ole remained very much a down-to-earth, professional, modest team player, despite the massive profile he'd earned through his dramatic winner at the Nou Camp. His European sensibility and lack of ego endeared him to the East Asia media; he talked eloquently about his team-mates and was confident and perceptive when discussing the forthcoming game. When talking about himself, he preferred to remain discreet and self-deprecating.

The team found it hard to acclimatise; they could not sleep as they had no time to adjust to the new time zone. Geoff Boycott had identified one of the failings of the England cricket team's poor showing in the 2006/07 Ashes Series, stating that they should have had at least a week to establish a decent sleep pattern. Stam concurred in his autobiography that in the training sessions they could just about drag themselves around the pitch.

Sir Alex looked to Ole and Sheringham to repeat their Champions League heroics as he started with them both up front in the Toyota Final. Neither of them scored, the only goal of the game coming on 35 minutes from the indefatigable Roy Keane, still providing the drive and energy. The star of the match, though, was Mark Bosnich, who played his finest game for the club, turning in a match-winning performance with a string of magnificent saves. If he could have maintained that form and avoided the pitfalls of fame, Bosnich may even have supplanted Schmeichel in the affections of the United fans and be universally acclaimed as one of the finest goalkeepers of his generation.

When he sadly slipped out of the game, the most precious memento of his time at United was the Toyota World Club Cup medal he won in Tokyo. Despite mouth-watering sums offered to him, he refused to auction it.

Ryan Giggs amazingly won the Man of the Match award and a new car. Bosnich should have been given the keys, but consoled himself with a samurai sword he bought in a souvenir shop. Sir Alex was delighted by the victory and the fact that his side had now confirmed themselves as the pre-eminent force in world club football.

There was no respite for the new Champions of the World, though, as the domestic season continued. Next up was Everton. Ole turned it on that day as he hit four goals in 31 minutes to devastate the Merseysiders. It was another thrillingly perfect display by the most clinical finisher in the history of the club. Ole became the first player to net four times on two occasions in the Premiership. In the

*Manchester United Annual 2007*, he says of his attitude, 'Always have the courage to score. Goalscoring is an instinct and is something you're born with; I've always felt that instinct and, no matter what positions I've got myself into, I've also felt I could score. But you need to possess a certain amount of greed and selfishness to do that. If you believe you can score from any position you have a great chance of becoming a top striker.'

That week, he certainly proved it, helping his team become the first British team to be World Club Champions and then shrugging off the fatigue incurred on a trip from the other side of the world to set a new Premiership goalscoring record.

The goalscoring continued unabated; four days later, again at Old Trafford, he scored the last goal as Valencia were dismantled 3-0. Having achieved so much the previous season, Ole was as thirsty for goals as ever, and the feeling of exhilaration at scoring was something that drove him on to deliver time and time again.

The twentieth century drew to a close with United just one point behind Leeds; they were to only lose one more Premiership game that season. Their domestic form was never in doubt, and the team consistently proved their superiority with fine performances. For Ole Gunnar Solskjaer, there was never to be another year like it.

The new millennium started with one of the most controversial events in United's long and sometimes chequered history. In October 1999, Ole and his pals had been told at a meeting conducted by Sir Alex that the team would not be entering the FA Cup. England was trying to host the 2006 World Cup and the decision rested with FIFA. They wanted United to play in the first World Club

Championship to be held in Brazil in January 2000. Immense pressure had been exerted by the Government and the FA for United to go. Eventually, an exemption was granted for United to withdraw from the Cup.

The machinations had been going on since the previous spring when United became the top team in Europe. A propaganda offensive was planned to tie in with the tournament. The late Minister for Sport, Tony Banks, threw his weight behind the political campaign to get Manchester United to go to Brazil, and the team found themselves in an impossible situation – they surely could not go against the wishes of the Government, FIFA and the FA, yet they knew only too well what a negative backlash there would be in the press if they chose to withdraw from the Cup. Little would be known about the pressure they were under to attend the tournament on Britain's behalf.

The truth was, the FA Cup had dwindled in importance over the years. In the first two seasons that Ole was at Old Trafford, they had gone out of the Cup to Wimbledon and Barnsley, sides they had comprehensively completed the double over in the Premiership. Until an automatic Champions League place was awarded to the Cup winners, then the superpowers would continue to regard it as a lesser competition, much like the Worthington Cup, significant only for a brief moment of domestic glitter and short-lived bragging rights. Wenger, Mourinho and Benítez had all come from backgrounds where the domestic cups were of little consequence. Wenger sarcastically referred to the United trip as their 'mid-winter break'.

A few days after Christmas, having just fought out a 2-2 draw in freezing Sunderland, United flew to Rio to compete in the FIFA World Cup Championship. The media circus was inescapable, and stories of the lads enjoying the high life and using the trip as a marketing opportunity were rife. Again, acclimatisation was a factor for the players – the temperature and altitude were enormously difficult to adjust to. Ole told Sky Sports, 'It was a good trip... we have been building team spirit and have learned something about another football culture.'

In the opening group phase, United were drawn against Necaxa of Mexico, Vasco da Gama of Brazil and Australian side South Melbourne. The first game was against the Mexicans in one of the most famous stadiums in the world, the Maracana, known as the home of Brazilian football. Situated in the centre of Rio, it had been graced by players with the hypnotising presence of Garrincha, Tosato and Socrates. Pelé had scored his 1,000th goal there. Ole was good but he had a long way to go to beat that particular total.

The stadium, like the fixture, turned out to be a huge disappointment. It looked like it had seen better days, a run-down version of its former glory, when it could hold 200,000 for Brazil games and concerts. That day, it was so devoid of fans the players could hear each other bellowing for the ball.

The game kicked off in the afternoon with the local side Vasco da Gama playing in the relative cool of the evening. The afternoon heat was intense, reaching over 40°C; to make it worse, Beckham lost the toss and Necaxa got to defend the shady end of the stadium. Within minutes, the Reds were saturated in sweat and physically drained. They just could not settle into any rhythm. The defence toiled vainly as the Necaxa forwards danced around them. Things became worse when David Beckham was sent off for a high challenge. The game ended 1-1, but United could have sneaked it when Dwight Yorke missed a penalty. Necaxa tried every trick in the book to disrupt the flow of the game and waste time with substitutions.

The disappointing start meant that United had to beat Vasco da Gama to progress out of the group. Sir Alex ranted at his players that they had travelled halfway across the world and had to improve their performance considerably. At no point had they reached the high standard achieved in the Premiership week after week. His words went unheeded as they lost 1-3 to the Brazilians. With Beckham suspended, Ole again played but he admitted to Sky that 'our match against Vasco was one big flop. I was very tired and never really got into the game. Just about everything went wrong for me and for the team.'

Everything did go wrong as the boys from Brazil raced into a 3-0 half-time lead. The home side's strike force of Romario and Edmundo were the main threats as they tormented the United defence in the blistering heat. Two errors by Gary Neville in a three-minute spell put Romario in for gifted goals and the English Champions never recovered.

Vasco continued to toy with United in the second half and put on a great technical display. Ole, it must be said, had a poor game as he struggled in the heat; the oval shape of the stadium meant that no cooling breezes ever blew across the pitch. Unusually, he actually missed a couple of chances that he normally would have converted. Nicky Butt did slot home a late consolation goal but it was game over and United were out of the competition.

Before the last game, Ole did some sight seeing with his room-mate Stam. Goalkeeper Raimond van der Gouw came along for the ride, which turned out to be a cable-car ride to the top of Sugar Loaf mountain. Stam, unfortunately, did not have a head for heights, and was teased by his team-mates for feeling a little queasy throughout the trip.

Ole came back to earth with a bump when he played against South Melbourne in the last game of the ill-fated expedition. It ended in an easy 2-0 win to United, with Fortune scoring both goals. Ole was guilty of missing some easy chances, but as he acknowledged on his website, there was nothing to play for, and the heat sapped any energy the players might have had, reducing the pace of the game to a stroll in the searing temperature. He remembers, 'We had absolutely no pace and the temperature was over 40°C. For the most part, we walked around the pitch. But so long as I create chances, there's a possibility that the ball will go into the net and I'm not too worried.'

United did not even make it on to the podium as they did not finish in the first three. As a PR exercise, the trip was an unmitigated disaster. United were dumped out of the competition early and attracted even more adverse publicity when Martin Edwards was linked with a bar girl in a sleazy nightclub. Beckham's dismissal also triggered a round of headlines dredging up his World Cup sending off against Argentina and questioning his stability.

Another story was run in the tabloids that a group of United players, including Teddy Sheringham and Nicky Butt, were given a sound thrashing in a game of beach football by a team of bare-footed kids. Ole, thankfully, was not present at this game and his services as sub were not required either.

Back in London, rumours were circulating that Rio Ferdinand, the West Ham prodigy, was going to end up at United, although his manager Harry Redknapp flatly denied them. The player dubbed the 'Peckham Beckham' was to join Leeds in November of that year.

Ole hardly had time to unpack before he was thrown into the Premiership fray. Despite their various problems on the trip, and the miserable results, the players did seem rejuvenated by the sunshine and set about the task of defending their Premiership and Champions League trophies. In their absence, none of their main rivals – Leeds, Arsenal, Liverpool or Chelsea – were able to capitalise on the domestic front.

To ease their return, United had two home games. In the first, they drew 1-1 with Arsenal in a game that they should have won but so nearly lost. The Arsenal goal was a bad mix-up – Henry headed on, a panicky Stam failed to clear and Ljungberg dispossessed him and ran through to beat Bosnich. The Arsenal fans among the record Premiership crowd of 58,293 chanted: 'You should have stayed in Brazil!'

A late equaliser from Teddy Sheringham, turning in Beckham's cross, secured a valuable point. The Champions played very sluggishly, their 26-day break in the sunshine soon forgotten. The pitch was a problem that season and its poor surface created bobbles which gave rise to errors in passing and dribbling.

Ole came on as sub in the next game, a narrow 1-0 win over Middlesbrough. With the score 0-0, referee D'Urso awarded a penalty to 'Boro when Stam tackled the Brazilian maestro Juninho. This incident enraged Keane, who confronted the ref with a look of absolute fury on his contorted face. The picture of this incident was beamed worldwide and added even more to the controversial image of the Reds captain. Bosnich, who had a remarkable record of saving penalties, made an acrobatic stop and, in the closing moments, Beckham grabbed the winner.

That fortunate win set up United for the title; they lost only one Premiership game out of the last 17, a 3-0 defeat to Newcastle. It was a bizarre game, in which Ole came on as sub, Keane walked for two yellow cards and United had 70 per cent of the possession but ended up losing heavily. Shearer grabbed two breakaway goals as United vainly chased the game.

Ole scored United's goal in a 1-1 draw with Liverpool and another in a 7-1 butchering of West Ham. Paulo Wanchope had given the Hammers an early lead, but the home team turned on an exhilarating display of attacking football. For Ole, already a United legend, it was further proof that he had that priceless ability of contributing with vital goals whenever required. Apart from Arsenal and Leeds, who fell away after United had beaten them 1-0 at home, there was no pressure exerted on United by any of the other Premiership sides as they strolled to the title.

The usual rumours started to circulate that Ole was set to quit Old Trafford as he was fed up being on the bench. The tabloids claimed that Sir Alan Sugar had a large war chest for Tottenham and that he had earmarked Ole as a major purchase. Another rumour was that Ole would figure in a future deal that would see Sol Campbell make the reverse journey to Old Trafford. Sir Alex had long been an admirer of the Spurs centre-back and the speculation rose that he would be the £8 million answer to United's defensive problems. With Ronny Johnsen, Gary Neville and Wes Brown injured, and Keane stalling on a new contract, they had a pressing need for a class centre-back.

Further rumours that Ole was set to quit Old Trafford were bandied about on a Norwegian website but were crushed by a statement from Ole himself stating that they were totally untrue. The *News of the World* continued to run a story that he was unsettled and needed to be playing more, particularly with the 2000 European Championships looming. The short-lived Sunday sports newspaper *Sports First* ran a front-page scoop that United were going to swap Ole for David Ginola. Sir Alex quickly reacted to the situation by telling Sky Sports, 'At the moment, it's not really worked out well for Ole Gunnar Solskjaer. He's not really had the same amount of football he had last year and I want to try and correct that over the next few weeks and make sure he gets plenty of football because he's important to us. He scored on Saturday [against Liverpool] and he could have scored a hat-trick on Saturday, and that's what the boy is made of – goals.'

The boy who was made of goals scored again a few nights after Sir Alex's tribute. The goal gave the holders a narrow victory over Girondins des Bordeaux. Despite Fergie's statement, Ole did not start the game in Bordeaux. The French Champions lost their striker Lilian Laslandes after 22 minutes for a second bookable offence following a clash with Beckham. Unexpectedly, they took the lead with a fluke goal from their Captain Pavon, his speculative shot slipping through Raimond van der Gouw's hands. The Dutchman had been curiously chosen ahead of Mark Bosnich but the mistake was elementary. Roy Keane equalised when he ran through a phalanx of French defenders to score with a looping drive. Sylvain Wiltord then came close, shooting wide when well placed.

Sir Alex put Ole on with five minutes left and once again

he proved to be the United saviour. A high clearance by van der Gouw landed at Ole's feet, who navigated his way into the box before slotting home past the Bordeaux keeper. The victory, coupled with Valencia's win over Fiorentina, meant that the Champions League holders topped their group. Keane harboured doubts, though, that United could retain the Champions League. The Irish midfielder was of the opinion that Bayern had 'bottled' it in the Final and handed the trophy to United. The Cork-born skipper was positive about Ole and his match winning performance, though . He told Sky Sports, 'That is what Ole is all about.'

Two more Group Two phase games quickly followed; the first was a 3-1 home victory over Fiorentina. Ole did not play in this match and watched as Batistuta put the Italians ahead but, after a shaky period, United bounced back for their win. Then it was off to the Estadio Mestalla to face Valencia. Ole played his part in helping his side obtain a 0-0 draw, which was enough to put them through to the quarter-finals and a plum draw against the Spanish multi-millionaires, Real Madrid.

United had gleaned four points against Valencia, who turned out to be the surprise package of the tournament by eventually winning through to the Final. They were a dangerous side, comprising the midfield playmaker Gaizka Mendieta and the pacy Claudio Lopez. Hector Cupar was their manager, having replaced the wily Claudio Ranieri. Sir Alex's ploy against Valencia was to deny them any space in midfield and neutralise their danger men.

United travelled to the Bernabeu in Madrid with a similar game plan. One of the greatest nights in their European history was the 3-3 draw gained there in May 1968. A superb George Best volley had given them a narrow first-leg lead, but that evaporated in a devastating burst of attacking play by the Spanish team. At the break, United trailed 3-1 on the night, 3-2 on aggregate. Inspired by Busby's half-time team-talk, they scored second-half headed goals from David Sadler and Billy Foulkes. The latter came from a chance brilliantly set up by Best. That made it 3-3 on aggregate and sent them to the Final at Wembley a fortnight later. There were 125,000 present at the Bernabeu in 1968; almost half that were in attendance over 30 years later. The fixture was woven into the history of the club. In world club football, few can match the intensity and significance of a Manchester United–Real Madrid tie.

United came away with a 0-0 draw which was a highly credible performance. Sir Alex decided to play it very tight and Ole was not utilised in the game. Bosnich had regained his place and was United's best player, denying Real with a string of fine saves, displaying great skill and nerve. Andy Cole put a simple headed chance over the bar near the end. If Ole had been on the pitch and had been presented with a similar opportunity, then United might have gained an advantage. Sir Alex thought they still had a great chance of getting through to the semi-finals.

Ole was on the bench for the return leg; a few days before, he had started the game in a 4-0 stroll against Sunderland at Old Trafford. Sir Alex brought in Ole, Nicky Butt and Henning Berg for the fixture as he rotated the squad with an eye on the Real Madrid return. All three scored, with Ole bagging a brace. A mistake by the Black Cat's Williams let in Ole for the first, rounding Thomas Sorensen and clipping home the fastest goal of the day. Sunderland fought back but, seven minutes into the second half, Ole scored again, cushioning the ball at knee height before re-adjusting his stance to rifle in a shot past Sorensen. Only a world-class save from the Danish keeper denied Ole from claiming a hat-trick. The Norwegian striker set up the third goal for Butt as he teed up Beckham's immaculate cross.

In his essay on *The Art of Goalscoring* in the *Manchester United Annual 2007*, Ole stressed the importance of timing. 'Not only is it important for strikers to time their runs towards the goal, it's crucial to have an understanding of timing with your team-mates. For example, when David Beckham was at United, you knew when his crosses were coming and where he would put the ball. The better your understanding with your team-mates, the easier it is to time your run into the right position.'

Bosnich was substituted at half-time with a hamstring injury; it was a cruel blow following his breathtaking heroics in the Bernabeu. The loss of the big keeper probably cost United the tie, as they went down 2-3 in a thrilling match to a great Real Madrid side. They had struggled earlier in the competition, twice losing to Bayern Munich in the qualifying stages, but that night turned on a wonderful display of creativity and tactical awareness.

Keane, of all people, gave Real the lead when he stretched at the near post to reach a cross and knocked the ball past Raimond van der Gouw. The goal was a freakish error and wrecked United's game plan. Two goals in two minutes by the sharp-shooting Raul early in the second half tore the heart out of United and the Champions League trophy was wrested out of their grasp. Redondo back-heeled the ball past Henning Berg to set up Raul for a simple finish. It was a wonderful piece of skill as he knocked the ball past the Norwegian and accelerated past him. Within a minute, Raul had made it 3-0, sweeping the ball home after a dazzling move by the quicksilver Real strikers.

United had never trailed by that score at home in a European game and threw everything into a series of attacks on the Spanish defence. Casillas, the Real keeper, kept United out, but Beckham reduced the arrears with a fine run past two opponents and a curling finish. Perhaps that was the time the Spanish scouts put his name on their shopping list.

Ole came on in a last desperate attempt to salvage the game but even he could not save the day. The last few frenzied minutes played out in front of the near-hysterical fans were perhaps the most exciting times since the Nou Camp sensation. Two minutes from time, Steve McManaman, the ex-Liverpool player, chopped down the rampaging Keane and Paul Scholes smashed home the penalty. It was 2-3, and the game was brought to a close when the whistle went, with United still camped in the Real penalty area and Ole screaming for the ball.

The loss of the trophy was a massive blow to Manchester United; at the time of writing, they have still not recovered it. The domestic league was won in a canter, yet the season United won the Champions League they had also been involved in a nip-and-tuck race for the Premiership with Arsenal. That battle went to the wire, the destination of the title only being decided on the last day of the season.

United had failed to build on the Treble – an impossible task perhaps – but the logical next step was to maintain their dominance in European football, and the way to do that was to win the Champions League on a regular basis.

United wrapped up the Premiership with a 3-1 win at Southampton. There were still four matches to follow but, with Liverpool's failure to beat Everton the night before, the victory gave them their sixth Premiership in eight seasons. Ole played and scored, collecting his third Premiership medal in his fourth season in Manchester.

The partying was kept to a minimum as United had a fixture on the Easter Monday against Chelsea. Ole played again and scored the second goal in an exciting 3-2 win over the Londoners. Yorke gave United the lead when Chelsea keeper Ed de Goey's clearance ricocheted off Yorke and into the net. It was surely the luckiest of the 97 goals Manchester United scored in the Premiership that season, the highest tally of goals scored, incidentally, by a Premiership-winning side.

Chelsea levelled when Ole's chum Tore Andre Flo sent over a cross, and Romanian Dan Petrescu fired a shot past Raimond van der Gouw. Petrescu then set up the second for Zola, who cleverly fired a volley into the ground which bounced over van der Gouw. Ole got into the act when he turned Petrescu inside out with some fancy footwork before firing a fierce low shot past him. It was 2-2 at the break, and the tempo dropped as the temperature rose and the celebrations hotted up. Yorke clinched it for United with his twentieth Premiership goal of the season.

Ole notched his twelfth goal (along with three in Europe) in another end of season party at Old Trafford against Tottenham. This finished 3-1 to United, and how Tottenham must have regretted not being able to have signed Ole as it was sixth goal against them since he had come to England. The rumours still persisted that Sugar would raid his savings to sign Ole and link him up with their talented Norwegian Steffen Iversen.

United had won the Premiership by a record 18 points,

still the largest gap for any winning team over their rivals, even when converted to the old system of two points for a win. Given everything that had happened in his four seasons at United, and bearing in mind how respected he was by fans and manager alike, Ole saw no reason to leave his beloved club. Then came the news that PSV Eindhoven striker Ruud van Nistelrooy had signed for United, and speculation intensified that Ole would leave the club.

# 7

# Champions Again

**'Money is not important. I can only live under one roof and within four walls. If money was important, I would not have played for United in the first place. My love for United is greater than my need for more money.'**
**OLE GUNNAR SOLSKJAER, MARCH 2001**

The season started with the news that Ole had been voted the club's Player of the Year by the official Manchester United website. Roy Keane had surprisingly been beaten into second place by the young striker. Keane was a colossus of a player, and rightly regarded as a modern legend, akin to the great Duncan Edwards. In retrospect, he had been the driving force behind the scooping of the Treble with a season of extraordinary performances. For Ole to beat him to the Player of the Year award was a stunning achievement, but how he had eclipsed Keane was puzzling to many.

Perhaps the answer lay in the players' demeanour and style, both on and off the pitch. Compare the snarling Keane haranguing referee Andy D'Urso in the 'Boro game to a smiling Ole greeting the Old Trafford faithful after notching his fourth goal of the game against Everton. There was always a serenity about him, the feeling that he would come through no matter what the odds stacked against him. He was a great player, at the top of his game, and playing for the team he loved. Playing in that spirit, with a smile on his face, naturally endeared him to fans and colleagues alike. He'd also been touched with genius by slotting home the winning goal in a Champions League Final. Few players could ever lay claim to that accolade.

Ole always played as though he thoroughly enjoyed having the ball at his feet, much like Ronaldinho, Zola and the emerging superstar Cristiano Ronaldo. That joy, the actual love of the game and the ability to transmit it to the fans was the rarest of gifts. Perhaps it was Ole's greatest achievement and the reason why he was held in such affection by the United fans.

The other endearing quality he possessed was his amazing ability – there's nothing quite like an undeniable talent to win the fans over. The stats indicated that for the previous season he had achieved an incredible 40 per cent goals-to-shots ratio. Another telling statistic was that his shooting accuracy was a phenomenal 77 per cent. Those figures must surely stack up well alongside previous United greats, who toiled in the times before any match analysis software such as ProZone or the Opta Index.

Speculation was rife that Ole would leave the club in the wake of the signing of Ruud van Nistelrooy from PSV Eindhoven. Chairman Martin Edwards was telling BBC television that a striker was likely to be sold to 'balance the books'. Andy Cole, whose goal tally had dwindled, was also in the frame to leave. Teddy Sheringham's contract was also up at the end of the new season 2000/01. It was then expected that the striker, born before England won the World Cup, would walk away from the Theatre of Dreams on a Bosman free transfer.

Leeds had been monitoring the Ole situation for some time with particular regard to his lack of regular starts. Sir Alex would never have sanctioned the move but, at that time, Leeds did seem to have emerged from the pack to challenge the United dominance of the English game. Ole's purchase price from Molde would have to be multiplied by nearly ten times if he was to leave Old Trafford. In his whole career, there had not been one instance of him agitating for a move.

Then the £19 million van Nistelrooy deal was put on hold when it was found out that he had cruciate ligament damage. Sir Alex was angry with PSV for leaking news of the deal before the details had been ironed out. The transaction looked dead in the water, but showing remarkable faith in his judgement and the medical staff, the United boss kept the deal alive. Eventually, van Nistelrooy joined Manchester United in the spring of 2001.

This took the immediate pressure off the quartet that had served their club so well in recent times. That season, the Sheringham–Solskjaer pairing was the most prominent partnership, finally deposing the once stellar Yorke–Cole combination. After all the permutations had been tried, Sheringham seemed to be the partner with whom Ole worked best. When it became public that, off the field, Cole and Sheringham did not speak to one another, perhaps it was not so surprising. The paper-thin dividing line between greatness and mediocrity was also a factor for Dwight Yorke, Cole's partner from the glory days of 1999. He was enjoying his time in the tabloids rather too much, and his relationship with the model Katie Price – aka Jordan – meant that he was making news on the front pages more often than he had done on the back.

In 2003, Ole told MUTV of his debt of gratitude to Andy Cole and Dwight Yorke. 'They are both great individual players but it was as a partnership that they really excelled. They gave us something extra and, during the Treble season, they were by far the best pairing in Europe. I learned a lot from both of them and, in a sense, we are still benefiting from that now, because at the time it was a new style, which we have taken on.'

Ole opened his account for the season with a goal in the pre-season friendly against Shrewsbury. Played at Gay Meadow, United hit eight goals. Ole scored the third with an acrobatic volley from a delicious cross provided by Jesper Blomqvist, who had damaged his right knee in August 1999 and had had two operations. The Champions League Final was the last competitive match he played in for United, as he joined Everton soon after the Shrewsbury game. Ole, like any other top-class player, was fully aware of the constant threat of a long-term injury that could jeopardise or even end his career.

Sir Alex had been very sympathetic to Ruud van Nistelrooy when he sustained his injury but his kindness of spirit did not extend to Mark Bosnich. In the summer, he had purchased Fabien Barthez from Monaco for £7.8 million. Some judges rated him the best goalkeeper in the world, and there was no doubt that he was vastly experienced and could emulate even Sir Bobby Charlton by producing World Cup and European Championship medals that he had won with France. Bosnich stayed on at United, though, vowing to win back his place. Sadly, he was never given the chance and was relegated by Sir Alex to third choice, eventually joining Chelsea in January 2001.

In another pre-season fixture, Ole scored a late winner against Real Madrid in the Bayern Munich Centenary Tournament in early August. Raimond van der Gouw started the move with a long clearance that Sheringham flicked on with his head. Ole ran on to the pass and turned the ball past the Real keeper Cesar Sanchez. The Cameroonian right wing-back Geremi and striker Fernando Morientes had fine matches. Before his match winner, Ole had been denied a further goal when Sanchez made a point-blank save from him.

Ole scored his first Premiership goal of the season at Everton in September. It was the sixth game of the campaign, of which four had been won and two had been lacklustre draws against Ipswich and West Ham. A three-goal burst in a ten-minute spell in the first half blew Everton away. Ole engineered the first goal for Nicky Butt when he was given far too much time and space out on the right and his inch-perfect pass was sublimely drilled home by the midfielder.

United doubled their lead when Ole headed a punted clearance from Barthez into the path of Sheringham, who ran through the midfield to fire in a powerful drive. Paul Gerrard in the Everton goal make a brave but futile attempt to save it and succeeded in parrying the drive, but it rebounded to Ryan Giggs who instantly scored with a low drive.

Walter Smith's Everton were in serious danger of suffering a heavy defeat when, in the ensuing moments, Sheringham and Ole both went close with attempts. After 39 minutes, Ole wrapped it up when he took a pass from Beckham and walked through the disintegrating Everton defence before committing Gerrard with a roll of his shoulders and stroking the ball home.

In the second half, the Red Devils dropped the tempo but Ole could have had a second goal when his attempted volley was cleared off the goal line. Paul Gascoigne and Mark Hughes were both in the Everton line-up but were jointly subbed after 70 minutes. This was a stark reminder to Ole of the brief spell players actually have at the highest level, no matter how brilliantly their star had once shone.

Ole's next goal came away to Leicester in a comfortable 3-0 victory at the old Filbert Street ground. The win, Leicester's first defeat of the season, put United back on top of the Premiership. Sheringham had put United two ahead from breakaways before Ole's pace created and executed the third. Dwight Yorke worked a neat one-two with him just outside the area, before the Norwegian unleashed a low drive into the far corner of the net. Tim Flowers, the City keeper, was absolutely powerless to prevent it. Sir Alex saw Ole's predatory performance as the perfect example of the benefits of a squad system.

Another example of the luxury of the squad system was the side that United fielded on Hallowe'en night in 2000, when they visited Vicarage Road to play Watford in the League Cup. Watford, managed by former England boss Graham Taylor, were at that stage top of the second-tier league, the Championship. The only recognisable first-team players in a side filled largely with reserves were Ole and Yorke up front and captain Phil Neville at the back. The gulf between Premier League and the lower leagues was now immense and growing all the time. Ole scored twice and Yorke notched another as the Hornets were trampled 0-

3. But despite the strength in the squad, United went out of the competition in the next round when they lost to Sunderland after extra time.

Once again, Ole was linked with a move to Tottenham. This time, the press were speculating that the Tottenham right-back Stephen Carr would be involved in the transfer. As always, Ole was top of the Tottenham wish list and Carr was a defender long admired by Ferguson. Nothing ever materialised, however.

Ole then hit a purple patch as he produced a steady flow of goals. In the run-up to Christmas, he nonchalantly scored the second goal in a 2-0 win over Tottenham. Then at Charlton, he scored again in a 3-3 draw. The goal he scored that winter's day was one of his best-remembered efforts. It started with a breathtaking lobbed attempt at goal from Ryan Giggs from near the halfway line, á la Beckham. The ball soared high in the air and finally crashed against the crossbar. Everybody in the ground seemed transfixed by the flight of the ball, except one player. Ole had raced into the box and, as the rebound dropped from the bar, he jumped to meet it, instantly driving the ball into the roof of the net. As he had shown many times before, Ole's laser-sharp anticipation, opportunism and pace put him in the perfect position to execute the killer blow, time and time again. This particular goal typified his style and personified his character.

On 23 December against Ipswich, Ole scored both goals in a 2-0 win, and on Boxing Day away at Villa Park, Ole scored the only goal of the match with a late header.

The only glitch in the fine run was a 0-1 home loss to Liverpool, who played it exceedingly tight, deploying their wide midfielders Nicky Barmby and Danny Murphy in front of their full-backs. Their game plan was simply to deny the United flank players Giggs and Beckham any room to weave their magic. This was the approach of every team that came to Old Trafford, packing more and more men in defensive positions and trying to counter on the break. The particular skills of Ole in taking half-chances – the goal at Charlton was a prime example – became increasingly important to United with space and time at a premium.

On the first day of 2001, West Ham United came to Old Trafford. Within three minutes, Ole had scored his first goal of the year courtesy of some slipshod defensive play by Rigobert Song. Perhaps the 67,603 crowd put Song under increased pressure, but his botched clearance rebounded back to him. Before he could control it, Ole raced in, took possession of the ball and immediately fired it past the West Ham keeper Hislop. It was a fine goal and finished second in an Internet poll for planetfootball.com for the best goal scored on New Year's Day.

United dominated the rest of the half as they totally outclassed a poor Hammers side without their star man Paulo Di Canio. After 33 minutes, Stuart Pearce deflected Phil Neville's cross into his own net. Perhaps he had it coming, as Pearce had made some aggressive tackles on Ole during the game, and had earned a booking for a foul on Scholes.

United took their foot off the gas at half-time but Yorke headed the third on the hour. Cruising to three points, they replaced Giggs and Keane with Jonathan Greening and Ronnie Wallwork. Frederic Kanouté headed a late consolation goal and Frank Lampard missed a fine chance.

Sir Alex was soon on Sky TV praising Ole for his recent superb form. 'I think that circumstances have acted against him in the past, but I think there is pressure on them all now. Ole has shown that he can play up front on his own and the goals he has scored have not gone unnoticed at the club.'

Another London side played United next when Fulham provided the opposition in a Third Round FA Cup tie at Craven Cottage. Ole put United ahead after just six minutes. As was the case with his previous strike against West Ham, it stemmed from a defensive error. Beckham robbed Lee Clarke when he dwelt too long on the ball and fed Ole on the edge of the area. Instantly, the Norwegian ace curled the ball into the far corner of the net to put United ahead.

In the division below at that time, Fulham fought back to equalise with a fine goal in the first half, Fernandes scoring with a free-kick. Fulham continued to trouble the United defence with their quicksilver forward Luis Saha proving a real handful for Wes Brown. Sir Alex was taking special interest in Saha's progress at that time.

One of the players he was looking to replace, Sheringham, scored the winner for United three minutes from time. Fulham's whirlwind attacks blew themselves out in the second half as United wrested control of the midfield. Fulham tired as the pitch cut up, and Sheringham capitalised when he pounced on a pass from Luke Chadwick to drive hard and low into the net.

The England striker was in wonderful form that season and ended up as Player of the Year for both the Football Writers' Association and the Professional Footballers' Association.

After the match, Ole told the *News of the World*, 'I am mentally prepared to be dropped again. The recent goals are very satisfying to me but, at a club like United, you always have to be prepared to be left out. The competition is so tough and your record does not mean anything. All that counts is what you can deliver at the moment. I feel my position is a little bit stronger now. I feel more comfortable and I'm in a better situation than I have been in a long time. I just had to grab the chance with both hands when I finally got it.'

United were hoping for another Cup run but it surprisingly came to an end in the Fourth Round against West Ham in front of 67,209 at Old Trafford. Di Canio scored the only goal of the game after Kanouté beat the offside trap to put him in for a bizarre winner. Instead of racing from his line to challenge the little Italian, Barthez stood his ground with his arm raised, vainly appealing for a whistle that never came. It was a formality for the maverick Italian striker.

Harry Redknapp had learned the lessons quickly from the 3-1 defeat a few weeks earlier. The young Joe Cole and Michael Carrick played brilliantly that day. Sir Alex had been charting their progress since they had both burst on to the scene when they starred in West Ham's resounding 9-0 triumph over Coventry in the 1999 FA Youth Cup Final.

Europe proved to be a happier hunting ground, at least in the earlier stages. Ole played as a sub in the opening match against Anderlecht, which ended in a resounding 5-1 home win. Then he travelled to Russia, where they played against Dynamo Kiev, the long trek ending in a 0-0 draw. Away defeats to PSV Eindhoven and Anderlecht meant that United had to beat Dynamo Kiev to stay in the competition. Sheringham put United ahead early in the game but, as the match continued, their nerves got the better of them and Kiev dominated. In the closing minutes, their Ukrainian striker Demetradze missed a golden opportunity that would have knocked United out.

## CHAMPIONS AGAIN

Roy Keane was exasperated by his team's form in Europe, their failure to step up to the next level and what he saw he saw as the complacency that had become part of their play. The United skipper also turned his attentions to certain sections of the Old Trafford support. After the game, he made his famous 'prawn sandwiches' outburst, which has become as famous as the Cantona 'seagulls' quote. He said, 'Away from home, our fans are fantastic, what I would call the hardcore fans... but at home, they've had a few drinks and probably their prawn sandwiches and don't realise what is going on out on the pitch.'

The second phase of the Champions League was not so problematic, United being pitched in against Panathinaikos, Sturm Graz and Valencia. The last two sides were very familiar as they had both been opponents in the previous campaign. Sturm Graz were simply dismissed home and away and Panathinakos were beaten 3-1 at Old Trafford.

Ole played as a sub in return leg which was a very difficult match. The Greeks had three strikers but only one played up front with the other two going deep just in front of their midfield. The United central defenders Wes Brown and Jaap Stam were at a loss as to who to pick up and were constantly dragged out of position. Only Barthez kept United in the tie as he acrobatically defied the Panathinaikos forwards, before eventually being beaten. In the last minute, Paul Scholes equalised but United were lucky to come away from Greece with anything.

Both the games against last year's beaten finalists, Valencia, were draws. Ole was sub in the matches as he came up against his Norwegian colleague, the giant striker John Carew. The teams first met on Valentine's Day 2001 at the Estadio Mestalla and played out a grim 0-0 game in almost torrential rain. The return was a week later in Manchester with the weather only marginally better. It was not a vintage performance; Cole put United ahead but a late own-goal from Wes Brown meant the spoils were shared.

Sir Alex was speechless with rage and furious at what he considered was a dreadful performance, completely lacking passion. Before the vital Premiership clash against Arsenal, he tore into his players, demanding that they raise their slipping standards before they ended up empty-handed at the end of the season.

The team responded with perhaps their most majestic performance since the Treble season. Arsenal on this occasion were without their twin defensive rocks – Tony Adams and Martin Keown. Yorke, whose season had been blighted by injury and loss of form, hit a first-half hat-trick. Keane smashed a blockbuster past Seaman but it was Ole who scored the neatest of the afternoon. Eight minutes before the break, he ghosted in at the near post after Nicky Butt had spun Gilles Grimandi.

Ole's strike killed the game; any lingering chance Arsenal had of getting back in the game was cancelled by the fifth goal. The manner of the finish – all speed, power and accuracy – had become an Ole trademark.

A crazy 5-1 scoreline after 37 minutes, Wenger's team had never taken such a beating. United were simply irresistible. No team on earth could have withstood the sheer power of their attacking prowess in that opening spell as they silenced the Gunners.

United coasted the second half, cruising among the wreckage of team that was to win the Double in the next 12 months. Igor Stepanovs in the centre of the Arsenal rearguard was run off his feet by Yorke. Henry had scored

Arsenal's equaliser with a characteristic finish after Robert Pires had carved out the chance. Sir Alex, always seeking improvement, was angry at Ole for not tracking back to block Pires.

Ole made amends by almost scoring again when he just failed to convert Keane's over-hit cross. Sheringham then came on as sub and scored the sixth. Ole had a chance to score himself, but Sheringham took the ball off his toes to thrash home. Never before in the history of the Premiership had the team at its pinnacle handed out such a beating to the team lying in second place.

Back in August, Ole had told Sky Sports that he considered Arsenal to be the biggest challengers to United that season. 'Arsenal are experienced at winning things. I think we will win it again. I am very comfortable in Manchester, and Alex Ferguson considers me an important part of the squad. I have learned a lot by working with him and have no plans to leave. I hope he will continue as manager here.'

That victory sealed United's third successive Premiership title in everything but name. Their dominance of the domestic league was undoubted, and every other team was virtually resigned to aiming only for the runners-up spot.

Once again, the Champions League beckoned – the challenge now was to dominate Europe in the same manner that they had the Premiership. Their opponents were Bayern Munich, against whom Ole had enjoyed his supreme moment of glory. The first leg was at Old Trafford, and it was a revitalised and strengthened Bayern who travelled to Manchester. Superbly coached by Otto Hitzfeld, they were anxious to gain revenge for 26 May 1999.

On the night, Bayern were clearly the superior side. Ole

played but there were no chances for him to convert and repeat history. A sub did grab the headlines, though – Bayern's Paulo Sergio grabbed their winner four minutes from time. Bayern's star player, Steffan Effenberg, curled over a free-kick, which Alexander Zickler flicked on, and Sergio tucked the ball home at the far post. The downcast United fans were already heading for the exits.

The United Treble-winning side effectively started to break up that night as difficult decisions were taken about the future by the brooding Ferguson. Keane still soldiered on, but the injuries were slowing him. Sheringham, despite having had a glorious season outscoring everyone, was to rejoin Tottenham in the summer. Beckham had lost form that season and his gradual decline as a player seemed somehow in direct proportion to his rise as an international celebrity.

In January 2007, his stock as a celebrity became stratospheric with news of his £128 million move from Real Madrid to LA Galaxy. Brand Beckham was truly global, and the Beckhams could now add Hollywood A-listers to their dinner-party circuit. A portfolio of lucrative sponsorship deals made him rich beyond belief, but as a world-class player, his moment had passed. Or had it?

After a long period in the doldrums at Real, without ever cementing his first-team place, the latter half of the 2006/07 season saw Beckham's stock as a world-class footballer rise again. Far from being the burnt-out has-been who sold his soul for an easy life in the US soccer playground, he became an integral part of Real's title win, and gained renewed respect for some brilliant performances on the pitch. He also attracted the attention of Steve McClaren, the England manager, who had originally dropped Beckham from the international side when he took charge. The Beckham story

– rags, to riches, to ignominy, to greatness, to untold wealth and celebrity, to ridicule, and then to even greater wealth and acclaim – still clearly has some chapters left unwritten. Who knows where the story will take him next?

None of the top Premier sides at the beginning of the millennium, though, had shown any interest in adding Beckham to their star-studded squads. Things must have weighed heavily on the United number 7, and perhaps he would have traded a large portion of the £128 million to still be wearing the red shirt. Ferguson, though, looked forwards, not back, and the offer from Real was simply too good to resist. Moreover, sentimentality did not figure in the formidable Scot's considerations – Beckham had become a liability in many ways, and the club could only benefit from severing its ties with one of the world's most recognisable male icons. No player, believed many at United, should ever be allowed to become bigger than the club itself.

As the maelstrom of manoeuvrings and transfers continued around him, Ole was one of the few at United untouched by the events behind the scenes of the world's most famous team. Ole continued doing what he did best – scoring goals. He did this again in the next home fixture against Charlton, firing in the winner in the 82nd minute after coming off the bench. It kept United on course for the Premiership and improved morale for the Champions League return leg in Germany. Once again, Sir Alex lavished praise on his Norwegian striker when talking to Sky Sports. 'Solskjaer must be the best substitute ever. Very few players have the temperament to go on in the heat of a game and remain as cool as he does. He has proved himself an outstanding professional. He accepted the situation tonight but was still dying to get on, and that's the sort of approach I want. He can score from anywhere. The way he made the most of what was hardly even a chance was fantastic.'

Ole was a sub at Coventry as United came from behind to win 4-2. The Coventry striker John Hartson gave Wes Brown a torrid time all afternoon and scored both Coventry goals. Later in the afternoon, Arsenal lost to Middlesbrough, thus ensuring that the Premiership remained in United hands.

Terry Venables had been recruited to try to stop the rot that threatened to relegate the 'Boro side that had lost its way under Bryan Robson. The ex-Barça coach did a brilliant job in reorganising and inspiring the Riverside outfit to climb back up the table. Beating Arsenal was the icing on the cake. It was a bizarre match with Arsenal conceding two own-goals as they went down 3-2.

The manner in which yet another Premiership title was won was a barometer of United's weird season. Predicable games and results had created a familiarity which, in turn, had bred a mild contempt. The dictates of TV meant that many of United's games had been shown at odd times to accommodate the schedules. This time, the TV companies were caught out as they failed to show Ole and his team-mates winning the Premiership live. It had become too easy for them in England as they sauntered to yet another title; they were undeniably a very big fish in a small pond. With Leeds about to go into free-fall, only Arsenal offered any serious challenge. Economics were to propel Chelsea into the role of serious challengers, but not for a while. Ipswich and Sunderland finished respectably in fifth and seventh place in a league described so eloquently by Keane as being 'piss poor'.

Nothing could take away the achievement of Ferguson, though, who had become the first manager in history to win three successive Premierships with the same club.

Rather more demanding was the task of lifting the Champions League trophy. Their next hurdle was to claw back the deficit they had incurred against Bayern. Keane tried to rally his troops before the battle, telling *Match* magazine, 'If we go out to Munich, heads will roll, no doubt about that. Players' futures, mine included, will be threatened. It might be time to inject new blood. When your time is up, that is it. Game over, so there could be a few P45s around.'

Sir Alex's last instructions to his side before they left the dressing room were to keep it tight and not to concede an early goal. Once again, Ole was named as a sub, to be held back for a final onslaught, just as he had done at the Nou Camp. David Beckham missed the game through suspension.

Ole spoke of United's European tactics to the *Inside United* magazine, saying, 'There are certain rules in European football that you have to follow. Away from home, you have to silence the crowd. It's a matter of reading the pattern of play as well. You know when you've got the opposition by the throat and you can pile on the pressure, but you can also recognise any team will have at least a ten-minute period where they create chances. At these times, you have to soak up the pressure, keep possession, and maybe the best medicine is to have a shot on goal to dampen the mood of their players and fans.'

United's best-laid plans were wrecked within five minutes of the kick-off. The continual United retreat into their own penalty area always caused problems as it meant that they defended too deep and invited constant pressure. A cross from Michael Tarnat skidded across the penalty box and the

Brazilian Elber evaded Wes Brown to fire home. It was a bitter blow to any hope of United salvaging the game but the away-goal rule meant that, if they still scored twice, they were through.

Near half-time, with the game still in the balance, Jens Jeremies burst into the box and crossed for the dangerous Elber to square to midfielder Mehmet Scholl, who turned the ball into the net. There was now virtually no chance of coming back from 0-3 down.

Keane talked at half-time about the Juventus revival. Hopes of a comeback flickered briefly when Giggs ran through to lift the ball over Oliver Kahn. The goal galvanised the Reds but the gritty Bayern regrouped and withstood a flurry of United attacks. Ole and Teddy were both on the field in the closing stages but there was no comeback and United slipped out of Europe at the same stage as the previous year. The season was over and the euphoria of the record-breaking Premiership hat-trick was replaced by the bitter taste of their dismissal from the European competition.

There were still five Premiership games remaining and United eventually won the title by a comfortable ten-point margin over Arsenal. Strangely enough, they only won one more game, a 2-0 victory over Middlesbrough in which Ole played. He also featured in the 1-1 home draw against Manchester City, who were teetering on the brink of relegation.

For a Manchester derby, it was a drab affair, suffering from the usual malaise associated with a lunchtime kick-off and a European hangover. The crowd seemed apathetic, too, and a tired-looking Scholes missed a penalty, but Sheringham scored from the second one awarded after 70 minutes. The game was only really remembered for Keane's spine-chilling tackle on Alfie Haaland, which led to the eighth red card of his career at Old Trafford. Near the end, Steve Howey scrambled an equaliser for City after Stam had failed to clear a deep corner. The season was ending not with the usual bang but a whimper.

United lost the last three games of the season – a dull 0-1 defeat at home to Derby, and away defeats to Southampton and Tottenham. Ole missed all of them because of a knee injury.He spoke of the operation he had to repair it when he told icons.com, 'In the end, the only way out was to have an operation. The doctor told me that there was a small cyst that he had to remove. I feel that the surgery was very successful. Hopefully, this will mean that the pain will be gone and that I will be able to start training again before too long. The pre-season training in England starts on 9 July, so I will be ready by then.'

Ole's long-term struggle with injuries became public knowledge at around this time, but it was not known then for how long he had suffered pain. One theory was that the original damage to his knee was incurred when he executed his famous knee skid across the Nou Camp pitch after scoring the most important goal of his life. Was it the case, then, that in the moment of supreme triumph, he suffered the injury that was almost to destroy his career?

8

# Strike Force

**'Ole is always going to score. He is a wonderful finisher.'**
**SIR ALEX FERGUSON**

Ole now had another Premiership medal to add to his growing collection. In five trophy-laden seasons at Old Trafford, he had collected four Premiership titles, plus the little matter of the Champions League and an FA Cup.

Ole had scored 10 Premier League goals in season 2000/01, finishing the club's second-highest scorer, five behind Teddy Sheringham. A further three goals in the domestic Cups had given him a total of 13 in 25 starts and 21 substitute appearances. And Ole was still not guaranteed a first-team place.

An interesting fact was that he had had 41 shots on target, more than Sheringham, Cole and Yorke. The 60 per cent accuracy of his shooting was the highest rating in the club. To his goals tally, four assists could also be added, but the statistics did not do him full justice. Ole was worth his place for his overall contribution; his link-up play was improving with each season in the top flight. His game had developed to such an extent that it not only provided him with goals, but almost guaranteed that those who partnered him would also be provided with chances.

Sir Alex had confirmed that 2001/02 was to be his final season in charge of United. One of his predecessors, Ron Atkinson, was predicting, though, that he would change his mind at the end of the season. Steve McClaren had left the club in the summer to take the job at Middlesbrough, replacing Bryan Robson. With the future uncertain, no proper replacement was named. This was to have a very destabilising effect on the club over the coming months.

In February 2007, the new West Ham manager Alan Curbishley talked about the 'Baby Bentley' culture among Premiership players. The ex-Charlton boss believed that there were too many cases of players putting self-interest ahead of their team's requirements. This had lead to a massive problem in motivating the young millionaires. The rewards were so massive and the downside of failure so high that it put players and agents in very strong positions.

Ole was the complete antithesis of the 'Baby Bentley' player; his only concern was for his beloved Manchester United. The man with the number 20 on his shirt did not court the limelight or indulge in excess off the pitch. Slowly, he was building a fantastic image in the game and was starting to receive recognition from unexpected quarters. UNICEF asked him to be an ambassador and he accepted immediately. Ole had worked for them before in an anti-smoking campaign in Shanghai, having been appalled to learn of the very high percentage of children who smoked. Delighted to be chosen, Ole told Sky Sports,

'I am proud to be a part of this. It is a declaration of faith in me as a person.'

Ole's lifestyle meant that he was in superb physical condition and the effects of this, in the later stages of his career, were to become even more apparent. The endless quest for goals went on unabated.

Another magnanimous gesture of his was when he won compensation from a betting firm that had illegally used his name. His image was used to promote their activities and Ole successfully sued to protect his name. Subsequently, he donated the money to his former club Clausenengen for the purpose of improving their youth development system.

Speculation continued to grow as the new season approached that Ole was to leave United; Aston Villa were the latest club to express interest in purchasing him and Tottenham were still sniffing around. United warded off the suitors by offering him a new two-year extension to his existing contract. It was a good move for both parties, United rewarding their gifted striker for his loyalty and consistent goalscoring, while Ole was pleased at the faith shown in him and his level of accomplishment. He told icons.com, 'I have become very fond of this club and the fans, and I look forward to new challenges and trophies with what I see as the world's greatest club.'

As expected, Teddy Sheringham left United in the summer to re-join Tottenham, now managed by Glenn Hoddle. The England striker went out on a high, voted the Football Writers' Footballer of the Year. Ruud van Nistelrooy arrived at Old Trafford in his place, now fully recovered from his notorious knee problem. The partnership between Ole and the 24-year-old Dutchman was to prove one of the most prolific in recent times. It had everything; they would score goals from distance and close range, left-footed or right, in the air and on the ground. Ruud was a very powerful player, strong, fast and brave, with Sir Alex deploying him as a battering ram to break down defensive walls. Ole was the 'bits and pieces' player mopping up behind, pouncing on whatever scraps fell his way. It was the oldest trick in the book. Brian Clough had employed similar tactics in his European Cup and title-winning sides. Going back even further, the great Tottenham Double-winning side of the early 1960s employed ex-blacksmith Bobby Smith as the centre-forward, with the greatest predator of them all, Jimmy Greaves, in the 'Ole' role.

The more mature United fans were already comparing van Nistelrooy to United's greatest ever centre-forward, Tommy Taylor. Taylor was the first £30,000 footballer, a wonderful header of the ball with an average of two goals every three games. He was 26 when he perished at Munich. The strike partnership with inside-forward Dennis Viollet, who survived the crash, was the stuff of legend.

Another acquisition that year was Juan Sebastian Verón from Lazio for £28 million, taking United's total outlay to over £50 million. Verón's father had scored against United in the World Club Championship for Estudiantes in 1968, and Maradona once described Juan Verón as 'the best player on earth'.

Sometimes, he looked it, but he had an unhappy spell in England and never really showed the Premiership what a truly brilliant player he was. Verón never settled in England; he could not speak the language and hated the Mancunian weather. Others, like Ole, had embraced the culture immediately. It helped to be multi-lingual before arriving in the UK, and for the Argentinian – a demi-god in his own country, and in Italy – Manchester, the English game and the fans brought him down to earth with a bump.

The season started with a 2-1 defeat to Cup-winners Liverpool in the Charity Shield. Van Nistelrooy scored United's goal to get him off the mark. Sir Alex then surprised everyone by selling defender Jaap Stam to Lazio. Stam had been given the run-around by Michael Owen in the Charity Shield and had a poor game against newly promoted Fulham in the opening Premiership game, van Nistelrooy scoring twice in a narrow 3-2 victory. The reasons for the departure of the Dutch defender were shrouded in mystery, but rumours spread that Sir Alex was unhappy with comments made in Stam's autobiography; another school of thought was that Stam was sold because Ferguson considered him to be in decline as a player following an Achilles injury. Lazio had offered £16.4 million for Ole's room-mate which was a healthy return on the £10.75 million he had cost. Another consideration was that the fee was a sizeable claw-back of the £28 million outlay for Verón.

The replacement for Stam was the former French captain Laurent Blanc on a free transfer from Inter Milan. It looked a good piece of business by the United boss but the downside was that Blanc was 36 and lacked the pace and the toughness to cope in the Premiership.

Ole was eased back slowly into the action following his knee operation. In a pre-season statement, he announced to Sky, 'This year, I plan to be stronger physically and mentally and have my best season for United. My goal is to be involved in all the big matches. I have looked after myself in the summer... I am free of injury after my knee operation towards the end of last season and I shall be more attacking.'

In the early matches, Ferguson paired Paul Scholes with van Nistelrooy as he tinkered with the line-up. Ole came on as a sub in the third Premiership game against Villa, which ended in a 1-1 draw, and then sat the next two games out. A well-taken goal in a reserve match against Liverpool put him back in contention for a place and he came on as a sub in the first Champions League match against Lille. A solitary goal from Beckham earned a rather shoddy victory in Group G.

Against Ipswich, Ole started and scored his first goal of the season in a 4-0 hammering of the Tractor Boys, one of the relegated sides that year. His first goal was the second of the match, drilled home after the Italian keeper Matteo Sereni had spilled Andy Cole's shot. Cole scored the third himself and Ole rounded off the game with number four. It was all a bit hard on Ipswich who played well for periods of the game. Sir Alex admitted after the match that it 'wasn't a 4-0 match'.

Deportivo La Coruña were to complete a Champions League double over United in the next few weeks. They became only the third European side to win home and away Champions League games against them. Ole was a sub in both games, a 2-1 defeat in Spain and a 2-3 defeat at Old Trafford.

Sandwiched between the Spanish defeats was a stunning 5-3 victory over Tottenham at White Hart Lane. What made it even more remarkable was that United were 3-0 down at the break and, to all intents and purposes, out. Ole did come on as a sub but did not score in the goalfest as Cole, Blanc (his first for the club), van Nistelrooy, Verón and Beckham all scored. It was a historic win and equalled a fabled recovery back in February 1910 when United had trailed 3-0 at Newcastle. Inspired by another Welsh wing wizard, Billy Meredith, United fought back to win 4-3.

Tottenham seem to have suffered irreparably from that crushing defeat whenever United come visiting, and have now lost their last six Premiership games at home to the Reds, culminating in the 4-0 drubbing by a Ronaldo-inspired United in February 2007.

United's form was patchy in the early Autumn of 2000; they leaked goals. A 2-0 victory over the talented Athenians, Olympiakos, restored the balance in the Champions League. This was followed by a 3-1 win over Sunderland at the Stadium of Light. Ole featured in both of these matches and also in a shock 1-2 home defeat to Bolton. This defeat enraged Sir Alex, who saw his side go down without a fight. He left his team in no doubt as to their responsibilities when they wear the red shirt, and would not tolerate anyone giving any less than 100 per cent for the club.

In the next three games, Ole almost single-handedly kept the season alive for his club as he scored vital goals. On 23 October, Olympiakos came to Old Trafford for the return match. Ole was on the bench for 73 minutes as he watched the Greek side put up heroic resistance. Their goalkeeper, Dimitrios Eleftheropoulos, had a marvellous game keeping United at bay for so long with a string of fine saves. Verón showed better form in the slower-paced European games than in the helter-skelter of the Premiership. Twice, he went close with fine volleys, and sprayed some accurate passes around. Eleftheropoulos made a great stop from Beckham, then later saved a penalty from van Nistelrooy. It did not appear to be United's night so, once again, Sir Alex turned to his best-kept secret weapon to break the deadlock. Ole went on with the clock ticking.

With just 11 minutes remaining, Ole latched on to a great pass from van Nistelrooy. He shook off his marker, held his head steady and lifted his arms to balance himself, as he scored with an ice-cool shot from six yards. Eleftheropoulos was finally beaten. Once again, the Supersub had come up trumps in an important European match.

Verón put Giggs in for the second two minutes from time with a beautiful through ball. The Reds were now building up a head of steam and van Nistelrooy arrived at the back post to crash in a third. It was a flattering scoreline, considering how United had struggled for so much of the match before Ole's introduction.

Four days later, United entertained a Leeds United side top of the Premiership and then unbeaten. Old Trafford was packed for the lunchtime kick-off; Ole was on the bench with van Nistelrooy the lone striker up front. Leeds boss David O'Leary watched his side being put under severe pressure from the start as United poured forward. Beckham's free-kick and a lobbed shot from Giggs were United's best efforts in a scoreless first half.

As the game wore on, United became increasingly frustrated and Ole replaced Butt as they reverted to a 4-2-4 system. Robbie Keane was lucky to stay on the field after pushing Beckham in the face after they had clashed in midfield. Leeds took the lead after Harry Kewell had cleverly set up a chance for his fellow Aussie Mark Viduka. That looked about it but, two minutes from time, Ole equalised with a superb header.

David Beckham appeared to overhit his cross which evaded everyone in the box except Ryan Giggs, who pounced on the ball, swivelled and chipped a perfect cross back to the far post. The 5ft 9in Ole Gunnar Solskjaer timed his leap perfectly, the ball flying off his forehead, across Nigel Martyn and into the bottom corner of the net. 1-1! The noise was overwhelming as the home crowd expressed their relief at salvaging a point from their old enemy. The script had been written for Ole and, once again, he had delivered the punchline in his own unique manner. The Champions moved back into the top three while hammering a message out that they would not relinquish their title easily.

For the third consecutive match, Ole was to save United again as they trailed once more. The Reds travelled to the Stade Felix Bollaert in Lens on Hallowe'en 2001 to play Lille. During the match, Ole scored one of his top-five, all-time great goals, as listed in the official *Manchester United Annual 2007*. He described it by saying, 'David Beckham's great ball put me in behind the defence. I knew exactly where I wanted to put the ball and fired it towards goal with my left foot. Sometimes, you know when you hit a shot that it's going in. I knew with this one even before it flew into the top corner.'

Ole was now the most mature of all the United strikers. The taking of chances was an inherent part of his game; he just wanted to do maximum damage to the opposition. He had no interest in playing to the galleries with tricks or flamboyant showboating. When Ole produced a stunning shot like the one against Lille, it was because he deemed it to have the best chance of success. On another occasion – for example, in the previous season's destruction of Arsenal – he scored the fifth goal with a straightforward side-foot from close range.

United's disappointing run continued, with the uncertainty over the future of Sir Alex doing nothing to help the situation. Ole did not start for the next seven games. They only managed one victory in that spell, a 2-0 win over a doomed Leicester City about to slide out of the Premiership and into obscurity. Successive defeats followed at the hands of the London trio of Arsenal, Chelsea and West Ham.

The Chelsea defeat was a particularly heavy 0-3 at Old Trafford, with Keane playing in a reshuffled back four alongside Blanc. They could do little to stop the audacious partnership of Hasselbaink and Gudjohnsen, who notched a goal apiece. Ole came on for Beckham after 76 minutes as United crashed to their worst home defeat in eight years. Claudio Ranieri's side had made rapid improvements in recent years and the side that had won so handsomely included the rising talents of Lampard and Terry. Slowly, the London club was becoming a force to be reckoned with.

Speaking on MUTV, Sir Alex suggested that his team could not now win the title. 'Every team makes errors, but we are making too much of a habit of it this season. I don't think we'll win the Premiership now because of the games we've lost.'

The following week, United went down at home 0-1 to West Ham, Jermain Defoe breaking the deadlock to score the winner. Defoe was another natural goalscorer in the mould of Ole, and Ferguson admired him. For United, it was their sixth defeat of the campaign, already equalling the number of games they had lost in the whole of the previous season. It wasn't even Christmas yet.

The problems stemmed from the defence; they had the second-worst defensive record in the Premiership. Their defensive stats were the worst for a decade and made sorry reading. Opta indicated that they conceded a goal every 51 minutes, almost twice as often as in the previous season.

## STRIKE FORCE

Sir Alex decided that attack was the best form of defence and opted to play Ole alongside van Nistelrooy. The partnership with Scholes had failed to gel as Ferguson had hoped it would; for whatever reason, they just weren't as successful together as their individual talents would have suggested.

Some fans were also saying that the addition of Verón to the squad had destroyed the midfield axis of Scholes and Keane, which had been the bedrock for so much of the team's success in recent years. By the end of October, the stats indicated that United had managed to score a meagre eight goals when they had van Nistelrooy as a lone striker. However, when a twin strike force had been deployed, it yielded 30 goals. Despite the patchy performances, though, United were still statistically the most potent attacking force in the land, regardless of the combination up front, having converted 18 per cent of all chances into goals.

The stats were borne out when Derby were crushed 5-0 at Old Trafford shortly before Christmas. Ole helped himself to a brace of goals, the first after just six minutes. It was another peach of a goal for the Norwegian; Mikael Silvestre whipped over a cross that Ole chested down and thumped hard and straight into the net.

Shortly afterwards, he turned goal-maker when he set up a chance for Keane to notch the second. The Irishman had started the move in his own half, which was carried on by Ole who cleverly slid the ball across the face of the goal for Keane to sweep in at the far post.

The third goal and Ole's second of the night came when Sunderland keeper Andy Oakes spilled van Nistelrooy's fierce drive. Ole simply ran the ball into the empty net, having anticipated the chance of a spillage. Not since Jimmy

Greaves had there been a player who could dispatch half-chances so clinically and economically.

Van Nistelrooy made it 4-0 and then Paul Scholes wrapped it up with the fifth as United coasted to the final whistle. Ole's assist for Keane's goal was his fifth of the season, three more than the jaded Beckham had managed so far. In the previous season, Beckham had more assists than any other player in the Premiership, but so far Ole had surpassed him with the minimum of fuss.

The Derby demolishing signalled the start of a decent run of form for United, who went on to win nine straight games. With Ole alongside him, van Nistelrooy set a new Premiership record by scoring in eight successive games. It equalled the record of the Busby Babe Liam (Billy) Whelan, who was also sadly killed in the Munich crash. Van Nistelrooy's run included a hat-trick in the 6-1 thrashing of Southampton at Old Trafford. Ole also scored in that game and grabbed a further goal in the 3-1 win at Southampton.

The pairing of Ole with Ruud in a central striking position not only gave them a great deal of fire power but it also meant that Scholes could revert to his usual role. With Nicky Butt replacing Beckham in some matches, the midfield was more structured and balanced.

Another amazing comeback by United was in the Third Round of the Cup away to Villa on a freezing Sunday night in the first week of January 2002. Villa were 2-0 ahead in the first 34 minutes, courtesy of some shocking blunders at the back. That was how it stayed with 13 minutes to go, until Ole popped up to pull a goal back. This was after a frantic mêlée in the Villa penalty box.

Then van Nistelrooy scored twice in two minutes to win the tie for United. The match was screened live by the BBC and made compelling viewing for the millions watching. When the equaliser was scored, there was a mini pitch invasion by excited United fans exhilarated by their heroes' courageous comeback.

Van Nistelrooy had been rested for the game but had been brought off the bench to turn the match. It gave him some clear insight into the unique role of his colleague Ole, as he told *Inside United* magazine, 'From the bench, I was watching the game like a fan. I just watch the games hoping we do well and getting excited by the chances we create. I think it's really hard what Ole does, the way he studies the game. I look in the books at the statistics of all the players and Ole's record is amazing. He's made so many sub appearances yet scored so many goals – I don't think I am made for that.' Indeed. Ole was fast becoming the goalscorers' goalscorer.

United's interest in the Cup did not extend past the next round where they rather surprisingly went out to Middlesbrough 0-2. Ole started the match but could make little impression. Their unbeaten run in the Premiership had ended a few nights earlier when they lost for the second year running at home to Liverpool as a result of a Danny Murphy goal. The defeat was a huge setback to United's title aspirations. The fans were surprised that Ole was consigned to the bench and Giggs took his place alongside the big Dutchman. It seemed a strange line-up considering Giggs was not as effective in that role. Ole came on in the dying minutes for Beckham, but to no avail.

All the while, Sir Alex was looking at ways of improving his squad, deciding to sell Andy Cole to Blackburn for £8 million, and Dwight Yorke was lined up to go to Middlesbrough for £6.2 million. At the last minute, Yorke pulled out of the transfer for financial reasons. This, in turn, meant that Sir Alex was unable to secure Di Canio from West Ham, which would have been financed in part by the Yorke transfer proceeds. It was a pity that a wonderful talent like Di Canio was never seen at Old Trafford. A Solskjaer–Di Canio partnership would indeed have been something to savour.

One player who did join United was Diego Forlán from Independiente for £6.9 million. He was not an unqualified success, scoring 17 goals in 95 appearances. Old Trafford presented a steep learning curve to the young Uruguayan, but learn he did. When he left United in August 2004 to join Villareal, he finished top goalscorer in the Spanish league. It was sink or swim at United, the expectation and pressure immense.

Explaining his transfer decisions, Sir Alex told Sky Sports, 'Teddy Sheringham left last year at 35, and I felt Andy Cole, at 30 years of age and on that length of contract, would not get picked in every game, and that was a worry for Andy, so I got Diego in at 22, and Ruud van Nistelrooy is 25. I couldn't believe Ole has just turned 29, as he looks 21 and he's fresh and he's such a young person.'

The following week, United travelled to the Reebok Stadium to take on Sam Allardyce's Bolton, who had won at Old Trafford in the early autumn after a truly slap-dash display by the Reds. Sir Alex recalled Ole to the starting line-up with Giggs reverting to his favoured position on the wing. Forlán made his début for United. The Norwegian repaid Ferguson's faith in him by scoring a hat-trick in a 4-0 romp. Bolton thought that they had United worked out – shut them down quickly and go in hard. Big Sam, born in Dudley, the birthplace of Duncan Edwards, liked to capitalise on dead-ball situations and long throws, which United dealt with easily.

It was Ole's third hat-trick for United. He had scored four goals against Forest and Everton and, on numerous occasions, he had bagged a brace of goals. After the victory, as reported in *Masters of Old Trafford*, Sir Alex stated, 'This is the time of year we really have to step forward. We need performances like the Bolton result and the genuine quality shown by Ole, who played the role of the quiet executioner to perfection.'

Ole followed on by saying, 'One game doesn't make a difference. We need to go on another seven or eight run of victories to make sure we are up there in April and May.'

Ole was on fire; in the next away game, United went to the Valley to take on Charlton. At the time of writing, Charlton have never beaten United in the Premiership, and they did not ever look like breaking their duck that February afternoon. Two goals from Ole was all that was required to finish off the Robins.

His first goal came after 33 minutes. It was a text book Manchester United break-away goal; Roy Keane spotted Ole's run on the Charlton flank and sent in a wonderful flighted ball that just skimmed the head of defender Mark Fish and fell to Ole. In one sweeping movement, he instantly brought the ball under control, feinted to deceive the recovering Fish and lifted the ball over keeper Dean Kiely. It was another superb goal created out of a half-chance and finished with the chilling efficiency of a master craftsman. Ole also showed a great deal of resilience and strength in that game, in which Charlton's back line tried to muscle him out of the game, but he just bounced back. Many had tried that over the years, but Ole's resilience and uncomplaining determination was remarkable.

Charlton, inspired by the talented Scott Parker, fought hard to get back into the game. The reigning Champions looked less than convincing in the second half. With 15 minutes left, Ole made it safe, though, with his second goal of the game. Beckham's superb cross found Giggs, who spun to crack in a tremendous shot. Kiely did well to beat it out, but Ole had anticipated the rebound and slotted home from a tight angle as England defender Powell tried to clear. Nothing looked on at the time because Powell was shielding the ball, but Ole managed to wrap his foot around the defender and the ball, and hook it home. Two strikes, and two perfect examples of opportunism par excellence.

It was a big week for United because Sir Alex had made a U-turn in his decision to stay at United. How fitting that perhaps his best signing and the man who had clinched his greatest managerial achievement now scored the goals that ushered in a new era. As one tabloid put it, 'SIR ALEX FERGUSON CAN'T FINISH BUT OLE GUNNAR SOLSKJAER CAN!'

In the next four games, United won three and drew the other 2-2 against Derby. Then came a tricky visit to Upton Park, which became even harder when the Hammers took an early lead, which was cancelled out by a Beckham equaliser, his 13th goal of the campaign. West Ham continued to press and Kanouté restored their advantage before Nicky Butt headed United level near the break.

Ole took command in the second half as he hauled United back in front. A wonderful run on 55 minutes took him past Thomas Repka and Nigel Winterburn before cutting the ball back for Scholes to crash home. Then he scored the fourth on the hour. Van Nistelrooy's clipped shot was brilliantly parried by England keeper David James, but Ole pounced to slot neatly home. West Ham fought on and

Defoe pulled a goal back before Beckham's last-minute penalty made it 5-3. The defensive instability among the United back line was to prove to be their undoing; conceding three goals to a mediocre side like West Ham underlined their fragility.

Ole was delighted that the man who had brought him to the Theatre of Dreams was still in charge after a change of heart. In the *Masters of Old Trafford*, he said, 'It means a lot to us that the manager is staying on, and it gives us a great boost. Now we know what is required of us and what is expected over the next few years. This club could not be in better hands.'

Ole celebrated his 29th birthday with two goals in the 5-1 destruction of French Champions Nantes in Group A in the Champions League. The previous week, the teams had drawn in France. For Ole, it was his first Champions League start as partner to van Nistelrooy. Frederic Da Rocha put Nantes ahead after 17 minutes after some shambolic marking, but Beckham's superb free-kick over the Nantes wall put them level within a minute. Sir Alex immediately switched Ole deep, back into midfield.

After 29 minutes, he put United ahead when he headed home a Giggs pass after van Nistelrooy had set up the chance. Mikael Silvestre headed in a third on 38 minutes from a Beckham free-kick. Ole was playing magnificently and created the fourth for van Nistelrooy in the second half. Barthez's massive clearance up field was helped on by Ole's delightful flick to the big Dutchman, who was chopped down by Fabbri and recovered to blast home the penalty. Shortly afterwards, van Nistelrooy was substituted and Ole switched back into the single striker role. Another wonderful free-kick from Beckham gave the Norwegian the chance to head his second and United's fifth, completing the club's biggest win in Europe for 22 games.

A scoreless draw against Bayern Munich at Old Trafford and an effortless 0-3 away win over Boavista (in which Ole scored) put United into the quarter-final against Deportivo La Coruña. The dangerous Spanish side was coached by Javier Irureta, who had already recorded two victories over United in the early autumn.

In the away game, United played superbly and won 0-2. It was a perfect example of different styles coming together on the pitch. Beckham, showing flashes of his early magic, scored the first with a marvellous dipping shot, and van Nistelrooy blasted home the second. Roy Keane pulled a hamstring in the first half and was ruled out for a month. Paul Scholes also picked up a booking, which ruled him out of the next game.

In the return leg, Ole scored twice in a 3-2 win. What is most memorable about the game is a two-footed tackle by Argentinian Aldo Duscher that damaged a metatarsal in Beckham's left foot and put him out for the rest of the season. It became the most famous injury in football as it cast huge doubts over his World Cup participation. The injuries piled up as Ronny Johnsen limped off with a recurrence of the hamstring injury that decimated his United career. It was to be Ole's fellow countryman's last appearance in the red shirt. His loss was another hugely damaging blow to the cause as his presence in defence always provided a steely strength.

The hard-bitten coach Klaus Toppmöller brought his Bayer Leverkusen side to Manchester for the first leg of the European Champions League semi-final at the end of April. Ruud van Nistelrooy scored twice, but the Germans came away with a 2-2 draw and the crucial away goals. The result was a bitter disappointment to Sir Alex who was desperate to get to the Final again for a number of reasons. It was to be played at Scotland's Hampden Park, the home ground of Queen's Park, where he started his career as a player in the same year as the Munich disaster. More importantly, the ex-Queen's Park striker wanted to win another European Cup to dismiss the charges that the 1999 triumph had been a fluke. The truly great European club sides – Liverpool, Real Madrid, AC Milan, Ajax and Bayern Munich – had all been frequent winners of European Cups, and he wanted Manchester United (only two wins so far) to be counted among their number.

It was not to be again that season, though. Roy Keane, now Ferguson's alter ego on the field, was back for the return leg against Leverkusen, and Ole was named as a sub. Keane blasted United ahead after 28 minutes to rekindle hopes of another final. Just on half-time, Oliver Neuville equalised and that proved sufficient to knock United out on the away goals rule. Keane summed it up by saying they got what they deserved – nothing.

The Premiership started to dissolve in front of their eyes, with Middlesbrough beating them by a solitary goal at Old Trafford. It was a bitter defeat; Steve McClaren was finding life at the start of his Riverside career as difficult as he was to find it at the start of his England tenure. His intricate knowledge of United, gained during his spell there, created the blueprint for the two shock defeats in a couple of months that sent their Cup and Premiership hopes crashing.

Ole was not giving up, though. In the next game, he showed Leeds exactly why they were willing to offer in excess of £10 million for his goalscoring services. He plundered two goals in an exciting 4-3 victory. Before the game, Ole observed in an interview with Sky Sports, 'We have been there and won it before and we have a squad that will not panic. The experience may yet get us through it. It is so close that it could yet come down to goal difference.'

The question of goal difference was highly significant as the Norwegian hit-man was turning this into a one-man war against the rest of the Premiership. In the next match, he netted the only goal of the game away to Leicester. That gave him a career total of 98 goals for United and he was anxious to get the hundred up before the season ended. Arsenal were slowly moving towards the Premiership title as they were top with a game in hand.

A goal at Chelsea in a 3-0 stroll put Ole on the magic 99. It was tucked away past his old team-mate Mark Bosnich, keeping goal for the Blues for £42,000 a week. The win at Stamford Bridge was only their second victory over a top-six side that season and ample proof of why they failed to win their fourth consecutive Premiership title. Chelsea were now haemorrhaging cash, yet to be offered the oil money that was to transform them into the occupying force at the top of the table.

A home defeat against Arsenal in the second-last game of the season clinched the title for the north London side. Keane described it as 'men against boys'. Sylvain Wiltord scored the only goal of the game, and Ole came on as a sub but failed to create anything. United's confrontational captain found it hard to hide his disgust at the season's failures, and his frustrations were about to spill over in his incendiary bust-up with Mick McCarthy at the World Cup in Japan-South Korea.

Arsenal, like the second-placed Liverpool, had recorded

the double over United that Ole had described as a '12-point switch'. In November, Arsenal had beaten the Reds 3-1 at Highbury. Paul Scholes put United ahead but a mistake by Gary Neville allowed Pires in to set up Freddy Ljungberg for an equaliser. Two basic errors by Barthez in the last five minutes then gifted Henry two goals. Defensive errors – that was the story of season 2001/02.

Ole's point about goal difference was accurate; the Reds finished as the highest goalscorers in the Premiership, notching 87 goals. The van Nistelrooy–Solskjaer combination contributed 40 of them, but they had conceded 45 goals, 50 per cent more than Liverpool. Arsenal, who eventually finished ten points ahead of United, had only a single goal superiority.

On a personal note, it was Ole's most prolific season during his time at United. He scored a total of 25 goals – 17 in the Premiership, seven in Europe and one in the FA Cup against Villa. Although he had no more medals to add to his collection, he could afford to be satisfied with his contribution, as he said to Sky, 'My life is really well at the moment. I'm as good as a regular for one of the world's best football teams. I score a reasonable amount of goals and have a terrific family.'

The young man who had arrived in Manchester five years before with his dreams of glory was to have one more season of joy before the bad times hit.

# 9

# Triumph and Disaster

**'If you walked into the dressing room and you didn't know who he was, you would assume Ole Gunnar Solskjaer was a lost YTS player.'**
**RIO FERDINAND**

Ole returned to Norway at the end of July in a pre-season friendly against Valerenga, forming part of the Reds' pre-season European tour. The game had been set up the previous February to mark the 30th anniversary of the Norway Cup. It was the world's largest international tournament for youngsters and the organisers had pulled a major coup in landing Manchester United.

A packed crowd of 30,000 in the Ullevaal Stadium saw their returning hero open the scoring for United. Ole scored from the penalty spot, the only recorded goal that he converted from a spot-kick in a competitive Manchester United game. He had scored penalties for Norway, the previous one coming against Turkey in a 1-1 draw the previous August. The former United triallist Pa Modou Kah equalised for a lively Valerenga in the second half before Roy Keane scored the winner.

Ole was concerned about the state of the game in his homeland; his major fear was that there was not enough young talent coming up through the youth sides. He told *VG*, 'Every time I travel home to Kristiansund, I am reminded that there is less and less football played in Norway. The football pitches are not fit any longer... many kids just sit around with their computers. We must not struggle with the recruitment. We cannot let the sport in Norway die out.'

On their day, Norway were a strong side and a team featuring Ole, Henning Berg, John Arne Riise and Jo Tessem had recently beaten the World Cup co-hosts Japan 3-0 in Oslo. The high spot of the evening was a great goal by Ole six minutes from time. It was a very small consolation for them not being able to sample the Japanese hospitality as they had failed to qualify.

Ole then took part in the Champions League qualifying match against the Hungarian side Zalaegerszeg. Having only finished third in the Premiership, the former holders faced the ignominy of having to play in the qualifying round. In the fourth minute, Ole had a great strike on goal but the ball rebounded off the foot of the post. That was the story of the game as United created and squandered a series of chances. Eventually, a last-minute goal by Koplarovic, after a silly mistake by Phil Neville, made the situation even more embarrassing.

Manchester United opened the new Premiership campaign with a turnover of £129.5 million and a wage bill of £49.97 million. On the opening day of the 2002/03 season, Ole finally scored his 100th goal for United in the home fixture against West Bromwich Albion. Fittingly, it was a late winner scored when he came off the bench. Trademark Ole.

West Brom defended stubbornly throughout the match and looked like they might steal a point. Ole came into the match on the hour to replace the tiring Verón, who earlier had treated the fans to some exhibitionist passing. Shortly after Ole's introduction, the West Brom skipper McInnes was sent off. Ten minutes from time, with United attacking for all they were worth, Keane and Butt combined to put in Ole. His perfectly placed, low shot from 12 yards left Russell Hoult stranded. A typical Ole finish, it was a week short of six years since he had scored on his début for United against Blackburn. Six years, a burgeoning collection of medals, a career of prosaic beauty and a ton of goals, many of them priceless. He had achieved so many of his dreams, but he never lost the hunger to score again and again and again. Ole's life could have easily slipped into tabloid hell and then mediocrity after the melodrama of the Nou Camp, but instead he was as rooted and focused as the day he arrived in Manchester. The rapid nature of his success meant that many of his targets had been achieved early, but soon enough, a new target was to present itself... and it could possibly be the greatest challenge of his career so far.

Ole scored another goal in the 5-0 trouncing of the brave Zalaegerszeg in the return match in Manchester. Any doubts about qualifying were quickly dispelled when United raced to a 3-0 lead in the opening 20 minutes. Van Nistelrooy, Beckham and Scholes were the scorers.

Scholes went off early in the second half to be replaced by Ole. The game was also noteworthy because Rio Ferdinand, newly signed from Leeds for £30 million, made his début.

The visiting goalkeeper was sent off after 76 minutes for a dangerous challenge on van Nistelrooy who blasted home the subsequent penalty. Two minutes from time, Ole made it five when he scored with a curling drive into the bottom right-hand corner. Forlán remained a virtual onlooker; he was yet to score for United and the pressure was building on him with each passing match. Luck plays a tremendous part in a footballer's career. The opening goal Ole scored in his United career takes on more significance with each passing year. The Norwegian instantly won over the crowd, while Forlán and Ferdinand found it much harder to gain acceptance.

Ole retained his place in the side when they visited the Stadium of Light four days later. Sunderland were in free-fall towards the bottom of the Premiership and some bleak years lay ahead in the cauldron of the Championship before Roy Keane galvanised the Black Cats and hauled them back into the Premiership in 2007. That day, Roy was not such a hero to the north-east fans. In the last minute, he was red-carded for elbowing his Irish team-mate Jason McAteer.

Ole set up the United goal after just seven minutes when he nodded on for Giggs to race clear and beat Thomas Sorensen. Giggs, along with Bolton stalwart Gary Speed, are the only players to have scored in every season of the Premiership. There was a chance for Ole to double the lead soon afterwards, but it was squandered.

Fellow Norwegian Tore Andre Flo scored a shock equaliser on 70 minutes, after McAteer teed the ball up for him to score his first goal following some pantomime defending by the United back line.

The Reds had got the season that promised so much off to a bad start. A van Nistelrooy penalty gave them a narrow home win over Middlesbrough, and there then followed two defeats. The first was against Bolton, who had inflicted their first home defeat of the previous season. Kevin Nolan scored the only goal of the game 13 minutes from time. It might have been a different story if Ole's first-half header had not been brilliantly saved by Jussi Jaaskelainen. The Bolton keeper, a rapidly rising talent, denied Ole again in the final minutes as United battered the Bolton goal. An apoplectic Sir Alex screamed at his players from the touchline, and the press rubbished their chances of regaining the title.

Leeds United beat them by the same score at Elland Road the following week. Ole featured in the match and picked up a rare yellow card. Last season's hero van Nistelrooy was going through the 'second season' syndrome, and goals were certainly much harder to come by. A rather shamefaced United team left the field at Leeds that day.

In an interview in the *Manchester Evening News*, Ole observed, 'We know we've got to sort it out now. When we perform, dig in and stay together as a team we're the best in England. But at the moment, it is not happening in front of goal. Sometimes we try to play too much. We all want to score nice goals but sometimes we have to be more direct, getting on the end of crosses and going back to basics.'

Shrewd words again from Ole and they must have helped in the next match, a 5-2 win over Maccabi Haifa. The Israeli side took a shock early lead when Katan picked up a careless pass to shoot through Barthez's legs. Giggs quickly headed United level and then Ole put them ahead from van Nistelrooy's killer pass, which he dispatched with power and accuracy.

Verón was the star of the night, revelling in the slower pace and the space afforded to him. The third goal was his, smashed in from point-blank range after a peach of a ball from Beckham. Then he put van Nistelrooy in for number four with an exquisite 40-yard pass between back and centre-half. Who knows how things would have worked out if the Verón–Beckham axis would have been allowed to flourish at Old Trafford? With the partnership of Ole and van Nistelrooy up front, it would have been highly interesting to say the least.

Diego Forlán had a good evening, too, finally breaking his duck and scoring the fifth from the penalty spot. The goal took the pressure off the Uruguayan and lifted some of the gloom that had descended over the club. The fans were still predicting that tough times were ahead, though. There was a general malaise in the air and the undeniable feeling that United were on the brink of decline, a slow spiral down to mediocrity. The media were of the opinion that United's cycle had run its course, and that their barnstorming days were over. As the seasons changed, they were drifting in ninth place in the table. Their third spot last season was the only time that they had not occupied a top-two position since 1991. Things were about to change for both United and Ole, but first there was another Premiership title to be won.

Tottenham were next on the agenda. Ole was in the starting line-up, much to Spurs' disappointment. For nearly four years, they had been trying to get him into the white shirt with the cockerel badge. In response, he had netted seven times against them. Teddy Sheringham was in the Spurs side and received a good reception from the United fans.

Ole did not score on that occasion but won the penalty which was duly converted by van Nistelrooy. On 63 minutes, Ole was sent flying by a crunching challenge in the box and his Dutch team-mate dispatched the penalty. Tottenham keeper Kasey Keller gave a brilliant performance, restricting United to just one goal. One particular save from a powerful volley from Ole in the first half was particularly memorable. Diego Forlán replaced Ole late in the match.

Ole's next goal came in the 4-0 defeat of Olympiakos at Old Trafford. The form came flooding back as the Reds blew away the Greek champions. An injury to van Nistelrooy meant that the diminutive Scholes was paired up front alongside Ole. They were two up in the first 25 minutes through Giggs and another fine goal from Verón. A Giggs cross was then diverted into the Olympiakos net by a Greek defender, before Ole struck with the fourth in a wonderful move involving Scholes slicing open their defence and the Norwegian striker curling the ball into the net. The result maintained United's 100 per cent start to their European campaign.

Everton were dispatched 3-0 in the next Premiership fixture at Old Trafford. It was another late, late show with all the goals coming in the last four minutes. Ole had come on as a second-half sub for Verón. For once, he miskicked a Beckham cross when well placed soon after being introduced. Scholes finally broke the deadlock with a left-foot shot after a poor clearance. Then Ole raced through with the goal at his mercy but was held back by David Weir who was instantly red-carded. It seemed a bit harsh as the infringement seemed to have occurred outside of the box. Everton felt even more aggrieved when van Nistelrooy smashed in the penalty. Scholes made it three when he scored with a searing shot that almost burst the net.

Everton had fought hard all night and were heartened by

the performance of their young striker, the Croxteth-born Wayne Rooney. Sir Alex was weighing up a bid for the prodigiously gifted youngster, who was already being hailed as the hottest property in the game. A few weeks later, Rooney scored his first Premiership goal to end Arsenal's 33-game unbeaten streak. The amazing run had been the cornerstone that had propelled them to the Double.

Throughout his career in English football, Ole had scored at all the London grounds – Arsenal, Tottenham, West Ham, Charlton and Fulham. The goal against the last of those sides had been scored at Craven Cottage in the FA Cup in January 2001. In October 2002, he equalised against Fulham, but this time the goal was scored at QPR's ground in Loftus Road, Fulham's temporary home. The Londoners had taken the lead after 35 minutes through Steve Marlet. United looked jaded after the midweek Euro 2004 qualifying matches and struggled to get into the game.

Ole had himself been in Romania with the Norwegian side, but he was bursting with energy. Yet again, Ole was to prove that he was the best last-minute weapon in football when he came galloping to United's rescue after 62 minutes. This time, he took advantage of a dreadful error by the towering Zat Knight to fire home from an acute angle. The Fulham keeper, Edwin van der Sar, had no chance with it, the Dutchman later denying a rampant Ole with a superb flying save. Steed Malbranque also missed a penalty near the end which would have won it for Fulham.

After the match, Ole told the *Manchester Evening News*, 'We just can't worry about what Arsenal or Liverpool are doing. We just have to win our games so we can't be pleased about the Fulham match. We didn't lose, but we shouldn't be pleased with one point. There has been a lot of travelling in the last week. It takes its toll. After breaks like that, you need to start well when you return to your next club match. We knew we had to start right and we just didn't.'

United qualified out of Group F in the Champions League with a 3-2 win over Olympiakos in Greece; Ole played no part in the victory. There were still two games to go, but United were already in the comfort zone. The return to the Premiership always seemed anti-climactic after their European jaunts, and the next game against Villa was no exception, with a scrambled 1-1 draw at Old Trafford. Ole played but, for once, the saviour's role went to Diego Forlán. The £7.5 million striker headed a late equaliser to record his first goal in open play for the club and produce a rabbit from the Manchester hat. Liverpool, who had put a strong run together since the start of the season, were at that stage eight points clear of United.

Maccabi Haifa beat United 3-0 in Israel to end the Reds' 16-match unbeaten run in the Champions League proper. Sir Alex used the game to field a mixture of battle-hardened foot soldiers like Ole and Scholes and blood the rookie Kieran Richardson. Forlán and Quinton Fortune also made the starting line-up. Ole could have scored in the opening minutes when Scholes played him in and he unleashed a fierce drive. The shot appeared to have beaten the Maccabi keeper Avate, but almost in desperation he kicked out and his boot deflected the ball around the post. Then the unthinkable happened as two blockbusting shots and a penalty sank United.

Ole's next goal was scored in the Manchester derby. It was a historic fixture, the last one ever to be played at Maine Road. In goal for the Sky Blues was an old friend of Ole's, Peter Schmeichel, who was enjoying a brief spell at

City. Peter's son Kaspar is currently on their books and, at the time of writing, he was on loan to Falkirk in the SPL.

In the tunnel before the game, the Dane shook hands with Barthez. Ole grinned across at Peter; the last time they had been on the same field was on 26 May 1999 at the Nou Camp. All that counted for nothing now. The sharpest reminder of this was when Schmeichel approached captain Gary Neville at the head of the team. Schmeichel offered his hand, but the United captain did not take it.

Actually, the snub to Schmeichel rebounded on Neville. The Danish giant kept his record of never losing a Manchester derby match, while, between them, the Bury-born Neville brothers, aided and abetted by Barthez, gifted City three of the easiest goals they ever scored in the fixture.

The game started frenetically and then speeded up. An appalling square pass by Phil Neville was intercepted by Shaun Goater, who burst through to shoot. The effort was weak but Barthez made a hash of the save and Anelka scored from a yard. Anelka had done so much to help Arsenal win the Double in Ole's second season in England, and his fearsome pace proved too much for Laurent Blanc that afternoon.

Ole was anxious that United took something from the pulsating derby and equalised within three minutes. Giggs supplied and Ole, at full stretch, turned the ball past his former colleague. That set United up and they should have gone on and sealed their dominance. The defensive failings that ruined their title hopes the previous year surfaced again, though, when Gary Neville made one of the worst errors of his career. The late Marc-Vivien Foe struck a forward pass, Neville tried to let it run out of play but Shaun Goater got behind him and robbed him of the ball.

Before the hapless Neville could recover, Goater flicked it past Barthez.

Early in the second half, the classy Berkovic latched on to another pass by Phil Neville to feed Goater who chipped Barthez for the third. United were in danger of being overrun by City, and it was only really Ole who saved United's blushes that day, a clever back-heel almost cutting the arrears, but Schmeichel was equal to it, making a brilliant save. Ole then carved out a simple chance for John O'Shea who should have done better than to head it over. It was United's third defeat of the season and the manner of it made the prospect of another Premiership title seem very distant.

United's next Premiership fixture was away to West Ham, a tie that had a history of being quite tricky. A brilliant piece of quick thinking by Ole set up a goal from van Nistelrooy on 37 minutes. The big Dutchman was jogging back from an offside position when Ole, out on the left flank, received the ball. In an instant, he threaded the ball through to van Nistelrooy who controlled it instantly before luring out England keeper James and rolling the ball home. The Hammers protested vehemently that the goal was offside, but the cameras proved that Ole's pass was weighted so beautifully that, at the moment van Nistelrooy collected it, he was back on side in line with the last Hammers defender. Jermain Defoe scored in the final minutes from a position which also looked suspiciously offside.

Around that time, Ole found himself involved in a dispute with the Norwegian magazine *Se og Hør*. This was over some photographs that were taken of his family vacation in Sardinia the previous summer. Ole lost the case as the press regulatory body ruled that the magazine had not broken any rules. They were of the view that the photographs had been taken in a public place and were not of a sensationalist nature. The magazine editor defended himself by saying that Ole was one of Norway's 'few international celebrities'.

Ole would have hated being referred to as a celebrity. Since his eye-popping final act at the Nou Camp, he had shunned the glamour and publicity and did everything in his power to keep his family out of the limelight.

Ole may not have wanted to grab the headlines in tabloids or magazines, but he certainly featured heavily in a rip-roaring 5-3 victory over Newcastle at Old Trafford. The fixtures with the Geordie boys were always high-scoring affairs that had the fans baying for more. This one was no exception, the centrepiece of it being a hat-trick by van Nistelrooy and a plethora of chances. Ole set up the opening goal with a dazzling piece of control as he pelted down the right and then cut the ball back for the onrushing Scholes to lash home. Given the perfection of the pass, the England midfielder could hardly have missed.

Newcastle equalised when a deep cross from Bernard looped over Barthez into the net. Back came United and van Nistelrooy scored twice before the break to put United in command. Alan Shearer reduced the arrears when he struck home a free-kick early in the second half. It was a historic strike because it was his 100th Premiership goal for Newcastle. In achieving this, he had created a unique double by becoming the first player to score 100 Premiership goals for two different clubs, his other century being for Blackburn with whom he won his solitary Premiership medal. How fitting that he should score the record-breaker against United who had vainly tried to sign him for so long.

Ole, Shearer's alter ego at Old Trafford, had also recently

passed his ton. Had Ole left Old Trafford that season for another Premiership club, his record surely suggested that he would be in line for another century.

Ole did not want to be upstaged and scored the fifth, with van Nistelrooy having notched the fourth to rack up his second Premiership hat-trick. Newcastle protested that Ole had fouled defender Aaron Hughes when he raced on to Silvestre's pass and slammed in the goal, but the linesman ruled that it had been a legitimate challenge and the goal stood.

After scoring, Ole was switched to midfield with Ryan Giggs moving into the attack. Sir Alex seemed increasingly interested in playing Ole in a withdrawn right-midfield role. Beckham's form had dipped again and already the wily Scot was looking for options. Still the goalfest continued and Craig Bellamy back-headed Newcastle's third goal.

After the match, Ole talked to the Norwegian Radio station P4 and confessed that he had not been happy with his form. 'If I had the answer to the problem, it would have been easy. Football is a complicated game and sometimes not everything goes your way. Small things that you don't even think about just then and there can be very decisive.'

The press was full of stories about who United would be signing in the next transfer window. Two names kept appearing – Eidur Gudjohnsen at Chelsea and Robbie Fowler then at Leeds. Sir Alex was a long-term admirer of both players. Fowler would have made a good foil for Ole in the same manner that Henrik Larsson did so briefly in 2006/07. Gudjohnsen, it was rumoured, was available for £10 million; Chelsea were yet to have their Russian injection of cash, and were thought to be £80 million in debt. Bearing in mind the success of the Sheringham–

Solskjaer combination, Sir Alex saw the blond Icelander as the perfect replacement for the Londoner.

Another Champions League goal was notched by Ole in the 3-1 victory over Swiss team FC Basel at the noisy Saint Jaakob Park. Basel were a useful side, managed by the ex-Tottenham boss Christian Gross. The Reds were a goal down within 30 seconds when Gimenez scored after the defence failed to deal with a corner. United went nearly an hour before equalising with a goal created by Ole for van Nistelrooy. Finding space on the right, Ole sent over a tantalising centre for his Dutch partner to score with a glancing header.

Within a minute, he had scored again from an impossible angle out on the goal line. Van Nistelrooy always regarded that strike as one of the finest in his career. The striker then turned provider after 68 minutes when he sent Ole clean through with a perfect pass. The Basel keeper raced from his line but Ole put the ball through his legs for an easy goal.

Ruud Gullit used to talk of the great Dutch striker van Basten being 'decisive' and that quality was what he was most remembered for. Ole had that rare ability; when it mattered most, he would take positive action.

Then followed a huge week for United, during which they could determine their own destiny with an away trip to Liverpool and a home clash with Arsenal.

Liverpool, as always, were worthy opponents but the honours went to United as they recorded their first victory over them in seven meetings. Forlán was the unlikely hero – thanks to the Liverpool keeper Dudek having one of the worst days of his career – scoring both goals in a narrow 2-1 victory. Slowly, he was coming good and overcoming the numerous problems he had encountered in his first season.

## TRIUMPH AND DISASTER

Ole was in the starting line-up at Anfield and mainly played in the withdrawn midfield berth on the right. Beckham had fractured a rib and Sir Alex saw Ole as the perfect replacement for David. The Norwegian told the *Manchester Evening News*, 'It's never been a problem for me playing right or left wing because I played so many games for Norway there and to adjust to that position is no problem. Sometimes, playing in that position, you face towards the goal more, rather than have your back to goal, and that might suit my game better.'

Sandwiched between the big two was a visit to Turf Moor to take on Burnley. Bitter rivals of the Reds in previous decades, they were now struggling in the Championship. It seemed a lifetime ago that Burnley had won the title in the early 1960s with a team of home-grown players. Despite the period of time that has elapsed, they compared very favourably with the class of 1992, featuring Beckham, Scholes and Co.

Ole was a sub in a team that once again comprised youngsters and combat veterans. With nine games in 35 days, the squad was severely stretched to mount campaigns in various competitions. The man in the 20 shirt came on at half-time for van Nistelrooy and scored United's second goal with a cracking shot on the hour. This was after some tight control by Luke Chadwick to set up the chance. The young prospect had beaten two men on the right and then fed Ole with a perfect centre. Marlon Beresford, the Burnley keeper, was rooted to his line as the power of Ole's drive left him stranded.

Forlán's confidence was now sky high after his lucky strikes at Anfield. Diego linked brilliantly with Ole in the second half, the interchanging between the two working particularly well. The Norwegian seemed able to pick out the Uruguayan in intricate moves that should have yielded more goals.

A good week for United was rounded off with a 2-0 home victory over their massive rivals Arsenal. Ole was included in the team and Sir Alex chose to recall Verón with the in-form Forlán dropped to the bench. Ole spent most of the game on the right flank in the Beckham role. Verón opened the scoring after 21 minutes, finishing off a high-speed passing movement. Scholes secured the points for United with a second-half goal after van Nistelrooy had put him clear.

For United, it was a marked improvement on the last time Arsenal had visited Old Trafford when they had tamely rolled over to the Double winners. Although the season had not yet reached its mid-point, the manner of those comfortable victories over their nearest rivals set them up for their eighth title in eleven seasons. The fact that Ole gave them another option on the right, positive in everything he did and still providing vital goals, was a major contributory factor to their continued success.

On the following Wednesday, Deportivo La Coruña were beaten 2-0 at Old Trafford to make it six straight wins in Europe since the hiccup in Haifa. Once again, van Nistelrooy was on target, scoring in each half as United took and called all the shots. Ole picked up another booking in this fixture.

West Ham, lying in 20th spot and subsequently relegated that season, visited Old Trafford next and were crushed 3-0. In the Saturday lunchtime fixture, Ole struck after 15 minutes with a near-post header to open the scoring. It was created by Gary Neville firing over a perfect centre for Ole

Ole is revered for his sense of fair play and sportsmanship. Here he congratulates Roberto Carlos after Real Madrid's win against Man Utd in the Champions League quarter final second leg match, April 2003.

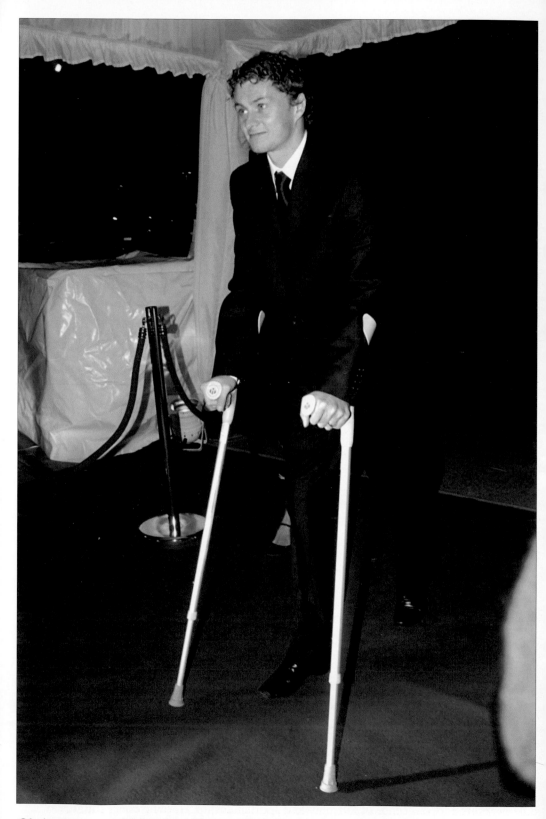

Ole is generous with his time. Here, performing his duties despite being injured, he attends the Unicef annual dinner at Old Trafford in September 2004.

Ole is a Manchester United stalwart and is as committed to his club off the pitch as he is playing for it.

*Left*: With the legendary Sir Bobby Charlton, holding Manchester United's Opus Book of History during a photocall at Old Trafford, 2006.

*Below*: Taking time to meet and greet the faithful fans at a shirt signing at Old Trafford.

*Above*: Solskjaer does it again: celebrating to the crowd after scoring another vital goal, this time helping United reclaim the title from Chelsea in 2007.

*Below*: Such is Ole's talent and integrity that he is bound to be involved with football in some capacity long after his playing days are over.

to head towards goal. The ball struck the Irons defender Tomas Repka and flew past David James.

Verón, in top form in those weeks, smashed in the second with a powerful free-kick; Schemmel, the Hammers defender, poked the third into his own goal in the second half. Another cross from Neville caused havoc in the Londoner's penalty area and, with Ole lurking, the error occurred. Beckham came on for Ole later in the game. The win lifted United into second place, and they had now gone ten matches unbeaten, the last five without conceding a goal.

The run came to an end in the Christmas fixtures with United losing two away matches to Blackburn and Middlesbrough. Ole featured in both of them and earned praise for his performance on the right flank in the match at Ewood Park. Blackburn's Swedish defender Nils Eric Johansson told the *Expressen*, 'I actually feel that Ole Gunnar Solskjaer is a more dangerous proposition than Beckham. Both Cole and Yorke told me how to deal with Beckham.'

While his goal tally had dropped only marginally, Ole's exuberant performances on the right wing were winning rave notices. The fact that he was now a regular in the side was raising doubts about Beckham's long-term future in England. The rumours that he would be going abroad in the summer were reaching new heights, with Madrid seeming the most likely destination. Sir Alex had already laid the blueprint for the development of the team and the 2004 model included Ole replacing Beckham in the long term.

In the 'Boro game, Ole set up Giggs's consolation goal with a defence-wrecking run and was a constant threat. Steve McClaren once again proved his credentials as he masterminded another victory over his old club. The defeat gave rise to another set of doubts about Sir Alex's side being able to recapture the Premiership. The usual clichés were hauled out – lack of commitment, loss of hunger, fatigue... United answered them in the best possible manner. They did not lose another Premiership game that season.

They resumed their winning ways with a 2-0 home victory over Birmingham in the last Saturday of 2002. Phil Neville replaced Ole in the match, ensuring that he got the first use of the bath. The match was only memorable for the wondrous pass that Verón provided for Beckham to chip in the second goal. Connoisseurs in the stands were gleefully comparing it to the 30-yard pass with the outside of his boot that Ole banged in for the second goal against Deportivo the previous April.

United then took on Sunderland on New Year's Day 2003. Verón headed a bizarre own-goal in the fourth minute to give relegation-bound Sunderland a shock lead. Ole had a chance to equalise in the first half but the Black Cat's keeper Macho made a breathtaking point-blank save to deny him. Macho put on a great show to maintain his team's lead and they went into the last ten minutes still ahead.

But memories of that night at the Nou Camp still lingered – two simple goals snatched the three points in dramatic fashion. Silvestre sent a tremendous punt up field in the hope that someone would get on the end of it. It was real route one stuff and most unlike United. The ball fell to Beckham, completely unmarked, who smacked it home. And in the dying seconds, Scholes tucked away Silvestre's cross.

After the match, Ole told *VG*, 'Now we play as we did a couple of years ago. We don't surrender before we are in the showers, and we won despite going a goal down. We could have lost this game, as we did against Bolton, but that would have been unfair. When we create as many chances as we did today, we deserve to win.'

At the start of 2003, Arsenal were five points clear and odds-on with the bookies to retain their title. In the interview, Ole lamented the six points dropped over Christmas but still thought that there was time left to close the gap.

That was, as always, Ole providing shrewd insight into United's present state of mind. After a 3-1 victory at West Brom, United had cut the deficit to just two points. The first goal went to van Nistelrooy and the second to Paul Scholes. WBA had taken an early lead through their classy midfielder Jason Koumas, and ex-United player Ronnie Wallwork showed flashes of his old promise as Gary Megson's West Brom fought hard to get back in the game.

Ole crushed the fight back with the third goal nine minutes into the second half. Gary Neville crossed deep from the right and the Norwegian ace allowed the ball to drop. Taking just one touch, maintaining his balance, he scored with a rasping drive past Russell Hoult. Fifteen more minutes were to elapse before Diego Forlán replaced him.

The International Federation of Football History and Statistics published their awards for 2002. Ole was positioned as the 12th most effective striker in Europe, according to goals per games, which, considering his limited number of starts, was an amazing testimony to the instant impact he managed to make when coming off the bench. Thierry Henry, considered by many to be the pre-eminent striker in Europe, if not the world, was three places behind him. Ole's strike partner, van Nistelrooy, was top of the list, just beating the Kaiserslautern predator Miroslav Klose. Whether or not van Nistelrooy would have been acknowledged as the best striker in Europe without the assistance of Ole as his source of supply is questionable.

The following week, Chelsea were beaten 2-1 at Old Trafford. Once again, United came back from the dead to snatch it. It was the 11th time that they had scored in the last 15 minutes of a match that season. Emmanuel Petit, showing the form that made him a megastar in his glory days at Arsenal, set Gudjohnsen up for Chelsea to take the lead after half-an-hour. Sir Alex was still seeking to bolster his strike force and the Icelander was top of his wish list.

Scholes headed an equaliser nine minutes later in United's first real strike on goal. The Chelsea keeper Carlo Cudicini bungled his clearance and Beckham instantly seized upon it to cross for Scholes to score. The game then hinged on substitutions, with Sir Alex bringing on Giggs still struggling for form and plagued by hamstring problems. Ole was then pushed up alongside van Nistelrooy. Chelsea manager Claudio Ranieri surrendered the initiative to United by taking off his most dangerous forward Jesper Gronkjaer and bringing on the defensive midfielder de Lucas.

United cranked up their attacks, tension pervaded the Chelsea defence and Ole hit the post with Cudicini helpless. The United boss continued to gamble, bringing Forlán on for van Nistelrooy. With just four minutes on the clock, he had one last throw of the dice, bringing on Verón.

Deep into injury time, the Argentinian administered the coup de grace when he picked out Forlán, who snatched the winner, the Uruguayan leading the celebrations with his trademark shirt-removal routine. Sir Alex danced a jig on the touchline, and the Premiership title loomed nearer.

Ole was limping near the end after a tackle by Marcel

Desailly, which resulted in him twisting his knee. He told Sky Sports, 'It's not good... I twisted my knee and we will see in the next days how serious it is.'

Ligament damage was feared at first, but Ole was back in the squad as a sub for the FA Cup clash with West Ham. It was noticeable, though, that his knee was now taking a battering in the hurly-burly of the weekly Premiership contests.

The hapless Hammers were put to the sword 6-0 as a ruthless United showed them no mercy. They extracted maximum revenge for their shock exit from the competition courtesy of Di Canio two years before. Ole scored the sixth after 69 minutes, driving the ball through David James's legs from a chance set up by his buddy van Nistelrooy.

The FA Cup has suffered in recent times, as we have seen, from clubs not taking the competition quite as seriously as they once did, and particularly when United withdrew a few seasons before. Purists claim that acts like that destroyed the very fabric upon which the Cup had existed for over 135 years. But the magic of the Cup was irresistible still, and could be found all over the country in the early rounds, whenever there was a whiff of a massive upset, or a highly dramatic struggle that would rarely be seen in league football. The Manchester United–West Ham game that season was one of those ties that kept the competition alive, and Sir Alex told the Hammers programme, 'It was a good performance from us today. You've got to give our lads credit for making sure that West Ham didn't gain anything, especially confidence in this match.'

February started with a 2-0 win at Southampton, which maintained the pressure on Arsenal. The game was over within 20 minutes as United scored twice through van

Nistelrooy and Giggs, who was clearly regaining confidence and confirming his return to form. Ole had created his goal with an excellent cross that Verón stepped over, allowing the Welshman to score at the second attempt.

A 1-0 victory at Birmingham and a 1-1 draw with Manchester City followed. Ole was a sub in both matches in which van Nistelrooy notched the goals. The home draw with City was particularly disappointing; Shaun Goater, who had starred in the débâcle at Maine Road in November, scored a late equaliser after a scorching run from Wright-Phillips.

Ole's hero Eric Cantona at that time talked to the *Daily Telegraph* about the Arsenal–United title race, saying, 'At this stage, no team is better than the other because all the players have ability. But I think Man United have the strongest mentality and that's why they'll win the League. They're able to handle the pressure. They have the experience.'

United still had a great deal to play for as the season reached its climax – they were already in the Final of the League Cup; snapping at Arsenal's heels in the Premiership; about to play Juventus in the Champions League; and now they were at home to Arsenal in the Fifth Round of the FA Cup. The Quadruple was soon reduced to a Treble, though, as Arsenal won 0-2 at Old Trafford. Ole was in the starting line-up but was closely marked for the entire game, and Giggs missed a sitter which was to prove crucial.

The match was typical Arsenal–United trench warfare; the fixture was portrayed as a face-off between the fiery Scot and the cerebral Frenchman who pulled the strings of the country's two best teams. In the first seven minutes, the names of Scholes, van Nistelrooy and Vieira all went into the book. Ole avoided the confrontations but, after the match, an incident occurred that was to go into the folklore of the club.

The story went that Sir Alex was spitting blood after losing to Wenger's side. A row broke out between him and Beckham after a mumbled remark. Ferguson exploded in rage, and allegedly kicked out at a boot, which hit Beckham in the face, causing a gash over Beckham's eye. Things were never the same between the two United icons after that incident, and Ferguson, now more than ever, had good reason to offload the 'liability' of Beckham's presence at the club. Another factor must have been that Ole had been acquitting himself extremely well out wide on the right, and Ferguson must have felt that sufficient cover was currently in place if Beckham were to leave.

In the *Red News* fanzine, Sir Alex's journalist pal Hugh McIlvanny was quoted as saying, 'Beckham has become a parallel industry, almost a parallel universe to United.'

United bounced back with home and away victories over their old adversaries Juventus. To their credit, the 'Old Lady' of Italy were severely weakened by 'flu in both games. Ole was sub for the 2-1 home victory and played brilliantly in the 0-3 win in Italy.

Sandwiched between the matches with Marcello Lippi's men was a lunch date with Bolton. Once again, Ole came to his team's rescue with a last-minute equaliser which kept their title hopes alive. The importance of Ole's contribution cannot be under-estimated – the inevitable hangover from a big European game is a recurring theme, and so is Ole's chameleon-like ability to adapt instantly and effectively to the circumstances around him. Time and time again, he comes up with the goods.

A defeat to Bolton not only would have earned them the double over United but it also would have been a massive blow to the Reds' confidence. Ole's talent for saving United in the final throes of a match was another reason for their indomitability. The goal was vintage Ole, pouncing on a defensive lapse in the dying seconds to bundle home Beckham's cross at the near post.

The Reds boss told Sky Sports news, 'There is plenty of evidence that we can find something when we need it. We did that again today. We didn't deserve a point but we got it. We managed to dig something out of an impossible situation.' In Ole, he had a player who fought for every last scrap until the final whistle.

The press were somewhat surprised that Ole was left out of the opening line-up for the Worthington Cup Final against Liverpool in Cardiff in early March. Sir Alex opted to go with van Nistelrooy in the lone striker's role. The England pair Steven Gerrard and Michael Owen scored for the Merseyside club but their star player was their keeper Jerzy Dudek. The 30-year-old Norwegian was sent into the fray with 15 minutes left but, on this occasion, his effort was in vain.

The cameras lingered on Sir Alex who was clearly incensed that his side had not managed to turn things around. After the match, Ole summed it up by telling *VG*, 'I was not involved and had no goal chances. I always want to play. But the manager put out the 11 players he thought was the best team. It's just the way it is. We didn't play badly despite the fact that we lost. You can't do something about their goalkeeper being terrific.'

Things brightened for Ole with the birth of his second child, a daughter called Karna, and then he suffered a bout of 'flu and missed the narrow 2-1 home win over Leeds. He was soon back in the team, however, for the visit to Villa Park. United had to win to stay in the title race and they squeezed home by the only goal of the game, scored by Beckham. Prior to his goal, Ole had created a chance for him with a neat cut-back, but the Villa keeper Stefan Postma made a great full-stretch save.

Around the Villa game were two meaningless Champions League fixtures, a 1-1 home draw with Basel in which Ole played and a 0-2 defeat against Deportivo in which he did not. Sir Alex fielded another team of 'babes' against the Spanish, including Mark Lynch, Danny Pugh, Lee Roche and Darren Fletcher. Only the latter is still with the club.

In the quarter-finals, United were drawn against Real Madrid, at that time the most expensive side ever assembled, and reputed to be the exponents of the most beautiful football artistry in Europe. But first it was back to Premier League action and United returned to the top for the first time in a year, even if it was only briefly, with a 3-0 drubbing of Fulham. It was an important psychological blow against Arsenal. Van Nistelrooy scored all three, with Ole earning the penalty for the vital opening goal. The Norwegian had turned sharply in the box but was impeded by Zat Knight, and a spot-kick was awarded.

Ole had his revenge over Liverpool for the Worthington Cup Final defeat. The men from Anfield were mauled 4-0 and Ole scored the last of them. After the match, he told Sky Sports, 'I am pleased with my season so far. I do not judge it on how many goals I score. I prefer to think about how I've helped the team. This season, I have played wide on the left and on the right, with not too many up front, so I have had to adjust my game and think differently.'

Three days later, United met the much-lauded Real Madrid in the Bernabeu and came away with a 3-1 beating. Real gave United a football lesson and humbled them in a manner no English team had managed in decades. The Spanish side had too many big guns – Luis Figo, Raul, Ronaldo and Zinedine Zidane – cherry-picked from all over the globe. A great goal from Figo, effortlessly lobbing Barthez with a shot-cum-cross after 12 minutes, stunned United, who never recovered their composure or discipline. Scholes was then robbed by Zidane, who instantly fed Raul to spin and shoot home number two.

Raul put them three goals ahead early in the second half before van Nistelrooy's 52nd-minute effort gave them a faint chance of a comeback in the return. Neville was later replaced by Ole who nearly scored from Beckham's cross.

Ole was concerned about the gap in class and lamented the lack of truly world-class talent playing in the Premiership. He told the television channel *Nettavisen*, 'I think that we played very well in the Champions League throughout the whole season. With the exception of one game – that one in Madrid. Then, we weren't good enough. We met an incredible team. I think we have too little chance to meet players like Figo, Ronaldo, Raul and, not least, Zidane. There are many good players in England, too. But no teams have four such good players.'

The fixtures continued to pile up and, on 12 April, United travelled to Newcastle. The United players were still licking their wounds after the Bernabeu battering. They responded in the best possible way, destroying the Geordies 6-2. It was a stunning victory as Newcastle were in third place in the table. More to the point, it showed the gap in class between the lesser Premiership teams and the best clubs in Europe.

Jenas gave Newcastle the lead after 20 minutes but Ole equalised within 12 minutes. Giggs chipped over the defence and Ole beat the offside trap to run on and bury his shot past Shay Given. It was a pivotal moment in Ole's career, scoring a vital goal that put United back on course for the Premiership after the morale-sapping thrashing in Spain. No one watching, though, dreamt that it would be his last goal in the Premiership for over three-and-a-half years.

Ole made the second goal, working a one-two with Scholes, who lashed a fierce volley into the net. The Reds scored two more before the break through Giggs and Scholes, as they turned the screw. Scholes then completed his dazzling hat-trick with an immaculate side-foot. Ole carved out a chance for Forlán late in the game, but he slipped as he was about to pull the trigger. United regained top spot in the Premiership that afternoon and stayed in pole position to the end of the season.

Three nights later, United travelled to London for the Championship decider with Arsenal. United obtained a 2-2 draw which gave them the psychological edge over Wenger's men and finally broke their resistance, virtually assuring them of the Premiership. They were three points clear of Arsenal who had a game in hand, but United now had the edge.

Van Nistelrooy put them ahead after 23 minutes with his 38th goal of the season, but another of the three great goalscorers on the pitch, Thierry Henry, scored twice to put Arsenal in front. Henry had been the most consistent factor in Arsenal's success over that period. By the spring of 2007, though, a succession of injuries and the resultant loss of form had left him a peripheral figure as the traditional Arsenal challenge to United faded.

Ole set up United's equaliser within a minute of the French superstar's goal. The Norwegian floated over a wonderful angled cross and Giggs eluded the packed Arsenal rearguard to flick his header down into the net.

That was how it stayed, but controversy followed when Sol Campbell was sent off after catching Ole with his elbow. Arsenal protested and Wenger questioned Ole's part in the incident. Campbell's appeal was subsequently rejected by the FA video advisory panel.

Sir Alex sprung to the defence of his striker, telling Sky Sports, 'The thing that angers me most is that, all of a sudden, Ole Gunnar Solskjaer is a villain. The Arsenal players are attacking him verbally and Thierry Henry apparently had a punch at him. I can't believe that reaction. It was quite clear on television that he has looked round to see where Ole is and has hit him with his elbow. Ole is one of the best professionals in the game. He is respected by everyone, yet I haven't heard one word from Highbury saying "How is your player?"'

Then it was United's sternest test so far that season – the return leg against Real Madrid. United's 93rd match in the Champions League and only their opponents that night had won more in the competition and scored more goals. United were already top scorers in the Champions League that season, having amassed 28 goals.

Sir Alex selected Ole ahead of Beckham – it was clear now that David was on his way out and Ole was the preferred alternative to step into the most publicised boots in world football. In the first match, Roberto Carlos, the Madrid left back, had eclipsed the England captain. The Spanish press had referred to Beckham as 'one-dimensional', and Sir Alex explained to Sky Sports his reasons for picking football's most famous sub in preference to its biggest name. 'It was quite straightforward. Solskjaer has been outstanding for us on the right-hand side, providing a real threat for us. I don't think you can take Ole out and regard him only as a substitute. I regard him as a first-team player who deserved his place. It was based simply on Solskjaer being fantastic in that position. I think the boy has progressed great and his form has been fantastic. I no longer regard him as a substitute, but a first-team player. There are only so many times you can hit a player over the head. Do you leave him out simply because David is a great player, too?'

The game was one of the most fantastic ever played at Old Trafford. Before it even started, the song 'Barcelona' was played over the PA system, a subtle reminder of the glory of that night at the Nou Camp, and a dig at Real by sounding out the name of their bitterest enemies.

United won an epic match 4-3, but slid out of Europe losing 6-5 on aggregate. They trailed three times to the Spanish conquistadors, but fought back to win an epic encounter. Ronaldo, the World Player of the Year, hit a fabulous hat-trick. The first came after 12 minutes when McManaman, Zidane and Gutti had created the opening.

Ole set up the first two goals for United. The first came on the break when Giggs seized on a poor clearance to find Ole, who crashed in a power volley. The Madrid keeper Casillas somehow clawed away his effort, but van Nistelrooy equalised from close range.

Madrid regained the lead four minutes into the second half when the marvellous Zidane set up Ronaldo for his second of the night. The game see-sawed and, within two minutes, United were level again when Ole slipped the ball to Verón whose mis-hit drive eluded Casillas.

United still had a chance; the atmosphere was similar to those incredible European, knife-edge nights of the 1960s with Best, Law and Charlton. Then Ronaldo ripped the heart out of Ole's dream of another European final. Ferdinand again allowed Ronaldo too much space; he looked to be too far out from goal, but sensationally scored with an arcing shot that went over Barthez's head. The tie was now over as a contest, United trailing 6-3 on aggregate. Ronaldo then departed the Theatre of Dreams, his work apparently done. With exceptional grace, the crowd of 66,708 awarded Ronaldo a standing ovation.

The drama was not over, though, as one current *galactico* was replaced by a future one – Beckham – who subsequently confirmed his status when he equalised on the night with a stunning free-kick. It set up a thrilling grandstand finish.

Beckham's curling cross was headed just wide by Ole, who was kicking himself for not having converted. There was no time for regrets, though. Beckham nearly blew the roof off Old Trafford when he grabbed his second of the game scoring from close range. As United powered forward in the dying seconds, the whistle brought one of the most exciting European clashes to a close. It was bitter-sweet moment as so often in the great club's history. An utterly amazing game with wonderful goals and superb action but, at the end of the day, United were out of Europe.

Not only was it a marvellous occasion, but it was one of the most pivotal moments in the modern game. That was the night that Roman Abramovich saw his first ever game of football. Orphaned at four, he was Russia's youngest oligarch before he was 40 and was on the look-out for a new thrill. In a way, United had stage-managed their own decline, albeit temporarily. Abramovich was so enraptured by the game that he fell in love with the sport and decided to buy a British club – or, as the late Tony Banks would have it, 'Abramovich bought a team, not a club.'

Some compensation for United was that they won their last four games to secure the title, but Real had removed the gloss. Ole had now won his fifth Premiership medal, a fabulous achievement by anybody's standards. Scholes, Giggs and the Norwegian were the kernel of Sir Alex's new vision of the team and the heirs to the dusty throne once occupied by Edwards, Best, Cantona and Charlton.

Nothing lasts, though, and tragedy struck Ole at the start of the 2003/04 season. Playing in a match against Wolves, he received a knock that all but destroyed his glittering career and threatened to consign him and his amazing talent to the pages of the history books.

# 10

# Down and Out

**'He has a determination that will hopefully help him. He has had one or two injuries in the past, but he overcame those and I am sure he will do so again. He is mentally strong... that's a great advantage.'**
**SIR ALEX FERGUSON**

The season 2003/04 started so well for Ole, one of the brightest stars of the United squad. His fifth Premiership medal had been won in low-key circumstances, after Arsenal's shock home defeat to Leeds. Interestingly, and perhaps coincidentally, the trophy was to head back to London and remain there for the duration of Ole's incapacity.

Ole confessed to *VG* that his celebrations were muted. 'I went and put my son Noah to bed and it only became a quiet celebration. Three of us were in the living room after he had fallen asleep. We didn't even have a glass of wine. It was very quiet and peaceful.'

The young Norwegian went on to say, 'I have been allowed to play in many vital games and feel I have contributed. But every season is special at this club. I have kept myself free of injuries and that is important.' Those were chillingly prophetic words that would come back to haunt him.

Transfers had made headline news that summer of 2003. David Beckham, as expected, had joined Real Madrid for £25 million. Ole's success in Beckham's role had swayed Sir Alex's thinking, and in an interview with the *Manchester Evening News* he explained, 'Ole is a great alternative as a striker, but his performances as an outside right last season were very, very good. He was outstanding in that position. It was something we maybe didn't expect of him. We have always regarded him as an out-and-out finisher. But he has such good intelligence of the game that you could see him developing as a footballer in terms of playing other positions. It was a real bonus for us, his performance on the right.'

The money from Real was used to purchase wunderkind Cristiano Ronaldo from Sporting Lisbon for £12.24 million – three years later, that deal must surely stand as one of the greatest in the history of the Premiership. He was signed after a devastating performance against United in a pre-season match that christened Sporting's new ground. Sir Alex was excited by the capture of the second most expensive teenager in the history of the game. He told the *Manchester Evening News* that the 18-year-old was 'one of the most exciting young players I've ever seen'.

Ole still figured prominently in the transfer rumours. Southampton, then managed by Gordon Strachan, denied that they had put a bid in for him. Celtic were also linked with a move for him. Ole was now 30 and still had three years on his contract to run; he was adamant that he would see it out. The most interesting of the deals he was linked with, though, was one for Ronaldinho, a player of uncanny instinct and ability, at that time playing in France for Paris Saint-Germain. It was suggested that Ole was part of the package.

The major transfer activity centred around Chelsea, who were taken over by Roman Abramovich on 2 July 2003. It instantly transformed them into the richest club in the world, capable of outbidding anybody in the transfer market. In a few days, Abramovich spent £150 million buying Chelsea, and over £110 million on players.

United travelled to America for a pre-season tour, the first match being against Celtic in Seattle's Seahawks Stadium. A huge crowd of 66,702 saw Ole make the first two goals for van Nistelrooy. Ryan Giggs scored the third, and Ole did enough in that game to prove that there was life after Beckham; the touches he demonstrated with his assists were as sharp and as accurate as anything the former dead-ball specialist could deliver. Henrik Larsson was playing for Celtic, the first time that he had crossed Ole's path in a club match.

Ole went to Hollywood on the next leg of the tour. This time they met a Mexican team curiously named Club America. The match was played in Los Angeles, which United won 3-1 with Ole setting up one of Forlán's two goals.

The last match of the tour was a 4-1 victory over Juventus in New Jersey. Verón set up two goals, one of them ably assisted by Ole. Not to be outdone, Ole scored the fourth with a tremendous strike. The match proved to be Verón's swansong as he joined Chelsea on the same day Joe Cole signed for them. Peter Kenyon, United's Chief Executive, arranged the deal. The fee of £15 million received for Verón was approximately half of what United had paid for him.

At first, Chelsea appeared to have obtained a bargain

with Verón when he scored on his début at Liverpool. It proved to be his only goal and he played only 14 games for the Blues before going back to Italy.

It had been a busy summer for Ole because he had also played earlier for his country in Euro 2004 qualifying matches against Denmark and Romania. Denmark's Chelsea winger Jesper Gronkjaer scored the goal that beat Norway in the Group Two game. Ole scored a penalty 15 minutes from time to give Norway a point at home to Romania.

The traditional season curtain-raiser took place at the Millennium Stadium when United locked horns again with Arsenal. The game finished 1-1 with United finally triumphing 4-3 on penalties. The bad feeling from their last Premiership clash spilled over into the match and Ashley Cole allegedly kicked out at Ole. Some consolation for him was that it was his first Charity Shield winner's medal.

Bolton visited Old Trafford in the first Premiership game of 2003/04 and were caned 4-0, the scorers being Giggs (twice), Scholes and van Nistelrooy. Cristiano Ronaldo made his début and showed flashes of his awesome potential with some high-speed dribbling. Only on the field for 68 minutes, Ole was replaced by Eric Djemba-Djemba, the new signing from Nantes for £3.5 million. Ole had a quiet game, operating in the right-midfield berth formerly occupied by Beckham.

The departure of Beckham and Verón meant that the squad was shorn of two world-class midfield players. The defence was also depleted with the loss of stalwart Laurent Blanc and the experienced David May. Ole related his misgivings about the squad and views on the game to NTB, saying, 'I'm not sure that the squad is better than last season. But at least it is bigger.'

Ole went on to talk about the performance against Bolton. 'We are really satisfied. This was a really good start for us. The first games are always even and close, so the most important thing is to take three points. This is the biggest win in a league start since I joined the club. I was not that involved but we are all pleased with the win now. I'm not injured, or anything like that. I could have played longer, but we have a big and good squad this season, so there's no need to play the whole game.'

The reference to not being injured seemed pertinent at the time, as well as the oblique reference to not playing for the full 90 minutes. Ole also played in the next game, a 2-1 victory over Bobby Robson's Newcastle.

On Wednesday, 27 August 2003, United had a home evening fixture against newly-promoted Wolverhampton Wanderers. Wolves were about to make the reverse journey, being relegated on 33 points. In their first two matches in the Premier League, they had been slaughtered 5-1 at Blackburn and 0-4 at home to Charlton. The gulf in class, quality and squad size was becoming ever greater.

In an exclusive interview with John Shaw of the *Red News* fanzine, Ole was asked if he would make any changes to his career, if he were to do it all again. Ole replied philosophically, 'If you know what you know today 15 years ago, how much easier would it be? I would have changed the last ten minutes of the Wolverhampton game, because that was the game where I got injured. I was tired. That's what I would change. That's the only thing that I would have changed.'

The game, as so often in these top-versus-bottom clashes, was anti-climactic. United were clinging to a narrow lead through a tenth-minute headed goal from John O'Shea, but

Wolves had missed some golden chances. In the closing stages, Paul Scholes sent Ole over a pass wide right. Ole took it, stamped down hard and twisted... that moment caused him years of anguish. Ole told the *Manchester Evening News*, 'The force of that step caused the damage.' The impact damaged the articular cartilage in his knee.

Six minutes from time, Ole limped off to be replaced by the Frenchman David Bellion, another summer acquisition. A substitute appearance in the 2-0 stroll over Charlton at the Valley in the second week of September was Ole's penultimate run-out for the Reds in 2003 before entering the twilight zone.

Ole's last Champions League match for three years was against Panathinaikos on 16 September, just a few weeks after he had sustained the first knock to his knee. The Greek side were crushed 5-0, four of them netted before half-time. Ole had notched the third, probably the messiest goal he ever scored for United. The unfortunate Panathinaikos goalkeeper Antonis Nikopodlidis had a nightmare game, gifting United the opening goals and freezing at vital moments. For a long time, it looked as if that messy goal would exist as the epitaph to Ole's Old Trafford glory days. Many pessimists were delivering the last rites to his career even then.

Giggs had the freedom of the midfield and found Ole in the box with a diagonal pass. The shot that the number 20 put in was not particularly powerful or accurate, but it was enough to beat Nikopodlidis and find its way into the far corner. That was virtually his last meaningful action for United as he received another knock to his knee. Grimacing with pain, he took a deep breath and scrambled to his feet.

Ole did not appear for the second half; In fact, he did not

appear again in a red shirt for five months. It could actually be said that the footballer that was Ole Gunnar Solskjaer did not reappear for three years. The player once called by his manager 'the sub from hell' was to go through his own private hell for a long, long time.

Exactly a week later, Manchester United issued a statement that Ole had undergone micro-fracture surgery on his knee that day. Their medical staff had waited for the knee to settle down before putting him under the knife. The bulletin went on to say, 'It is something we have tried to correct over the last few weeks but it is important that Ole now has this operation so he can concentrate on the rest of the season. Ole will be assessed after the operation to determine how long he will be out for.'

In November, a recuperating Ole told the *Manchester Evening News*, 'It is five weeks since the operation. So it is has been about patience, working in the gym and working hard. It had to happen because I was playing on with it and it wasn't doing me any good. I have been lucky with injuries in the past, so it is a learning experience. I will just start with walking I suppose. And then it will be a case of taking it one day at a time.

Significant changes were also afoot at Old Trafford. Malcolm Glazer, an American businessman who owned the Tampa Bay gridiron team, upped his stake in the club in the same month Ole scored against the Greeks. Peter Kenyon defected to Chelsea, going on 'gardening leave' as the clubs thrashed out a compensation deal.

Sir Alex had his fair share of problems in the Premiership with the loss of Ole, Arsenal's dazzling form and Chelsea's limitless spending. Off the field, he also became embroiled in a bitter dispute with United's largest individual shareholder, John Magnier, over the 2000 Guineas winner Rock of Gibraltar.

Back on the pitch, United struggled to score goals without Ole. Diego Forlán showed flashes of brilliance and Sir Alex stated that he would develop as well as Ole, but at Old Trafford he couldn't find any consistency. Sir Alex had pioneered the four strikers policy in 1998 when he added Yorke to the mix of Cole, Sheringham and Ole, but now he found that his options were severely limited. The Reds went down to a Lampard penalty at Stamford Bridge on the last day of November. In that match, United looked decidedly short of strike power.

Meanwhile, in the early phase of his recovery, Ole was spending hours on end in the swimming pool and then cycling. He told the *Red News* fanzine, 'It's quite hard and not hard at the same time. When I was in the pool, I could see lads coming in to training and I'd been in there for 20 minutes already in the pool swimming, and they come walking in, ready for training in 40 minutes or whatever and then, when you do your weights, you can see them leaving and they have finished for the day's work. It's all part of the rehab. It's all part of the mental build-up as well. I did not ask to go home at 12.00pm or whatever. I just knew I had to do it. You need a foundation first, so then you focus more and more towards the football.'

Ole was already aware that it was going to be a long job and was digging in mentally for the task that lay ahead. The only way he would make it back to the big time was with the same raw self-discipline that had taken him there in the first place.

Just before Christmas 2003, it was announced by Sir Alex that he had pencilled in a reserve game at Birmingham on

15 January as Ole's comeback. This was halfway through the transfer window period and already a reasonable chunk of the rainforest had been converted into newspaper speculation about which players would be going to Old Trafford. The names were a veritable *Who's Who* of the game's top attacking players, from Henrik Larsson (who had impressed in the pre-season game against Celtic in Seattle) to the young PSV flanker Arjen Robben.

Sir Alex was excited by the imminent return of Ole; not only would he boost their goalscoring but he would strengthen their right flank. The news then broke of Rio Ferdinand' s ban from the game for eight months. It was one of the strangest events of recent years. The United and England defender had left the Carrington training complex before giving a sample to drug inspectors carrying out a spot-check on 23 September. The England defender said he could not be contacted later as he was out on a shopping spree and had switched off his mobile.

Ole was the model professional; you somehow knew that he would be very unlikely to find himself in a similar situation. When Ferdinand joined the club, Schmeichel had commented with apprehension about the new breed of player that was entering the game. Keane had already made comments in his book about players who were more interested in Rolexes, cars and fashion than winning things for their club. None of these comments were aimed directly at the young Ferdinand, who, it must be said, overcame this incident to become one of United's key players in their renaissance season of 2006/07. For the first time since he joined the club, Ferdinand played alongside the same players for a long period which helped him greatly.

In the last game before Christmas, United won 2-1 at

Tottenham to go back to the head of the Premiership, one point ahead of Arsenal and Chelsea. As 2004 unfolded, Ole was back working with the first team, training without any great exertion but back with the chaps. Sir Alex's compliments were ringing in his ears at the time. One of Ole's greatest fans and a staunch supporter of his value to the team, Sir Alex was telling the press something they already knew, what a great professional Ole was. This was another marvellous piece of astute management by the Scot, as he sought to improve the confidence and self-esteem of his striker. Not for a moment had Ole let the situation get to him, though.

Sir Alex then told the *Manchester Evening News* about Ole's potential as a future manager. 'I think people might be surprised, but I think Ole would make a good manager.'

Jim Solbakken, Ole's personal adviser and agent, expanded on this and told Nettavisen, 'Solskjaer wants to try himself as a manager when his career is over. He was about to start a coaching course when he picked up his injury. Some people may say he needs to go back to Norway to start a managerial career, but I do not think he has to do that. I hope he can have a coaching role with the national team when he retires. Ole agrees with the Norwegian FA's ideas and would love to work with them. But the real target is to get him fit again. He doesn't have any spare time at the moment; he works 100 per cent to get back after the injury. It's important, as it will make the difference between playing or starting on the bench. This is the most important period in his career.'

Ole had to regain his fitness – as Solbakken said, it was the most important period in his life. The first of the numerous setbacks that dogged his recovery happened around that time. The comeback game was put on hold as Sir Alex sent him away on holiday.

It was concern over Ole's long-term fitness that gave rise to the acquisition of Luis Saha from Fulham for £12.5 million, a player who has yet to win over many United fans.

Ole had been read the riot act about overdoing things and was given very strict orders to rest. The punishing schedule that he had set himself was taking a huge toll on him. By a strange quirk of fate, the Birmingham game was postponed because of serious injuries sustained by youth player Phil Marsh in a car crash.

When Ole returned to Carrington to continue his rehabilitation, the team flew out for a five-day break for some sea and sand in Dubai. The hero of the Nou Camp reassured his fans through the club's official website that he was OK and, as if to prove it, Ole made his first tentative steps back to the first team in a match against Aston Villa Reserves. The game was held at Altrincham's Moss Lane in a Barclaycard Premiership Reserve League (North) fixture. More than 1,200 fans turned up on a rainy Thursday night in the first week of February 2004. They saw a real treat, better than some of the dull, negative affairs played out in Europe or the Premiership. The previous week, Sir Alex had pulled an enthusiastic Ole out of a match against Rossendale United because he feared that the freezing ground would be too hard a surface for his convalescing knee.

Aston Villa Reserves were doing something that their first-team cousins were incapable of doing in the Premiership – running away with the league. They had been unbeaten all season and were defending a huge 13-point lead. The United side was not too short on pedigree itself, though – eight of them had had Champions League experience, and one of them had actually scored the winner in a Champions League Final; another, Kleberson, was a World Cup winner.

In the first 90 seconds, Ole ran through the Villa defence to bring a great save out of Villa keeper Stefan Postma. After a quarter-of-an-hour, though, Ole set up the first goal when he broke out of his own half to find new boy Bellion. The ex-Sunderland winger scurried into the box and crossed for Richardson to score easily. The knee was then tested when Ole swivelled on three occasions to fire in random shots which cleared the bar. The travelling Ole fan club were delighted when he executed a fancy back-flick to create a chance for Mads Timms, whose promising career was soon curtailed when he was later jailed for 12 months for dangerous driving. For Ole, though, it was so far, so good and, considering he had not played for five months, Ole looked sharp and focused.

The initial plan was for Ole to play just the first 45 minutes; he felt so good, though, he completed the hour before being pulled off by the Reserves boss Ricky Sbragia. United went on to win the match 3-0. Everyone was pleased with his first match back, nobody more so than Ole, who told the *Manchester Evening News*, 'My injury felt good and that is what is most important to me. It's still quite a big step until I feel I am fully match-fit. I need a lot of hard work and match training. There is another 10 to 15 per cent left before I can play for the first team, but feel really good about the injury. I am on the right track but do not know when I will be ready. One of my positives is that I have always been there when the manager needs me. Soon I will be available again.'

# DOWN AND OUT

The impressive performance by Ole temporarily put an end to some of the rumours that had been sweeping the city of Manchester. The principal one was that he would need another op as the first one had not worked. Others in circulation around the bars claimed that Ole's career was over as he would never recover from the injury, and that his knee had been too badly damaged.

The Premiership comeback game was against Leeds United in a Saturday lunchtime encounter that the Reds simply had to win to stay in contention for the title. Ole had played a further 60 minutes in a reserve game against Liverpool as he strived to obtain fitness.

In a drab, lucklustre performance, United struggled against Leeds who had lost six out of their last seven games and were about to crash out of the Premiership. Scholes eventually put United ahead in the second half, but Leeds fought back and their England striker Alan Smith headed a deserved equaliser. Smith was later to join United and, like Ole, was to sustain a career-threatening injury that he successfully overcame.

Ole came on for Phil Neville after 70 minutes but found the going tough as Leeds closed up shop. Considering the length of time he had been out and United's stuttering form, Ole deserved more than the 5 out of 10 rating in the *Manchester Evening News* and the clipped comment, 'Adrenalin alone wasn't enough.'

Perhaps this was the first clear indication that his return would not be plain sailing and the nagging doubt also remained that the knee was not right.

Wolves Reserves were next on the agenda for Ole while his team-mates flew out to Portugal for the first leg of the first knockout stage of the Champions League against

215

Porto, managed by the brightest young coach in the game, José Mourinho.

The Portuguese coach was eventually to become Sir Alex's nemesis, but on this occasion there was cordial politeness between the two men. Two goals from Benni McCarthy in response to Quinton Fortune's opener left United with an uphill task. Roy Keane was sent off for deliberately treading on the Porto keeper and was automatically suspended for the second leg. His loss would weaken United's midfield bite considerably.

Mourinho, a master at playing the media, stoked up the war of words by telling the press about his post-match spat with Sir Alex. 'You would be really sad if your team gets as clearly dominated as that by an opponent who has been built on maybe 10 per cent of the budget.'

Ole was called into the squad for the FA Cup quarter-final tie against Fulham at Old Trafford, which was another lunchtime kick-off. United had cruised into the Sixth Round with effortless victories over Villa, Northampton and Manchester City. A Steed Malbranque penalty gave Fulham an early lead, but goals in each half from van Nistelrooy put United into the semis. Two minutes from the end, Ole replaced Ronaldo. There was no time to make any impact but, once again, he received a wonderful reception from the crowd. The lift it gave to the player, team and the supporters was very moving, and it reaffirmed the special place that Ole had in the hearts of the United faithful. He may have been away for a while, but he was far from forgotten.

In an interview he gave to the *Manchester Evening News*, he explained, 'For me, it is great to be back playing and every minute I have to the end of the campaign will be a bonus. I just want to contribute something to the season.

The last five months have been about me because I have been focusing on myself and my fitness. Now it is about getting into the team and helping them. It is about us and not me. The easy bit has gone now. The easy bit was to get to where I am now... the hard bit is to get back in the team and back up to 100 per cent match fitness and performing how I was. But I am confident I will do.

'It has been more difficult for me in recent weeks because the closer you get, the more you want to be there and the fact the team haven't done so well increases that feeling.'

Roy Keane was a great inspiration to Ole; he intuitively sensed his difference from other players. It would be hard to find two more disparate natures, but there existed a bond and mutual respect between them. Keane had his ups and downs, but always maintained a dignity and harsh ethical code by which he lived; this was crucial to his philosophy. Ole, when faced with a difficult day during that turbulent period, would remind himself of one of his skipper's maxims: 'Rome was not built in a day'.

One Roman was trying to build in a day, though. Abramovich's spending carried on unabated and Chelsea progressed further in Europe as the Russian-funded Londoners began to get the best out of their starry squad.

Three nights later, Porto knocked United out of Europe by scoring a last-minute goal; to Sir Alex, it had all the hallmarks of a United last-gasp winner, and the irony was not lost on him. It made the score 1-1 on the night, but Porto went through 3-2 on aggregate. Mourinho could not stop himself from dancing on the touchline in celebration, and it was to prove a significant early rung on a very long ladder of success for him.

Two European knockouts for United helped revolutionise

the English game. Not only did they change the course of Manchester United's history, but also that of Chelsea Football Club. We have already seen how the valiant, thrilling exit to the *galacticos* of Real Madrid, witnessed by Abramovich, triggered his purchase of Chelsea. Having fired his imagination, the acquisition of an English football club became an obsession for Abramovich, and it wasn't long before his deluxe helicopter was touching down within spitting distance of Stamford Bridge.

The exit of United to Porto triggered the next chain of events. Porto, master-minded by Mourinho, went on to lift the Champions League in Gelsenkirchen. It remains one of the biggest shocks in the competition's history. Within days, Mourinho had quit to join Chelsea. With a combination of Mourinho's self-proclaimed talents, Abramovich's money and Kenyon's input, the Premiership was annexed for consecutive seasons. The worry for all those who loved the national game, was whether football could cope with the changes at Stamford Bridge, and still offer fans what they wanted – a fair and level playing field. The monster had already been created with TV money and ever-rising players' salaries... with Chelsea's acquisition, was the monster now permanently out of control? To the Stretford End, Mourinho had instantly become public enemy number one.

As the 'public enemy' patrolled the touchline agitatedly during the game against Porto, United appeared to be going through on the away goals rule. Paul Scholes had scored after 31 minutes with a header to level the aggregate scores. Ricardo Carvalho was Porto's best defender, nullifying the threat of van Nistelrooy and brilliantly marshalling his defence. Just on half-time, Scholes had a perfectly good goal ruled out for offside by the assistant referee. The decision was one of the most blatant errors ever made in a Manchester United game by an official. It most certainly cost them the tie as Porto would have found it hard to have come back from two goals down.

Sir Alex was amazed that Scholes's effort was ruled out and told the *Manchester Evening News*, 'To be honest, I couldn't believe it. You can understand it maybe if there's one defender and the linesman doesn't see it, but when there are three playing him on-side you cannot understand it. That would have put us into a very, very comfortable position.' Ole reiterated the gaffer's view, saying, 'We went out to Porto when Scholesy is two yards on-side when he scores.'

While there remained only one goal in it, Porto still had every chance of getting that golden away goal. Seven minutes from time, Ole was sent on for Ronaldo. The young winger had only been on the field himself for some eight minutes as a sub for Fletcher. The ruthless Porto defence was quick to spot the danger and hacked down Portugal's finest prospect. Ole did not receive any support as United withdrew deep to run down the clock. The game was almost over when Phil Neville rashly fouled Edgar Jankauskas on the edge of the box. The Reds defence, without the presence of Ferdinand, was momentarily paralysed and vulnerable. Benni McCarthy, who only a few weeks before had been banished to the bench by Mourinho, lashed in the free-kick. United Keeper Tim Howard, who had replaced the erratic Barthez, could not hold the shot and Costinha smashed home. That was it. The well-oiled Porto roadshow, displaying brutal efficiency, went on to lift the Champions League trophy by thrashing Monaco who had knocked out Chelsea in the semis.

Already, Mourinho was building up a sizeable portfolio of critics who despaired of his 'negative' tactics. One Spanish journalist scoffed, 'They say Gelsenkirchen is cold and flat. It's the perfect place for FC Porto to take on Europe with their brand of anti-football.'

Ole was philosophical about the defeat to Porto, telling *VG*, 'We have got a taste of our own medicine. We have won so many games in the dying seconds in the past. Now we have got to experience how it is to lose in the same way. For them, it must have been the best way to win. For us, this was really bitter. I am very disappointed. Sometimes football is brutal. This was one of those times. It was very quiet in the dressing room after the game. None of us had got much to say. I couldn't find the right words to use.'

The press found the right words as they attacked Sir Alex's faltering empire. The departure of Beckham was highlighted as one of the reasons for their decline. Much was made of the fact that the injury to Ole had robbed them of the ideal replacement.

Things went from bad to worse as a powerful Manchester City side beat them 4-1 on the following Saturday. Ole came on for Ronaldo 18 minutes from time but had no chance of putting things right.

Things improved with a 3-0 home win over Tottenham in which Ole started a game for the first time since his lay-off. The speed of thought of the Norwegian marksman was slowly coming back. Then followed two monster matches against Arsenal, the first in the Premiership, and then in the semi-finals of the Cup.

The Premiership game at Highbury ended 1-1 and Ole played his part by coming on as a sub after 72 minutes and setting up the equaliser for Saha. Thierry Henry had put

## DOWN AND OUT

Arsenal ahead early in the second half with one of his specials. Ole's low cross eluded the Arsenal back line in the closing minutes and the unmarked Saha tucked home from close range.

The best game that Ole played in that injury-ravaged season was in the semi-final clash against Arsenal on 3 April 2004. It was a return to Villa Park, the venue for the epic 1999 tie decided by Giggs's wonder goal, which had proved to be the springboard for the Treble.

The game never matched the drama of that night but then games as special as that come round once in a blue moon. With van Nistelrooy ruled out with knee trouble, Ole operated as the lone striker and did a fantastic job. Considering his level of fitness, it was even more remarkable. Unable to train fully because of the pain, he still put in a stellar performance against one of the greatest teams to grace the Premiership. Once again, he had a tough battle with the Gunners defence, but Ole's thoughtful passing, brisk movement and clever positional play pinned the Arsenal back four down and did not allow them time to build from the back. The array of his passing was a great asset to United, playing it short or long depending on who was available.

For the first time since his injury, the United fans saw flashes of the old Ole as his confidence slowly flowed back. Paul Scholes scored the only goal of the game on half-an-hour with a right-footed drive from Giggs pass. This was enough to put them into the Cup Final against Millwall, the surprise finalists that year. The United fans gave their team wonderful support that afternoon, and made sure that the Arsenal fans were reminded that their chance of emulating the Treble had gone.

Ole was rejuvenated by the win and told the *Manchester Evening News*, 'You can not pick your confidence out of a refrigerator, so those two games against Arsenal will mean a lot to us. The confidence can kick in now. What does the Villa Park win mean? That means the season for us. We know we are too far behind now in the league, but we now have a trophy to play for at the Millennium Stadium.

'Since we drew Arsenal, I think we were looking forward to the games against them and prove that we are a good team. It was not about them and the Treble. It was about pride for us. We have our pride to bounce back and that's what we did. The atmosphere was just brilliant, our fans were fantastic. You could notice the difference between the two ends and that helped us. The supporters never let us down and the Final is great for them as well.'

Molde had approached Ole's adviser Jim Solbakken about the possibility of him returning to Norway for a loan spell in a bid to aid his fitness. The Norwegian club's director Espen Silseth thought that they could have given him good match training in the spring and summer. United, though, wanted him to stay in Manchester and get 100 per cent fit for the 2004/05 season.

United's Premiership challenge fizzled out as the unstoppable Arsenal team went through the whole season unbeaten, becoming the first team in 115 years to achieve such a feat. United had lost nine games in the campaign, finishing a poor third, 15 points behind the Gunners. In the last eight games following their semi-final victory, the deposed Champions won four, lost three and drew 1-1 with Chelsea. Ole came on for Ronaldo in the last three minutes of the match against Claudio Ranieri's side. The affable Italian was already calling himself 'the dead man walking', and had prepared himself for the sack. This was after leading Chelsea to second spot for the first time in their history, and also to a Champions League semi-final.

As the season drew to an end, many feared for the future of the game, and whether anyone would be able to live with the new-look Chelsea side that was hastily being supercharged – money no object – in time for next season. Ranieri's last act as manager was to sign goalkeeper Petr Cech and, much to the chagrin of Sir Alex, the brilliant Dutch winger Robben. More purchases were to come in the close season.

The beauty and purity of the game had, though, still been evident in the way that Arsenal had raised the bar stylishly by playing a brand of football that, at times, was breathtaking. They played with volcanic energy and great teamwork, yet they gave nothing away. Could United compete at the new level?

If so, the Reds would need the cold-blooded specialist Ole even more than ever. Something was still not right with him, though. In ten appearances since his return, he had failed to find the net. Nobody expected him to set the world on fire but it was patently obvious, even to his most devoted fans, that he was a long, long way from recapturing his killer touch. There were further murmurings in Manchester that the knee was damaged severely and restricted his manoeuvrability.

One of the matches United lost in April was at home to Liverpool. Near the end of the game, Ole failed to steer home a cross from Ronaldo that would have avoided defeat against their old rivals. At the end of season 2003/04, United had no ammunition left. After the match, Ole told the *Manchester Evening News*, 'I am very disappointed I didn't get a connection on that cross from Cristiano. That shows I need some match practice. I lack a bit of sharpness. But this season was always going to be about rehabilitation and recovering from that operation. Hopefully, next year I will be better. It is important to play every time you put the Manchester United shirt on. It is not about getting into the FA Cup Final team. You play for your pride, the badge and Manchester United.'

Ole came on in the closing minutes of the Cup Final as United, 3-0 up, cruised to victory over Millwall. It was one of the most one-sided Finals in living memory, with Millwall unable to live with the quality of United's play. Ronaldo, who grew in stature as the season wore on, opened the scoring and van Nistelrooy scored twice in the second half.

For many fans, Ole's brief cameo seemed to be the end of his United career. It was a magnanimous gesture by Sir Alex in rewarding his loyalty and bravery with his second FA Cup medal. The United boss knew what the FA Cup Final meant to his striker. When he was growing up in Norway, Ole would always watch the live Cup Final, the traditional showpiece as the last game of the season.

His appearance in the lap of honour as the massed ranks of United fans displayed their passion for the team was seen as being a farewell. Question marks continued to be raised about his future. SPL Champions Celtic had expressed interest in signing him but, ironically, it was to replace their legend Henrik Larsson who was Barcelona bound. The Celtic boss Martin O'Neill was keen to bring Ole to Celtic Park and had admitted to being a Solskjaer fan. Both Jim Solbakken and Sir Alex told the press, though, that Ole would be staying at Old Trafford and working hard all summer to regain his fitness.

# DOWN AND OUT

Ole himself told *Dagbladet*, 'I'm wanted by the boss so I will not change club. He has not quit in believing in me. Rumours about players leaving the club can affect the fans. Now I am in great shape, at my best if only I get to play games. The time when you could take six weeks' rest just to get a tan in the sun is over. We have got an important Champions League game at the start of August. We must use our days off well.'

Ole never made the team for the Champions League qualifier against Dinamo Bucharest. The 31-year-old suffered a recurrence of the knee problems in pre-season training and experienced severe twinges of pain. He told the *Manchester Evening News*, 'On the first day back in pre-season training in July, I was OK during the session but when I cooled down afterwards I was in bits. The knee was so sore.'

United flew to America to train at the NovaCare Complex, home of the Philadelphia Eagles, before their three-match tour. However, Ole headed to Sweden. A United spokesman said, 'In Gothenburg, he underwent an arthroscopy that unfortunately confirmed persistent damage to the articular cartilage of his right knee. He will undergo further treatment but it is likely that Ole will miss the whole of the season.'

Sir Alex was extremely distressed at the news and the gravity of the situation. In an interview with the *Manchester Evening News*, he said, 'When Ole went to get treatment at the end of the season, he saw a Swedish specialist, who is reputedly the best in the world. There was a proviso from the specialist there would possibly be a second step. That's the second step we are taking now. It's not a shock, only a disappointment. There were no guarantees [after the operation]. It was a trial and hopefully there would be success. But we feel now that it has not been 100 per cent successful and that he should take the second phase and go back and see him again. It is just unfortunate that a player of that calibre and such a great professional is missing out on the best years of his life. It is only in the last two or three years he has become a consistent performer for us. He was always the player we brought off the bench because he was so good at it. He was probably the best substitute of all time. He could analyse football by watching it, understood exactly his role when he came on, understood the tactics of the game. He is a rare bird.'

Glowing praise from perhaps the greatest manager of all time but, at that point, it remained to be seen whether Sir Alex would ever have the luxury of seeing that rare bird fly again.

# 11

# The Long and Winding Road

**'I cannot just lay down and cry. I am only 31 years old.'**
**OLE GUNNAR SOLSKJAER, SEPTEMBER 2004**

Ole did not kick a ball in season 2004/05; premature retirement was never so mockingly near. United purchased Wayne Rooney from Everton while Forlán went to Spain where he resurrected his career.

By some strange quirk of fate, United travelled to Stamford Bridge for the first Premiership game of the season. José Mourinho was newly installed, and he set out his stall from day one as far as his tactics went – a ruthlessly efficient back four in front of the best goalkeeper in the world were shielded by a gritty, grafting midfield. The long-lost art of goalscoring could take care of itself. It pretty much did, as his team became the masters of the one-nil win. Seen by many as 'anti-football', no one could deny its efficiency – they dominated the season with an imperious and terrifying arrogance, stamped very much in their new manager's image.

The Reds had a fair chunk of the game but lacked penetration and guile in the penalty box. Chelsea won by the only goal, which was hooked in after 14 minutes by Sir Alex's long-term target Eidur Gudjohnsen.

Ole had his second operation in August 2004; it was performed by the Swedish surgeon Lars Peterson, who was acknowledged in the medical profession as one of the foremost experts on that type of injury. The United physio Rob Swire watched the operation, as had been the case for the first one. To repair Ole's damaged cartilage, a sample of cells was taken from his knee and used to grow fresh cartilage. This took about three weeks in a special laboratory. They were subsequently inserted back into the injured tissue. Ole then spent the next three months in bed. A slow recovery period followed during which Ole manoeuvred himself on crutches. For months, he was unable to drive his car and, in the meantime, he started using a mountain bike.

Ole had to wear a CPM (continuous passive motion) machine which was a kind of brace with rollers attached. This contraption would rock the knee back and forward. This was worn for 12 hours a day for 3 months. It was even worn in bed. From time to time, his youthful good looks were contorted with pain as he struggled to get about. The simplest of movements – walking, turning – became a real effort, and improvement was painfully slow.

In November 2004, he told the *Manchester Evening News*, 'You always need dreams, and my dream is to lift a trophy again with Manchester United. I am starting from scratch and I know I have to do everything right because the goal at the end is such a massive one. But at the end of this season, I will be looking forward to the new campaign. It feels like this is the start of the rest of my career – and that is going to be at United. I never got back to full fitness after the operation last year. For now, my training is Sunday walks with my wife.'

Chelsea hit the top of the Premiership in November 2004 and stayed there until the end of the season. Nobody really got close to them, as they ground out result after result. The only Premiership game they lost all season was in Manchester, to City, with an Anelka penalty enough to settle the game.

United were always a poor third, the high spot of their domestic season being a 2-0 victory over Arsenal in late October. This brought an end to the north London side's run of 49 unbeaten games. Rooney celebrated his 19th birthday by sealing the victory with the second goal in the last minute of stoppage time.

In the autumn of that year, the chants of Ole's name and the famous 'You Are My Solskjaer... ' refrain started to reverberate around the Theatre of Dreams. No matter what happened on the field or how much time had elapsed, the fans never forgot Ole. Not only for his priceless goals, but also for the composed dignity and unflagging loyalty that he displayed throughout his career. Above all, they recognised his readiness to sacrifice his own career and health for the sake of Manchester United. On the Stretford Road End, the legendary tribute '2O LEgend' first appeared in public. They sang for Ole in the same way they had done for Eric Cantona. Beckham was respected and missed, but never commanded the level of adoration that Ole did from the *aficionados*. He told one publication, 'On the Stretford Road End, they have hung up some banners with my name and my squad number. At every game, they sing my song. That gives me enormous motivation.'

José Mourinho was triumphant at Old Trafford for the second time in nine months when Chelsea won 2-1 in the Carling Cup in January 2005. Damien Duff, another player that United had been linked with, scored the winner after a mistake by Tim Howard. Ole could only look on in horror.

By the early spring of 2005, Ole was back at Carrington doing the lightest of jogging. It was a tiny step forward, but a huge leap for the Norwegian, who was taking his rehabilitation extremely seriously, and very carefully. The Swedish medical team had informed him that the earliest he could even contemplate playing would be August 2005. Pleased with his progress, Ole told the *Manchester Evening News*, 'I have no pain with the light jogging but I still have to force some discomfort through the knee to stimulate it. I could have gone 12 months without feeling anything but then when I started playing again it would have been sore. So you have to force a little bit of pain because that is the nature of this injury. The transplant is maturing and now, for the next two or three months, it needs stimulation forced through it gradually. The light jogging has been the next step, but I am not jumping or sprinting yet. The next step will be to run 100 metres. But when that happens, you do not know. There is no specific timescale. You are governed by how it reacts each day. It is a slow process and you have to be very patient.'

Ole's burning dream was to lift another trophy with United. That was his obsession and would drive him on, despite the hard days and setbacks. Ole revealed that if he had not been injured for nearly two years, then season 2005/06 would have probably been his last in English football, as he had plans to retire to Norway.

Ex-United players were already advising Ole to quit.

Stuart Pearson was a 1970s hero back in the Tommy Docherty era, and whose career was truncated by a knee injury sustained while on international duty with England in the USA. He told the *Manchester Evening News*, 'The situation with Ole sounds very similar to mine. I had surgery and it was never right, even when I started playing again. I went from being an England player, missing a year out of the game, to having a knee which was never the same again. What Ole has to consider is, while this may not be the end of his playing days, it could be the end of his top-level football. I had lost a little bit of pace and my knee was never as strong. You were always subject to that tackle from behind when it gives way, and you are out for a few more games. You just get frustrated with yourself.

'I finished when I was 32. Hopefully, Ole will have earned enough and looked after it and there will also be some sort of insurance package to help him on his way.'

Without Ole, United struggled to score goals; in the first 12 Premiership games in 2004/05 they found the net just 11 times, compared with an average of 25 goals for the previous seven seasons during the same period.

One plus that came out of the injury was the fact that Ole got to spend more time with his young family. When the weather was good, he would sit with his wife and kids in the family stand next to the tunnel. Noah was learning fast and, according to his father, the little guy was already highly knowledgeable about the game.

Ole loved meeting the fans and, on Valentine's Day 2005, it was announced that he had become a patron of the fans' group – Shareholders United. Some of the hardcore fans had become increasingly disillusioned with the spiralling cost of tickets, lack of atmosphere and bizarre kick-off times. Ole told the *Manchester Evening News*, 'I am honoured. I think it is important that the club remains in the right hands... I am absolutely on the supporter's side. I am a United fan myself and only want what is best for the future.'

United's push into Europe ended in the first knockout round with two 0-1 defeats to AC Milan. The first setback was at a frosty Old Trafford. The goal was fortunate, coming 12 minutes from time. Hernan Crespo scored the winner after Roy Carroll had spilled a Clarence Seedorf drive. Crespo was still on Chelsea's books but had been shunted out to Italy on loan by Mourinho. Sir Alex's counterpart did not see a place for him in his new-look, all-conquering side. Andriy Shevchenko, at that time the deadliest marksman in Europe, had missed the game for Milan with a fractured cheekbone.

Jaap Stam, Ole's ex-room-mate from the Treble season, was now playing for Milan but was injured in the warm-up. The pair were still in touch with each other and Ole enjoyed catching up with the Dutchman. Nights like that must have been particularly hard for Ole. Always cheerful on the surface, deep down he hurt, and how he would have loved to have taken on the masterly Milan defenders Nesta, Maldini and Cafu, who completely shackled Rooney, Ronaldo and van Nistelrooy.

Nearly 10,000 United fans travelled to the San Siro for the second leg to see a reprise of the first match, Crespo scoring the only goal after 30 minutes, Milan slowly choking the Reds to death as they packed their midfield. Ole was very disappointed at the exit and had told *Red News*, 'We had AC Milan and I felt we could win. It was two close games and I thought then they would go on and win it. Obviously, we all crossed our fingers and hoped they would win it, but they did not. We have been very, very close. In the year we won it, we played well but we were 2-0 down to Juventus, and we came back. Against Inter, we had Henning save off the line. There are defining moments which go one way or the other. It is not about the team's got worse or the other teams have got so much better – any out of eight teams can win the Champions League.'

It was a season of general disappointment; they returned to Cardiff for the FA Cup Final against Arsenal, in which United were clearly the better side but crashed out on penalties, the first team in the history of the competition to lose a Cup Final in that manner.

Ole sat in the Millennium Stadium wearing the grey Cup suit. Once again, he could only watch sadly as United keeper Carroll failed to get near any of Arsenal's spot-kicks. As Vieira buried the winning penalty, he could not help wondering if he would ever play again in a high-profile game for United. What he saw left an indelible imprint on his mind and drove him even harder to regain fitness. Events like that committed him to the rehabilitation programme even more.

A few days earlier, United had suffered another night of disappointment. The new Champions, multi-million-pound Chelsea, had won 3-1 at Old Trafford. The duopoly of United and Arsenal had been torn apart by Abramovich's mountain of cash. Chelsea's new Chief Executive, Peter Kenyon, felt it necessary, though, to assert 'we have not bought the title'.

Roy Keane and his troops, their confidence punctured, formed a tight-lipped guard of honour to clap the newly-crowned Champions on to the pitch. The Irishman's face was a picture as he tried to mask his thinly-veiled contempt at the situation.

Van Nistelrooy put United ahead after eight minutes from Rooney's pass. It was the first goal that the Dutchman, plagued by an Achilles injury for most of the season, had scored in open play at Old Trafford. Chelsea bounced back, though, through Eidur Gudjohnsen and the massively influential Joe Cole. Once again, Sir Alex's early transfer targets had demonstrated to him what good buys they would have been for United.

The stats weren't looking terribly healthy for United – it was the first time in four years and 103 Premiership games that United had taken the lead and were subsequently beaten. They had lost their home record and finished 20 points adrift from Mourinho's title-winners. It was the biggest gap since 1991 when George Graham's Arsenal had won the trophy. The 1994 records set by United of points amassed and games won was eclipsed by Chelsea that night. No further proof was required that there had been a quantum shift in the balance of power in the domestic struggle. The football world now wondered if Chelsea's dominance – both in footballing and spending terms – would ever again be challenged.

Despite the undoubted spending power of the north London club, and the tactical nous of Mourinho, other clubs could still make their mark if their squads performed on the pitch. The press soon pointed out that Sir Alex had splashed out a not inconsiderable £68 million on his strike force – Rooney, Saha, Smith and van Nistelrooy – who had only scored a meagre 41 goals between them. He may not have an Abramovich behind him, but the boss had no excuses for his front line misfiring in the way they were.

Since his horrific knee injury, Ole was severely missed by United. Not only had he been carving out a career for himself in the Beckham role, but the squad was depleted without him. The first XI could still give anyone in the Premiership a game; indeed, they had recorded doubles over Arsenal and Liverpool. The problems arose when the squad required rotation for tactical reasons, or because of injuries. It was then apparent that they were sadly lacking in depth. The fringe players were simply not living up to their reputations – Saha scored only one Premiership goal and even Wayne Rooney, the much-vaunted wunderkind from Everton, only managed 11. They were – or had been – great players, but they lacked the mental and physical toughness that Ole brought to the team.

The United team did a humiliating 'lap of honour' to an almost deserted Old Trafford. Only a handful of Reds fans stood their ground to honour the badge. Ole, briefly alienated, stood at the back of the family stand watching his chums walk slowly down the tunnel, their heads down, the crude taunts of the Chelsea fans burning in their ears. The slow decay of Manchester United was painful for him to witness, and he knew that if he made it back to full fitness, he could do something about it. He also felt that he owed it to the club's devoted fans, who paid their money and cheered the team on through good times and bad. He had made it back this far by setting himself short-term and long-term goals, and now he was faced with the giant task of getting back into the first team and scoring again.

In *Red News*, Ole explained how he felt when he heard the 'You Are My Solskjaer...' chant sung at away games when he had been watching on TV with his family. 'I have been watching and we can hear it in the background. I say, 'Sssshhh... sssh... listen, listen... it is my song. It is my song. It warms your heart and is good for my son Noah. "Dad, they are singing your song, but you are not playing." He has been really buying into this as well.'

The road Ole travelled was a long one with no promise of hope, or guarantee of a future. One step forward, two back... that's how it felt sometimes, but still he walked it. After a few months, he told the *Manchester Evening News*, 'It is frustrating. You want to play football. When I was injured, it was maybe my first season as a regular first-team player who started the first game and was expecting to play a few games. But then again that is what happened and I just get on with it. I am not a laid-back character, but I just deal with what is the truth and reality now. You cannot dwell in the past or look too far forward.'

Chelsea were a triumph of form over content. Mourinho had thrown down the gauntlet but there was to be another season of despair and hardship for Ole and United. The colossus that was Manchester United had to rediscover its humility for a while, and become a little more mortal again.

In the summer, Ole continued with his rehab and busied himself with a one-week soccer academy in his home town. The United ace had set the academy up in 2003 to promote the game in Norway. It consisted of 50 youngsters – 25 boys and 25 girls – who were watched by scouts from the Norwegian international set-up. United also sent scouts over, and five of the youngsters would win a trip to Old Trafford.

Ole had long harboured dreams of becoming a manager and saw the academy as a good starting point. Working with the young hopefuls was good for him; it took his mind off the slow progress he was making and also increased his determination to play again. The enthusiasm and energy around the kids was infectious. It wasn't long before the academy was reaping dividends for United when, in August 2006, attacking midfielder Magnus Eikrem signed for United.

The big news of the summer was the takeover of the club by the Florida-based Glazer family, themselves billionaires like Abramovich. Nobody could match the financial clout of Chelsea, though, as Abramovich pumped yet more cash into the club's coffers, with spending exceeding £200 million. Chelsea were desperate to emulate some of the greatness of their London neighbours, and that of the north-western clubs such as Liverpool and Man United, and they felt that Michael Essien, from Lyon, would help to take them that little bit closer to pre-eminence domestically and in Europe. As the Blues were to discover, though, the cash alone would not guarantee instant success – players with the commitment and heart of an Ole Gunnar Solskjaer are not bought, they're nurtured and then deployed in the best possible formation to allow their talent to shine. Mourinho had done wonders, no doubt, and his team had been winning, but they were far from thrilling. The huge array of multi-millionaire stars were a long way off understanding what it meant to play for each other, and to play for the badge.

Despite his long absence from the top-class game, Ole took some comfort from the fact that his long lay-off might actually extend his career in the long run. In August 2005, it was reported that he was back in training with a faint possibility that he may be fit for the start of the season. Further speculation had arisen that United may have been prepared to end Michael Owen's exile at Real Madrid and bring him home. His comeback was postponed indefinitely, though, by his doctor, when he suffered a tear in his knee. It was another sledgehammer blow and, again, rumours emanated from Norway that Ole would never return to the big time. Even Sir Alex, for the first time, expressed doubts, when he told Sky Sports, 'I am not sure he will play for the first team again. You cannot be sure when a guy is 32 and has been out a year.'

Gary Neville was more upbeat, though, telling MUTV, 'I hope we have him back soon. I sit next to him in the changing room and he is genuinely one of the nicest lads you will ever meet. For 12–14 months he has slogged in that gym like you would not believe from nine in the morning 'til three. That might not seem like long hours but to be in a gym every day for 12 months, when you are a football player, he is just giving it his all. If anyone can come back from the injury he has had, it will be him, because he has been so professional and has done everything perfectly.

'He scored the winning goal in the European Cup Final... he will always be one of the legends of Manchester United. There are spine-tingling moments that this place can give you, and I am pretty confident he will have that moment [of coming back]. I can see him scoring a goal for United again.'

Ole played down the news of his latest setback by telling the media that it was unconnected with the original injury and that he hoped to be back in training in November. The specialist, he said, was pleased with the progress that had been made so far.

After United had drawn 0-0 away to Liverpool in the middle of September, they trailed seven points behind Chelsea, who were an astonishing 4-1-on to retain their title. United beat them 1-0 in November, which ended their 40-match unbeaten run, just as they had done to Arsenal just over a year earlier. Darren Fletcher's looping header after 31 minutes gave United only their fifth win in their past 31 home league games against the west London side, and Sir Alex recorded his first win over Mourinho in seven attempts.

The crowd were fantastic that Sunday afternoon at Old Trafford as they roared on their heroes; the match-day atmosphere at Stamford Bridge was disappointing, by comparison. It must have dawned on Abramovich, returning to the scene of his initial exposure to the sport, that despite the £200 million spent, he had failed to purchase the very essence of what had lured him there in the first place.

The result was unexpected in many quarters as United had gone down to a heavy 4-1 defeat to Middlesbrough the week before. Once again, Steve McClaren had masterminded the victory; he had the remarkable record of having beaten United in each season since he had departed from Old Trafford. Those results were a major factor in enhancing his reputation and eventually landing him the England job.

The rest of November was not so good for United as two legends departed. Roy Keane left for Celtic, his ageing, battle-scared body unable to withstand the demands of the Premiership any longer. Ole would talk in awed terms of the nine fantastic seasons that he had played alongside him. In *Red News*, he was quoted as saying, 'Roy has been the most influential one, he is the one I listen the most to. He has the wisest words to tell. The things you see on the pitch is only half, not even half, of what Roy is all about. He was always setting standards high, asking 100 per cent from him and from us.'

On Friday, 25 November 2005, George Best died in a London hospital at the age of 59. To those lucky enough to have seen him play, he was simply the greatest talent the British Isles has ever produced. He was also unquestionably one of the greatest players ever to have worn the red shirt.

Best's contribution to United's European Cup Final win over Benfica in 1968 earned him the accolade of European Footballer of the Year... and a place in the hearts of every Manchester United fan for ever more. If Ronaldo was the speed of sound then Best was the speed of light.

Ole was chosen as the players' representative at George's funeral in Belfast. He told *Red News*, 'I never saw him play football. I have seen a few clips. It was just being there and representing the players... that's something that I will always remember. I met George Best a few times. It was a great honour to be there. I felt the players should be represented.'

Ole's attendance at Best's funeral must have been one of the most poignant moments in his career. Like Best, he had scored in a European Cup Final. Like Best, he had played on numerous occasions for his country. Like Best, now the most revered player of them all, he held a tremendous affection in the public eye. Best had a talent doomed to be squandered; Ole had a talent that fate almost squandered. Following his injury, Ole was met with thumbs up and good wishes wherever he went.

The similarity ends there – Best destroyed his career and eventually his own life. Ole, in the words of his adviser Jim Solbakken, 'never made a wrong move'.

Ole remains a very private person, never chasing fame or courting publicity, just the sanctuary of a happy, carefree family life. The Ferraris, Kristal champagne, Rolex watches and nightclub infidelities could be left to his team-mates... he simply got on, quietly, with returning to the stage he loved so much.

## THE LONG AND WINDING ROAD

United crashed out of Europe before Christmas when they failed to qualify from their group. They only won one home match and sustained defeats against Lille and Benfica, which torpedoed their chances. Ole told the press that the Champions League was a 'major, major disappointment'.

He received an early Christmas present when, in the first week of December, he made his comeback in a reserve game against Liverpool at Hyde United, which Liverpool eventually won 2-0 with Neill Mellor and Ramon Castilla scoring. It was his first game since he had come on in the Cup Final against Millwall, 19 long months before.

Ole described his comeback in the *Red News*, saying, 'I did not really set any standards or pressure on myself to perform. I was just going to go out there and enjoy it. I knew that I had not played for two years so it was not going to be a good game. Obviously, you think it can be if the team plays well and you get chances. I can score four or five goals, but it can also happen that you mis-control every ball so it can be either/or... and it was more "or", to be fair! It was a bad game, it was the first time the reserves had not scored in a game and that's the game I played up front.

'I really, really enjoyed it and coming there with all the crowd was amazing. Jim Ryan, the assistant manager, he always comes to the reserve games. He was 15 minutes late because he was stuck in traffic. There is never that much traffic round there. There were about 3,000 there. It was a bit disappointing not scoring a goal in your comeback because you still have hope.

'I will show them what they have been singing for... it just did not happen. I will score again.'

This heartened Sir Alex because, a few weeks before, he had again expressed doubts about Ole's return. This time he told the BBC, 'We are all hoping he can make it back and we keep praying. The first thing I ask the physio is, "How's Ole?" and it is always, "Just the same, just the same... " I could not put a time on it, but it is a worry.'

But Ole did come back, against Birmingham City at St Andrews, after nearly two years out of the red shirt with the number 20 on the back. Three days after Christmas 2005, and seven minutes from time, he came on as a sub for the next legend-in-waiting Cristiano Ronaldo. The reception he received from the travelling United fans was little short of rapturous. It would have been nice to say he scored the winner, which would have kick-started a run that would have overhauled Chelsea, who at that time were 11 points ahead. However, the game ended 2-2 without Ole getting on the score sheet. It was a game United should have won after twice leading through van Nistelrooy and Wayne Rooney. However, for Ole, it was a triumphant return after facing such hardship. With so little match practice, it was another remarkable performance by him.

In an interview with the *Manchester Evening News*, Ole said, 'The fans have been fantastic. It is surreal in a way and maybe a bit unrealistic. They have seen me come back now but, hopefully, they will see a few better performances from me. It was a great feeling just to get back on the pitch again and to be able to wave to the supporters at the end. I am back in the squad now and available if the manager needs me. But it is going to take time to get the proper match fitness back.'

There were still hurdles to overcome, but Ole's next appearance was in the FA Cup away to Burton Albion, which ended 0-0. In the replay, United crushed Burton 5-0 in a powerhouse display of attacking play. It was a huge moment because Ole captained United in front of 53,564.

He explained how he felt to *Red News*: 'Yeah, of course, it was great. If you had said to me halfway through my rehab that I would be captain at Old Trafford in front of fifty-odd thousand in the Third Round of the FA Cup, I would have been delighted. Even if it was Burton Albion, it was still a proud moment for me.

'When you are captain of Manchester United, what more can you ask for, really? And we won 5-0. That was one of the things that I have always had as a dream or a realistic target as well, really, because I always thought I could get back to playing at Old Trafford. But I have not been there in a major game, which is the ultimate target.'

Ole still had the belief that he could make it back to the very top, playing and scoring against the élite. That had been his dream for so long, he never lost sight of it as the blood pounded in his veins.

Ole might have scored that night had Gary Neville linked with his old pal with a simple square pass rather than firing wide when he burst through in the closing minutes. It would have capped a near-perfect night for him as his two kids were watching. The returning hero joked that he would be having 'a quiet word' with Mr Neville.

Two of United's Cup goals had been scored by the young prospect Giuseppe Rossi, snapped up from Parma and rated a 'goal machine' by Ole. The American-born youngster had greatly impressed Ole; he had that unique predator's quality of thinking about scoring before he received the ball.

United's interest in the FA Cup ended in the Fifth Round at Anfield when they went down by a solitary goal, although the afternoon was marred by the horrific broken leg sustained by Alan Smith.

Another setback hit Ole when he was out for three weeks

with a hamstring injury that he sustained in training, perhaps because he was just a bit too eager to push himself beyond his limits. In the scheme of things, three weeks was nothing to the years he had been injured. At that stage of his comeback, it was very poor timing. Ole's game plan then was to play as much as he could for the reserves and as many minutes as he could in the Premiership. His drive to succeed and score for United was as strong as ever.

Ole returned for the reserves again in February against Aston Villa Reserves of all people. Villa beat them 3-0, with their prospect Gabriel Agbonlahor grabbing a first-half hat-trick. Ole headed wide early on and Rossi had a goal ruled out. A poor result, but another step along that long road to full fitness as he tried to resurrect his career.

Things looked brighter for Ole than they had for a long, long time, but football has a nasty habit of smacking you in the face when you least expect it. Lo and behold, he then fractured a cheekbone in a reserve game against Middlesbrough. The Norwegian was accidentally caught by defender Ugo Ehiogu after just seven minutes, and the injury ruled him out for the rest of the season. A United spokesman confirmed that the injury would put him out for six to eight weeks but the loss of match fitness would preclude him for any remaining games.

Once again, Ole's United future at Old Trafford was at a crossroads; he had done so much to find himself on the brink of a regular first-team place, and then fate dealt him another cruel blow. His contract expired in the summer and he hoped to negotiate at the very least a pay-as-you-play deal. The injury threw a huge question mark over his future, and few gave him much hope of turning out again for United in a competitive match the following season.

The future, though, was decided very swiftly, and it gave Ole some good news at last – United offered him a new two-year contract. Details were not specified, but it was thought to be dependent on how many appearances he made. The United Chief Executive David Gill had reassured Ole about his future at Old Trafford, and there was further good news when he was told that he was now eligible for a testimonial. Ole was now officially the longest-serving foreign player in the history of Manchester United. Sir Alex wanted to use Ole as an ambassador and leader at the club for as long as his playing days continued, and afterwards perhaps as a coach. Suddenly, the future was bright again.

Unfortunately, the present wasn't so bright for the team as a whole – the season ended with Chelsea retaining their title and eventually finishing eight points in front of runners-up United. This had been achieved by playing a brand of football that was diametrically opposed to the attacking verve and flair of the United trademark approach. On their run-in, they had beaten the Reds 3-0 with Joe Cole, their most improved player, scoring one of the goals of the season. Since Abramovich's arrival, the gap between the two sides seemed to be widening, and few could see how any of the other big hitters in the Premiership could compete with the financial excess that was driving the Blues onward. They had achieved a great deal in a short amount of time, but at what cost? And if that continued, one wondered for how long football fans would put up with it, and whether they might desert the game in favour of something a little more competitive and meaningful.

Ole told *Red News*, 'If you look at the points tally and the way we have played, I think you cannot criticise the team, because they have played really well. Chelsea have done fantastically well; they have raised the bar so much. In a normal season, say of my ten seasons here, the points tally now would have been enough in six or seven of them at least to be top of the league.'

It was not all doom and gloom, though. United lifted their first trophy since Ole's absence by beating Wigan 4-0 in the Carling Cup. Rooney had the run of the park and scored twice. Ole was not fit enough, though, to warrant a place in the squad at the time.

Winter turned to spring, and Ole trained harder than ever. Now aged 33, he had not scored a goal for three years and he knew that he was not going to be given many more opportunities to do so. The clock was ticking.

# 12

# Return of the King

'If I do not win anything more I will be disappointed. Then I will go home and I will feel that since my injury I have been a failure. That is what I will feel.'
**OLE GUNNAR SOLKSJAER**

'For all the ravages of time and injury, Solskjaer remains a masterful finisher. Pure class.'
**HENRY WINTER, *DAILY TELEGRAPH***

Ole did play again for United in the 2005/06 season, appearing as a substitute against Sunderland on Good Friday. United fired blanks, though, as they could only draw 0-0 with the doomed Black Cats. The last faint hope of recapturing the title went that night but Ole was far from a marginalised figure. Soon, his long wait would be over – Ole was on the way back.

In July 2006, Ole scored his first goal in United colours since the Panathinaikos match in September 2003; the first, and then his second as well, came against Orlando Pirates in Durban, the first match on United's three-match tour of South Africa. It was played in front of a large, noisy crowd. The first goal was set up by the young Giuseppe Rossi and his mentor Giggs. Ole finished the move with a screamer of a half-volley. The second of his goals was a clipped effort, also down to Rossi. It gave him a great boost to realise he had lost none of his finishing prowess.

With the out-of-favour van Nistelrooy departing to ply his trade with Beckham at Real Madrid, Sir Alex was delighted to welcome Ole back into the fold. Ole was the main reason that he opted not to sign a replacement striker. Never one to lavish praise without very good reason, the gaffer admitted to the *Manchester Evening News*, 'Ole is a terrific option for us. He has this great natural talent and is the type of player who warms up in front of goal, rather than freezes.

'If you go back three seasons, he was really starting to excite us in that wide right position. He has this amazing understanding and awareness. He was a revelation at the time and there are still great possibilities for him there. At the moment, though, it is just fantastic to have him back. There are many examples of players who have dedicated their lives to recovering from injury, pushing themselves through gym sessions sometimes four times a day. Ole is one of them.

'He always said he would come back. I do not want to push him too much too soon and 45 minutes is enough for him at the moment. But he has worked incredibly hard and now we just hope he gets some luck.'

'Luck' was the key word here. Buoyed by his goals, Ole scored in further pre-season matches against Preston and Porto.

Norway came calling again for his specialist talents and, a few days before the 2006/07 season, he played against Brazil. The game finished 1-1 and Ole played for 45 minutes. In September, Ole scored twice for Norway in their 4-1 victory over Hungary in Budapest, a UEFA Euro 2008 qualifying game. The Norwegian boss Aage Hareide told the *Manchester Evening News*, 'I was criticised by some people in Norway for trying to get him back into the Norway line-up so quickly. But I had seen him against Porto in the Amsterdam tournament. His fitness levels were incredible. United were down to nine men but Ole was running all over the place and scored a goal out of nothing. His touch and movement were remarkable.

'I knew what I was doing and knew what he was capable of. Just to have him in the squad is fantastic because he lifts everybody. He does a great job encouraging others. His love for the game is fantastic and I am so happy he has come back in such great form.'

Eirik Havdahl, Norwegian soccer writer, observed, 'The ex-Manchester City player Hareide was Ole's former manager at Molde and signed him from Clausenengen FK back in 1995. Hareide was keen to sign Ole two seasons before, but the young striker insisted on serving his apprenticeship with the Third Division outfit. How typical of Ole; he wanted to perfect his striking skills before making the step up. He resisted all overtures to leave Clausenengen before he felt it was right.

'Ole showed the same single-mindedness in overcoming his injury. Nobody could shake him from his deeply-held belief that he could make it back to the Premiership. They say he kept a diary of his comeback and only filled it with positive thoughts... what a guy. A true hero.'

The memorable 2006/07 Premiership season commenced with a home game against Fulham. The expectations were high, as always, at Old Trafford; and part of that feeling was driven by Michael Carrick, who had joined the club from Tottenham for £18 million. However, as had been the story since Abramovich's arrival, Chelsea were again ominously the high-rollers. They were inexorably attracting and retaining some of the biggest names in football. In the summer of 2006, they snagged the world-class talents of the Ukraine striker Andriy Shevchenko and Michael Ballack. They came to Stamford Bridge on £121,000-a-week contracts, which did little to dent Abramovich's vast reserves. The German captain had turned down an approach from United the previous season, but he had finally fallen to temptation. It all looked great on paper for Chelsea – Mourinho just had the small task of turning his galaxy of stars into a functioning team. Once again, having seen Ballack hanging up his kit bag at Stamford Bridge, Sir Alex was left ruing the loss of a massive talent to the Londoners.

It was easy to be pessimistic about the new season if you were a United fan, but hope was about to surface. A clueless Fulham were crushed 5-1; Ole came off the bench to replace Saha in what was an impressive start for the Reds.

Ole's first goal on his return to the Premiership came in injury time at Charlton in United's imperious 3-0 win. Charlton had been a lucky ground for him in the past, but this was a wonderful moment in his career. Those of a red persuasion were absolutely delighted for their favourite striker, who had spent the last two years working with the single aim of getting his body back to decent enough shape to compete again on the pitch, and put the ball in the back of the net for the club he loved and respected. And he'd done it. He told the *Manchester Evening News*, 'I have been dreaming about this day and now it has finally arrived, I just feel relief. I waited a long, long time to celebrate with the fans after scoring a goal. The prospect of doing it was one of the major things that has motivated me over the past three years. Throughout all that time, the fans and the manager have supported me. They have shown patience and the gratitude I feel for that is difficult to put into words. Maybe, in an ideal world, I would have scored the goal at Old Trafford. But that does not really matter. I have a goal on the board now – and that is the important one.'

To score at Old Trafford was the next target for Ole, his morale boosted further by the Charlton goal. He did not have to wait long, scoring the winner in the 3-2 victory over Scottish champions Celtic. Their first Champions League Group F match of the season – aka 'the Battle of Britain' – was played throughout in a cauldron of noise. The crowd numbered 74,031 - 42,000 more than watched Chelsea play Werder Bremen in their equivalent European opener.

It was the type of goal that characterised Ole's career – the product of commitment, speed of thought, and executed with simple efficiency. Sir Alex told the press that the moment the first shot was struck by Saha, Ole was 'on the move'. This time, as he celebrated, he was treated to a display of the '2O LEgend' tribute banners in the Stretford Road End and saluted the fans. It was his 20th goal in Europe in 76 appearances – 34 starts and 42 substitutions – and he was now 16th on the all-time United goal-scoring charts. For the man who had apparently come back from the dead, Ole was now not prepared to sit back and wait for things to happen. He was living now on borrowed time, and however long he might have to wear the red shirt, he wanted more than ever to win something else, and prove that he could help his team to more glory. The giants of English football were clawing their way back to greatness, and Ole was an integral part of their renaissance, just as they had been an integral part of his.

Ole described how he felt after his Old Trafford goal to the *Manchester Evening News*: 'The feeling when the ball went in was just fantastic. I am not a believer in making up for lost time, but I do think I need to pay the fans back. They have sung my name so many times when I have been sat in the stand, it has become a little embarrassing. It is so nice to be back on the pitch again and to score in front of the Stretford End is particularly special.'

A special guest of Ole's that night was the Norwegian skiing legend Kjetil Andre Aamodt who was a huge inspiration to him. Shortly after Ole had first injured his knee, Aamodt severely injured his ankle and ligaments in a skiing accident while training. Ole had two major operations on his knee but the Olympic gold medallist had to undergo four. Written off by the media, Aamodt made a fairytale comeback and won a further Olympic gold in Italy in February 2006. In his darkest hours, Ole had taken enormous encouragement from the way that Aamodt had overcome similar hopeless odds.

Arsenal inflicted the first defeat on United when they won 1-0 at Old Trafford on the Sunday following the Celtic game. Ole came on for the disappointing Rooney after 77 minutes. The Gunners' stand-in striker Emmanuel Adebayor won it with a late goal, but Ole almost saved a point but for an incredible flying save from Jens Lehmann. Arsenal defended stoutly as United threw everything at them. The game was watched by 75,595, a new Premiership record.

Ole said of the new-look team, 'This is as good as the side I was in before I got injured. It is a bit different because we have lots of pace, we are good at counter-attacking and, obviously, with Wayne Rooney and Cristiano Ronaldo, we have players who can beat men and do things on their own. We are in a team that works together. There are no personal agendas or individual targets. It is winning something as a team.'

Sir Alex was urging Cristiano and Wayne to learn from the wonderful example set by Ole in his career with particular reference to his humility and down-to-earth nature. When he was striving to get back from injury, Ole asked Manchester United TV for a DVD of all his goals so he could picture himself scoring again. Rooney, in particular, could have done with a lengthy spell viewing it.

When Ole arrived at Old Trafford, he was advised by Pallister, McClair, Schmeichel and, of course, his original mentor Cantona. Now Giggs, Neville and Ole had become the senior statesmen of the dressing room. Ole understood that this was part of the natural evolution of a team. If you stuck around long enough, you were naturally going to become a role model for the younger players.

The period he spent playing in the reserves, as he battled to regain his fitness, was another learning curve for him. He enjoyed being able to impart his vast knowledge at first hand to willing lads like Rossi. Ole knew, too, that even at his age he could learn from world-class talents like Ronaldo and Rooney.

There was still a lot he had to give to the senior squad, though, and on the first day of October 2006, Ole scored both goals in United's 2-0 win over Newcastle at Old Trafford. It was an intoxicating afternoon of muscular football and the heartfelt faith of the United crowd. The first goal came on 40 minutes when the brilliant and bold Rolando's long-range drive crashed against the post and Ole swept home from six yards. The Portuguese flanker was in devastating form and terrorised Newcastle all afternoon.

Three minutes into the second half, Vidic fired in a goal-bound shot and Ole raced in to deflect it with his right knee – the knee that had been injured for over two-and-a-half-years – past Steve Harper and into the net. Ole said afterwards that he was trying to get out of the way but it had just hit him. The Norwegian claimed it, though, showing the mentality of a true striker.

Newcastle could not come back from that and United cantered to an easy victory and top spot. It was Ole's first Premiership goal at home since he had scored against Liverpool in April 2003. Slowly, bit by bit, the goals were coming back.

Ole did not have to wait long for his next one, either, as he scored the last goal in United's 3-1 romp at Wigan. Paul Jewell's side had taken a shock lead at the JJB Stadium, but goals by Vidic and Saha put United in front. Sir Alex was not employing Ole in the front line but as a wide man, in the Beckham role that he had filled so well three seasons earlier. Ole's goal was another gem, taking the ball on and smashing it high into the net. It was fast becoming a football cliché, but Ole could nearly always make the keeper work because his aim was unerringly accurate.

There was a belief now in the Reds camp that United could put in a sustained bid for honours and enter the first serious challenge to Chelsea since the Blues' emergence as a superpower. There had been a change in tactics following the departure of Keane. In the seasons that they had been without Ole, and with Keane slowing, they had adopted a more cautious 4-3-3 system. Following Keane's move to Celtic and the return of Ole, Sir Alex had switched to the free-wheeling 4-2-4 and the goals had flowed. Keane was now bossing Sunderland and had turned them around in a remarkably short space of time. The ex-United skipper was a huge admirer of Ole and was dismissing reports that he was set to sign him in the January transfer window.

Another huge admirer of Ole's courage and talent was Alan Smith, also slowly finding his way back. The big man paid tribute to Ole in the *Independent,* saying, 'Ole is an inspiration. If you wanted to talk about attitude, Ole's the man to look to. Two years ago, people were talking about him having a testimonial, yet you look at him and he still seems as though he is 19 or 20. I mean, that is good for everyone.'

Crewe away at the rain-lashed Gretsy Road in the League Cup was the scene of Ole's next goal as his comeback gained momentum. As had been the case in previous matches in the competition, the Carling Cup holders' line-up was the usual blend of youngsters, fringe players and old campaigners, and the side was captained by Ole.

Youngster Richard Jones set up the opening goal with a strong run to the by-line which was fiercely stuck home by Ole from eight yards after 26 minutes. It was a long way from the Nou Camp, but the feeling was the same as the ball hit the back of the net. He was proving to the world that he was anything but a shadow of his former self. It was his sixth goal in ten appearances and already Sir Alex was setting him a target of fifteen goals for the season.

Dario Gradi's side put up stubborn resistance and, 17 minutes from time, they equalised through Varney. The game went to extra time and, with penalties looming, 18-year-old fledgling Kieran Lee won it for United with a Solskjaer-type strike. It was a hard-fought victory but Ole valiantly completed the full two hours in difficult conditions.

The next first-team appearance for him was the away leg with Copenhagen on 1 November 2006. A freezing

Copenhagen was to prove to be far from wonderful for both Ole and United. Sir Alex rang the changes from the first X1 and brought in Ole for Giggs. The pitch was awful, having been churned up by a Bruce Springsteen concert the previous weekend. A pedestrian United dominated the game from start to finish. Rooney, who had scored a hat-trick in his previous match against Bolton, could have had another one in the first half-hour if his shooting had not been so wayward. The game looked to be heading for a stalemate but ex-Villa man Allbäck headed a late winner, with the United back four static. Worse was to follow when, in the last minute, Ole limped off holding his leg. United fans in the Parken Stadium and the millions watching on TV held their breath. At first, everybody thought his knee had gone again, but they were relieved to find out that it was a hamstring strain. Sir Alex was particularly pleased that it was not a recurrence of the knee problem. However, he would be without his Norwegian striker for the next five weeks.

The games came thick and fast during Ole's absence. The holders relinquished their grip on the Carling Cup when they went out to Southend by a solitary goal. The Essex side were languishing with Leeds United at the bottom of the Championship.

United also suffered a defeat by the same score line in the return match with Celtic at Parkhead. The kept up their realistic challenge in the Premiership with a string of victories over Blackburn, Sheffield United and Middlesbrough away, and home wins over Portsmouth and Everton. The only game in which they failed to take maximum points was a 1-1 draw with Chelsea. The draw left them three points clear of the London side, and

# RETURN OF THE KING

Cristiano Ronaldo voiced his annoyance that Chelsea had escaped from Old Trafford with a point when he told the *Sun*, 'I feel we ended up with two points lost after our exhibition and the chances we created. We played better and, because of that, this draw leaves a bitter taste.'

Sir Alex could barely conceal his disdain when asked to comment on Peter Kenyon's predictions that Chelsea would eventually overtake United as the biggest club in the world. United's boss did concede, though, that the Premiership would develop into 'a two-horse race'.

Ole was back in the squad for the Benfica game. He was desperate to gain revenge for the humiliation the previous season when United were knocked out in the qualifying round. Ole told the *Manchester Evening News*, 'Every game is a big one for United but to get through in Europe is especially important when you remember what happened last year. The defence is as good as it has been for several years. We are defending very well and we are really difficult to play against. That is the foundation for any good team.'

Benfica took an early lead with a spectacular goal, but Ole need not have worried as United powered back to win 3-1, enabling them to join the last 16. Ole made an appearance as a replacement for Paul Scholes but it was Ronaldo who dominated the game. The Portuguese winger put on a show against Benfica which brought comparisons with Best's performances against the same club four decades before.

Ole's first taste of Premiership action was when he came on as a substitute at West Ham for Ryan Giggs. In one of the shocks of the season, United went down to a late goal from Hammers skipper Reo-Coker after a mistake by ex-West Ham skipper Rio Ferdinand. It was West Ham new boss Alan Curblishley's first game in charge following the departure of Alan Pardew, who later was to swap places at Curblishley's old club Charlton. Chelsea, thanks to a last-gasp win at Everton, cut United's lead to two points. They had both played 18 matches and the Reds had amassed 44 points. Slip-ups at West Ham had cost United titles in both 1992 and 1995, and the manner of the defeat raised doubts about their current credentials.

One good bit of news was that Henrik Larsson watched the match after agreeing to join United on a short-term loan deal. The former Celtic and Barcelona legend arrived on a ten-week loan spell from Helsinborgs. Like Ole, Henrik did not become a professional footballer until he was 22. The Swede had also endured a stint in the military doing his National Service. Again, like Ole, his earlier hardships had made him even more determined to make a go of his chance in football.

United bounced straight back to form with an effortless 3-0 away win at Villa. Ole took no part but was lucky enough to see Paul Scholes volley home a goal of incredible power. It won the December *Match of the Day* Goal of the Month contest in a competition in which the standard was incredibly high. In their lucky win at Everton, Lampard and Drogba had both scored tremendous long-range goals to enable Chelsea to come from behind to snatch the points.

Then Ole hit a rich vein of form as he scored in the next three home games. The first came in the 3-1 Boxing Day victory over Wigan. The man of the moment, Ronaldo, scored the first two goals and Ole ran in the third. It was his first goal since his strike at Crewe in the Carling Cup. A late penalty from Baines gave Wigan a flattering score line. Sir Alex was still confident that Ole would attain his 15-goal target for the season and told the *Manchester Evening News*, 'Ole is an incredible finisher... I said before he got his injury at Copenhagen, he is definitely capable of getting us 15 goals a season. I am still certain of that.'

Goal number seven of the season was notched by Ole four days later when he scored the opening goal against Reading. By a quirk of fate, it was scored on that magical 33rd minute slot. It was the climax of a wonderful move between him and Ronaldo. The Reading defenders Murty and Little on the left decided to block off Ronaldo and forced him inside. To a one-footed winger, this would have presented a problem, but Ronaldo is no ordinary player. Naturally two-footed, he whipped over a perfect cross with his 'weaker' foot. Ole outwitted his marker to get in front of him and nod into the net. The Norwegian number 20 only needed a split-second to shake off his man and score.

A spirited Reading side had drawn at Stamford Bridge on Boxing Day and again showed their fighting qualities when they equalised five minutes later. On the hour, Ole regained the lead when he raced on to Rooney's pass. He simply outpaced Sonko and ran across the face of the box, before unleashing a shot that crashed against the post. Ronaldo, at full pelt, met the rebound first time to hammer United back into the lead. Ronaldo then grabbed a third from Giggs cross. Ole had a fine match and might have had a hat-trick, nearly netting a rebound from another Ronaldo shot and later hitting the woodwork.

Reading scored their second in stoppage time; when the whistle blew, the news filtered through that Chelsea had dropped more points at home to Fulham. Slight cracks were starting to appear in the Stamford Bridge citadel. Cech had suffered a serious head injury and then Terry started to pick up injuries. Lampard's form was being questioned for the first time but the most worrying thing for Chelsea fans were rumours of a rift between Abramovich and Mourinho.

At Old Trafford, the garden, for once, was apparently rosy. The third of the crucial Christmas matches ended in a 2-2 draw at Newcastle, another game from which United should have taken three points after leading twice. Talking of Ole's lack of involvement in that match, Sir Alex explained to the *Times*, 'I did not take Ole to Newcastle because he has played two games in four days and I thought he would be better resting for Sunday's match against Villa. He will play along with Larsson.'

Actually, Rooney started with Larsson in the Third Round FA Cup tie. The Swede scored on his début for United, breaking the deadlock ten minutes into the second half. Baros equalised for Villa 15 minutes from time and it looked like a replay. Sir Alex then gambled by replacing one legendary Scandinavian striker with another. Ole came on for the tiring Larsson 12 minutes from time and, once again, in front of millions of BBC TV viewers, Ole won the game for United with a low shot in the dying seconds of injury time.

Evra started the build-up with a pass to Ronaldo, who found Rooney, who then found Ole, who squeezed the ball beneath the body of the Hungarian keeper Gabor Kiraly. Sir Alex did not see Ole's ninth goal of the season as his view was blocked. He heard the deafening roar from the crowd, though, as their favourite son did what he does best.

Alan Shearer was watching the game in his capacity as a pundit and made the valid point that Ole's outstanding virtue was that he hit the target almost every time. The tabloids had a field day, making great capital out of the fact that the combined age of the Solskjaer–Larsson combination was 68. They claimed that the 91st-minute winner was an omen dating back to the Treble-winning season when Ole was so influential.

Villa went down again by the score of 3-1 the following week in a Premiership game, Ole again replacing Larsson, although neither of them scored on this occasion. Then Arsenal beat them at the Emirates after Rooney had put them in front. Again, late goals undid a cautious Reds side, Henry heading the winner in the fourth minute of injury time. Ole did not feature in the match, which would have put them nine points up on Chelsea had they had won it.

Portsmouth were United's next FA Cup opponents in a Fourth Round home tie. The 68-year-old strike force started the game. Andy Cole played for the south coast side for just over an hour, the duration of Ole's time on the pitch. Sol Campbell denied Ole a goal with a superb interception during that period. A great back-heel from Ole set up a chance for Larsson who shot narrowly over. Rooney replaced Ole and scored twice in the last 15 minutes to earn United a home tie with Reading.

Sir Alex had demanded that Wayne become more of a 'fox in the box' and sniff out the straightforward chances. The two senior 'foxes' in the game, Ole and Larsson, could not have been better examples to emulate.

In the next match, Larsson came on for Ole for the last 25 minutes and scored in what turned out to be a 4-0 pasting of Watford. United then maintained their sprint for the title as they butchered Tottenham 4-0 at White Hart Lane and then rolled Charlton 2-0. With Larsson in the squad, Sir Alex was able to rest Ole in a bid to safeguard him for the later stages of the season and the FA Cup ties. The

Norwegian captained the side against Reading in a 1-1 home draw, in which Carrick gave United the lead with a cracking 25-yarder just on half-time but Reading equalised after 67 minutes.

Ole was particularly unlucky not to get on the score sheet that evening. He had what appeared to be a perfectly good goal disallowed and then the Reading keeper Adam Federici made a fantastic save from him. Ole cracked in one of his specials, but the young Aussie keeper somehow kept it out with his legs. Federici was rated the best goalkeeper to come out of Australia since Mark Bosnich, of whom Federici said in the *Evening Standard*, 'I followed Mark's career when I was growing up and he was the best goalkeeper in the Premiership at one time. I looked up to him and that was when people in Australia started to watch more of the Premiership. He was a brilliant keeper and everyone looked up to him, especially when he went to Manchester United. He was a national icon at the time.'

Federici was blitzed when he played in the replay at the Madejski Stadium on 27 February. United scored three times in the first six minutes effectively to kill off the tie. Gabriel Heinze drove in the first with a shot that Federici should really have saved. Then Louis Saha scored with an angled shot as United poured forward. Ole grabbed the third after he had raced clear of the Reading defence. It was an incredible shot as he picked his spot to leave the keeper helpless.

The replay was televised again and Shearer was once more spellbound by the quality of Ole' s finish. At that stage, it looked like the Reds could have run up a record Cup score but they shut up shop. A goal in either half from Reading made it more of a contest than it should have been.

# RETURN OF THE KING

The future looked bright again for Ole. At that juncture, his club were nine points ahead of Mourinho's Blues, who had a game in hand, they were in the last 16 of the Champions League and through to the Sixth Round of the Cup where Middlesbrough lay in wait. For Ole, it had gone better than he had dared hope for. The comeback king had reached double figures in the goalscoring stakes, and had started 11 games and been a sub in 10 more. Another setback befell him, though, and he was ruled out for the next month when his knee was 'cleaned out'.

The most pleasurable moment for him during that further period of inactivity was when United played a celebration game for charity. It was against an all-star European X1 to celebrate 50 years of European football and also the 50th anniversary of the Treaty of Rome. More than 74,000 watched United triumph 4-3 with the gate money going to the Manchester United Foundation. There was a *Who's Who* of United legends in attendance, including Bobby Charlton and Brian Robson. David Beckham was also there but, like Ole, he was injured and could not participate in the game. Beckham received a great reception but even that was eclipsed when Ole walked on to the pitch in a United tracksuit holding the European Cup aloft. For a footballer to receive the adulation of the crowd, things could not get much better for Ole.

As the sharp end of the season loomed, United knocked Middlesbrough out of the Cup after a replay. In his last game before his loan period ended, Henrik Larsson scored the winner against Lille which put them into the last eight against a powerful Roma side.

In the Premiership, a last-minute goal by O'Shea gave them three precious points against Liverpool at Anfield, which were vital to keep Chelsea at bay. Still rumoured to be racked with back-room unease and boardroom strife, the Londoners had put together a long winning run and were maintaining a relentless pursuit.

Ole was back as a sub on the last day of March for the visit of Blackburn to Old Trafford managed by Mark Hughes. Rovers took a shock lead, before United absolutely destroyed them with a second-half display of majestic attacking fire-power. Ole scored the last goal in the closing minutes. Down south, Watford looked like holding Chelsea until another late goal gave them three points to maintain their challenge.

Then United travelled to Roma for the first leg of their quarter-final match, which they lost 2-1 with Paul Scholes being sent off for a second bookable offence after 30 minutes. Ole started the game and set up United's goal with a perfect cross for Rooney to score. It was the England striker's first goal in the Champions League in 18 games. Ole might have scored himself before he went off after 72 minutes to be replaced by Fletcher. This was just after the Roma sub Mirko Vucini had scored the winning goal.

A bad defeat – 2-1 at Portsmouth – put a dent in United's Premiership hopes and enabled Chelsea to cut the deficit to a mere three points with a fortunate win over Spurs. A crazy own-goal by Rio Ferdinand sealed United's fate in a lacklustre performance. Ole came on as a sub towards the end and created United's goal with a fierce shot that the immaculate David James could only block. John O'Shea then ran in the rebound, but it was too late to alter the result.

Roma came to Old Trafford for the second leg three nights later. Sir Alex had said in Rome that he believed they would go through if they scored, although even he would not have dreamed that they would score seven in one of the all-time great European nights for United. The final score was 7-1, giving them an amazing 8-3 win on aggregate. Ole did not score but came on as a sub after an hour, by which time they had rattled in six. To destroy one of the finest teams in Italy in such a fashion hammered out a warning across Europe. Only Chelsea, it would seem, now stood between them and another Treble.

# 13

# A Perfect Finish

**'I think for us it is the club's greatest achievement.
We looked at the squad and we knew there was
enough ability. We had a foundation of players
like Giggs and Scholes, Neville and Solskjaer.'
SIR ALEX FERGUSON, SPEAKING TO
*THE SUN* A FEW DAYS AFTER CLINCHING
THE 2006/07 PREMIERSHIP TITLE**

United were drawing 1-1 with Middlesbrough at Old Trafford with only a few minutes left to play. Ole Gunnar Solskjaer, alert as ever, waited for Mark Schwarzer to settle himself to launch yet another hopeful ball up field. As the keeper steadied himself to kick the ball, Ole darted forwards, flicked the ball away, and rolled it into an empty net. For a brief second, he beamed with delight, and then he heard the whistle. The goal had been disallowed, and Ole was booked. Opportunistic, cheeky, technically astute and clinical... and the goal was simply too fiendishly executed for the officials to take in what had happened – a typical Ole moment to savour.

The destination of the 2006/07 Premier League title could have been determined in that moment. The game petered out in a 1-1 draw and a weary United watched two precious points slip away from them. It could have been worse – 24 hours later, Chelsea's amazing run of nine straight wins in the Premiership ended when a stubborn Newcastle side held them to a goalless draw.

The Middlesbrough game had started brightly with Richardson giving the Reds an early lead; for a while, it looked like they would pound Southgate's nondescript side into oblivion. Fatigue and injuries were slowing down the United challenge, though, and, as the match dragged on, there was a growing feeling that this would not be their day. Mark Viduka took advantage of the Reds injury-hit back four to equalise in first-half injury time.

The second half was dour, attrition football, with Ole replacing Smith near the end. When Ole executed his smash-and-grab on Schwarzer, comparisons were drawn with a similar experience George Best had suffered when he played for Ireland against an England side with Gordon Banks in goal.

United had swept to the FA Cup Final a week earlier when they had brushed Watford aside 4-1 in the semi-final at Villa Park. When United had thrashed Watford 4-0 in January, their manager, Aidy Boothroyd, had said the contest was akin to 'Muhammad Ali v Jimmy Krankie...' That comparison was also appropriate for the Villa Park clash. Watford were relegated a few days later and the difference in class was immense. Wayne Rooney had a magnificent game and scored twice with that wrecking ball of his right foot. Ole entered the game after 83 minutes when he replaced Ryan Giggs. Shortly afterwards, the perpetual understudy, Kieran Richardson, criss-crossed through the midfield and lobbed the fourth to confirm United's return to Wembley.

# A PERFECT FINISH

Things were looking good for United – Cristiano Ronaldo had signed a new deal to ward off the persistent interest of Real Madrid, and Ole was now back to his devastating best, and intent on securing further winner's medals.

The next day, Chelsea scraped through to the Final with a win against Mark Hughes's Blackburn, courtesy of a late Ballack goal in extra time. If Ole's Norwegian team-mate Morten Gamst Pedersen had not missed a simple headed chance with seven minutes of normal time remaining, it might have been a different story. The tepid contest was played at Old Trafford with Chelsea failing to sell out their allocation by thousands. Roy Keane sat a few seats away from Abramovich and left before extra time, disappointed at the quality of the match. He saw nothing that would leave him worried about the future.

It was now set up for the 'dream' Cup Final, a fitting climax to a memorable two-horse-race of a season. In the ten matches that the clubs had met in the FA Cup, United had won eight and drawn one, Chelsea's only victory coming in a Sixth Round tie in 1950. The Reds were now bidding for their 12th Cup Final win, the sixth for Sir Alex.

Sandwiched between the Watford semi-final and the 'Boro game was a home tie against Sheffield United, another potential banana skin, but goals from the England pair Michael Carrick and Wayne Rooney saw United home. Strangely, both goals were scored four minutes into the start of each half. Ryan Giggs made his 500th League appearance and was replaced by Ole nine minutes from time. The Welsh winger wasn't particularly pleased about this, and glared at Sir Alex as he left the pitch.

Ole did not have time to make any impression on this occasion. Despite the win, United fans were concerned about their increasing catalogue of injuries. Sir Alex was mustering every fit player he could to repel the Chelsea challenge. A bad tackle forced Patrice Evra off and Richardson was introduced as a makeshift left-back. Rio Ferdinand was still injured and Edwin van der Sar, injured against Watford, was replaced in goal by the efficient Kuszczak.

Chelsea kept up the pressure by trouncing a stuttering West Ham the next evening at Upton Park, and it was also announced that Mourinho had settled his differences with the Chelsea owner and board, and he'd be staying... for now, at least.

Ole also announced that week that season 2007/08 would be his last as a professional footballer. The 34-year-old had a contract with United until the summer of 2008, but he told the Norwegian Paper *VG* he could see no future beyond then. 'I will most likely stay here. I have one year on my contract and I am aiming to do as well as possible to carry on. I will have to see how I feel... I could suddenly say enough is enough. But I will stay here next year in any case. I am almost certain I will be here next season. Then I will have this season behind me after two or three years out.'

Ole was confident he could play in the Premiership again in 2007/08 and there was every reason to believe he would after his astonishing comeback. As to what would happen after that was open to conjecture. Sir Alex was keen to use him in the ambassador's role for the club, knowing that the Norwegian club hero would be a huge asset to United off the field as he was on it.

Norway beckoned, too; speculation was rife that one day he would manage his national side. And there was always a chance of a job in the game in England, possibly working with Roy Keane or Mark Hughes.

## A PERFECT FINISH

Around 1.30pm on Saturday, 28 April 2007, Chelsea were effectively level on points with United, having appeared to have caught up with them. Chelsea led Bolton 2-1 while United trailed 0-2 at Goodison Park. Within an hour, though, United had stretched their lead to five points with just three games left.

It was another nerve-shredding afternoon for United fans as the pendulum swung first one way and then the other. Both teams kicked off at the same time on Saturday lunchtime. Everton tore into United and went ahead in the first half with a deflected free-kick from Alan Stubbs. Ole started the game on the right flank, and he, like his colleagues, struggled in the unseasonable heat.

That was how it stayed at half-time, when the news filtered through that Chelsea, after falling behind themselves to an early goal, had turned things round to lead 2-1. United's lead would be wiped out if it stayed like that. When Manuel Fernandes lashed Everton further ahead after 50 minutes, things looked desperate for the Reds. Then, Ole won a corner on the right with an hour gone.

The heat was telling on the 34-year-old as the camera tracked him in the penalty box; he looked exhausted as Giggs floated over the centre. Ole darted to meet it, but the kick was poor and it looked like an easy catch for the young Everton reserve keeper Iain Turner. Instead, he let the ball slip from his grasp. Ole was at the far post and tried to reach it, but John O'Shea was nearer and crashed home.

That goal sparked United into life. A half-fit Ronaldo came on for Alan Smith as Ferguson's side, smelling blood, poured forward. Seven minutes later, a desperate mêlée occurred in the Everton penalty area. With four Manchester United men up front – Ronaldo, Ole, Rooney and Giggs –

the Toffees cracked under pressure. Phil Neville, veteran of over 300 games for United and now captain of Everton, tried to steer the ball to safety but, with Ole lurking, he could only turn the ball into his own net. 2-2.

Rooney put United ahead with a brilliant piece of skill as he converted Ronaldo's cross. Once again, Ole was ready to pounce on any rebounds or deflections but he was not required as Wayne's finish was so precise. Four minutes from time, Ole went off, looking as if he had run a marathon, to be replaced by young Chris Eagles, who rounded off the afternoon by curling in the fourth. When the whistle blew, an excited Sir Alex greeted his troops with confirmation that Chelsea had dropped two precious points. Ole immediately congratulated Eagles on his fine goal, showing what a fine professional and team player he is.

Then it was off to the San Siro for the return with AC Milan. The heat of Everton was replaced by a monsoon as the rain lashed down. History was against United – Milan had won all three of the two-legged ties between the sides. They had also triumphed in nine out of their eleven semi-finals in the European Cup and Champions League. Another telling stat was that the only team to overcome a first-leg deficit against United were the Rossoneri winning 4-0 after losing 1-2 in the first encounter. This had happened in the first European fixture after the Munich disaster in 1958. Dennis Violett, a player with whom Ole was often compared, had got the winner at Old Trafford.

The day before the match, Liverpool beat Chelsea on penalties in the other semi, much to Mourinho's disgust. Sir Alex was disgusted himself, feeling it necessary to defend the reputation of Cristiano Ronaldo, whom Mourinho had decided was ripe for some typically controversial treatment.

## A PERFECT FINISH

United, though, never made it to Greece to play Rafa Benítez's side in what would have been the greatest clash of all time of British clubs in Europe. The semi proved a game too far for them, as the collective artistry of Milan made United look clumsy and slow. Ole took no part in the proceedings, just peering from the bench at his team's plight as a storm raged above.

Ronaldo set the tone for the evening when in the first 20 seconds, he tried a flick that bobbled wide of any United player. The crowd hooted and the Premiership leaders struggled to get started. Soon, Kaka was racing on to a smart header from Seedorf to smack home the first. The years of playing together gave Milan a great fluency in their teamwork and the ability to change the pace of the game at will.

Seedorf put Milan ahead in the tie after 30 minutes when he held off Fletcher's challenge, rode Vidic's mistimed tackle and fired in the second. That is how it stayed at the break. United had to score a goal to put them back in the game and, early in the second half, they had a good spell but never looked composed enough to score. If Ole had been brought off the bench, things might have been different. He may have been able to show his team-mates what it really meant to be in the right place at the right time.

Milan never allowed United to play as they did in the Premiership. Twelve minutes from time, Wes Brown gave away the ball to Ambrosini who put in Gilardino for the third. The Brazilian striker was in acres of space and only needed two touches before shooting past the advancing Edwin van der Sar. It finished 3-0, and Ole's dream of another European Cup Final was washed away in the Milan rain.

The Reds regained the Premiership, though, four days later. Chelsea could only draw at the Emirates as Arsène Wenger's disappointing side held them. That was enough to return the title to the North-West for the first time in four seasons. The day before, Ronaldo's penalty had been enough to beat City in the Manchester derby. Ole sat the game out and watched as the newly crowned Footballer of the Year drilled home from the spot after 36 minutes.

It was United's 16th League title, the 9th won in Sir Alex's 21-year reign. Only Ryan Giggs had the full Fergie set, and Ole had six. This one meant more than the others because, for a long time, it looked as if he would never play top-class soccer again, let alone play a major part in a Premiership-winning team.

The sale of van Nistelrooy at the start of the season was one of the most crucial factors in United's amazing comeback. Sir Alex stuck with Ole and played with no recognised centre-forward. Instead, he juggled with interchanging Ole, Saha and Smith and, for a short spell, Larsson playing off the hub of Rooney and Ronaldo. The quartet featuring Ole all suffered injury problems, which limited their appearances but, by the very nature of their interchange ability, it gave rise to a very fluid style.

Compare this to Chelsea, whose solitary spearhead Drogba had a highly successful season (scoring over 30 goals in all competitions), but the long ball game became very predictable towards the end of the season, and was highly effectively dealt with by Liverpool in the semi-final of the Champions League, when it really mattered most. Mourinho, it seemed, had no plan B.

Chelsea hosted United on a rainy, cold evening on 9 May in a dead rubber of a game. Neither side wanted to show their real hand with the FA Cup Final at the new Wembley ten days away. Ole started and finished the game, which saw several changes to the United first XI. There was a début for Dong Fangzhou, who partnered Ole up front, and starts for Chris Eagles and Kieran Lee.

Although there were only really bragging rights at stake, Chelsea were keen to beat United to establish moral superiority before Wembley and also claw back a modicum of pride. They fielded a strong side including Terry, Makelele, Wright-Phillips and Essien, and Joe Cole played the second half.

A substantial amount was bet on Chelsea to win the fixture, their selection that night being the stronger and more experienced. The new Champions, though, comfortably held the runners-up to a scoreless draw. The most satisfying moment for Reds fans was when Chelsea had to clap the new Champions on to the pitch. Ole was ninth on to the field, and smiled and nodded to his Chelsea colleagues. He held his hands aloft as he passed through the guard of honour to acknowledge the polite applause of the fans, and he then turned to greet the large contingent of United fans camped in a corner of the Shed End.

It was a champagne moment for Ole. His mind must have strayed back to one day approximately three years before when the United players had to perform a similar function, greeting Chelsea's first title win in 50 years and the first of the Abramovich/Mourinho regime. Ole had had his own demons to deal with; he had shattered his knee the previous September and years of pain, frustration, effort and setbacks lay in front of him. But now he was back on his own terms, a proven winner, and a legend while still serving the club he loved.

Those players not participating walked around the pitch – Giggs, Ronaldo, Ferdinand and the captain, Neville – and reaffirmed their place as great players who served one of the greatest clubs in British football. In Alex Ferguson, whose record was extraordinary by any standards, they had a manager who let his actions speak louder than his words. The Chelsea manager that night would have done well to take note. And if Sir Alex's achievements were not enough to silence the carping from Mourinho, then perhaps the United fans that night might have got through to him. They kept reminding Mourinho that he was no longer 'special', and even carried a huge banner with the Premiership trophy on it saying, 'We're Here Today... To Take It Away'.

Ole had no chance to seal his moment with a goal and shatter Chelsea's unbeaten home record. For most of the game, he played on the right of midfield, tidying and probing, just happy to be part of the occasion. United should have had a penalty when young Eagles was cut down. As the whistle blew, Ole swapped shirts and pleasantries with Michael Essien, who had put in a performance that was a cut above any of his team-mates.

After the match, United used their visit to London as the opportunity to hold their celebratory dinner. The function was held in one of the dining rooms of the private member's club Les Ambassadeurs in Hamilton Place, Mayfair. Ole sat at a table hosted by Sir Alex; behind him, Giggs and Ronaldo also hosted tables. Late into the night, the event broke up and the coach headed back to Manchester.

One of the guests that evening was the West Ham star Carlos Tevez, at the centre of one of the most controversial incidents of the season by virtue of his transfer irregularities.

## A PERFECT FINISH

The muscular Argentinian almost single-handedly kept West Ham in the Premiership as they won seven of their remaining nine games, the last of which they won at Old Trafford. It gave them a sensational double over the new champions, and United had failed to score against them in both fixtures. Tevez has scored the winner in first-half injury time when Wes Brown had failed to deal with a high ball.

Ole retained his place in the side, starting up front with Alan Smith. Ole played throughout the game and infiltrated the Hammers defence on a couple of occasions, but was unable to add to his goal tally. The nearest he came to scoring was when Yossi Benayoun cleared off the line and he just failed to hook it back.

A crowd of 75,927 were there to see the new Champions collect their ninth trophy. In a nice touch, Munich survivors Albert Scanlon and Bill Foulkes helped carry the trophy on to the pitch. Sir Alex, his dynamic chewing reaching new heights, could barely conceal his anger at losing to Curbishley's outfit, his will to win as strong as ever. His moment of glory had been tarnished a little, and deprived United of a record-breaking 29 wins over the season ... but it was a slip that he could afford, with only pride at stake for United, and Premiership survival at stake for West Ham. Regardless of the result, he finally had the Premiership trophy in his hands to make him feel better.

Two days before the Cup Final, Ole spoke to Stuart Mathieson of the *Manchester Evening News*. 'The players have it all. The only limit for them is what they limit themselves to. If they let themselves go on, there is going to be a lot to come from these players. And I am not just talking about Cristiano Ronaldo and Wayne Rooney. We know they are going to be, or rather are, two of the best players in the world. But there are others here who still have another couple of gears in them.

'This side is a very, very exciting team to be part of... it has pace. It is back to the old United that I used to watch back home before I came to Old Trafford. It is back to the speed of Andrei Kanchelskis, early Ryan Giggs and the Lee Sharpe era.'

In a hugely disappointing final, United went down to a solitary goal scored by Drogba four minutes from the end of extra time. Ole had come on after 112 minutes and hardly saw the ball in those last frenetic moments.

The game was played on a windy, chilly afternoon in the world's most expensive stadium, the perfect stage for the Premiership's two best teams to slug it out. When Sir Matt Busby was made a Freeman of Manchester in 1967, he said, 'There are two aspects of the game that have always impressed me. I love its drama, its smooth playing skill – and its great occasions, for example the Cup Final in the great arena at Wembley. I feel a sense of romance, wonder and mystery, a sense of poetry. On such occasions, the game is larger than life.'

The 2007 Cup Final lacked poetry, romance and, most of all, excitement. Chelsea must shoulder most of the blame for that, by employing their tried and tested long-ball-to-Drogba approach, and stifling any creative flair in midfield. They had looked burnt out in the closing weeks of the season, unable to win any of their last five games. Their game became much more direct, centring around winning the ball and hitting Drogba with it.

Drogba is a wonderful athlete, capable now of exploding with awesome power. The transformation from the overweight playboy toiling away in French football to the

Premier League top goalscorer has been amazing. It was Drogba who dashed United's Double dreams when he ran through the middle to dink home Lampard's neat side-footed pass, his one telling contribution throughout the entire game. Only Scholes came out of the game with any credit for United, with all the greats – Ronaldo, Rooney and Giggs – appearing to have mislaid their golden touch. Giggs appeared to have scored in extra time but Cech was adjudged to have been bundled over the line. Apart from that one incident, there was little for United fans to cheer about.

Ole was second up to collect his loser's medal, to be placed next to his two winner's medals. He smiled that Ole smile, and was one of the few United players who could walk away with his head held high that day, grateful and proud that his career had been given that second lease of life.

Sir Alex was philosophical about the defeat, still clearly proud of his players' achievements that season. 'You can't do much about it when they score as late as that... my players were too tired to launch a challenge. We had two or three players who looked tired from the first half. We looked jaded. It has been an exhausting season with a lot of matches and that is understandable.'

Ole told the *Manchester Evening News*, 'I always thought I could still be part of this, despite everything I had gone through. I am not getting any younger but, if the gaffer wants me to be a part again of this squad for 10, 20 or 30 games next year, then I will be delighted.'

In the official Opta stats for season 2006/07 there was a 'minutes per goal' section. Topping the table as 'the most effective striker in Europe' was Ole Gunnar Solskjaer of the Champions Manchester United. His average was a goal every 131.9 minutes. In a career that combined the heights of a European Cup-winning goal with the despair of two years out of the game, there was no denying the skill, determination and sheer class of Ole Gunnar Solskjaer – the Baby-Faced Assassin was well and truly back at the top, where he belonged.